They Don't Want Her There

They Don't Want Her There

*Fighting Sexual and Racial Harassment
in the American University*

Carolyn Chalmers

For Meg, my friend
& great friend
and a fine reader!
Carolyn

UNIVERSITY OF IOWA PRESS ❖ IOWA CITY

University of Iowa Press, Iowa City 52242
Copyright © 2022 by University of Iowa Press
uipress.uiowa.edu
Printed in the United States of America
Cover design by Kathleen Lynch / Black Kat Design
Text design and typesetting by Sara T. Sauers
Printed on acid-free paper

Library of Congress Cataloging-in-Publication Data
Names: Chalmers, Carolyn, 1946– author.
Title: They Don't Want Her There: Fighting Sexual and Racial
    Harassment in the American University / Carolyn Chalmers.
Description: Iowa City: University of Iowa Press, 2022. |
    Includes bibliographical references.
Identifiers: LCCN 2021028953 (print) | LCCN 2021028954
    (ebook) | ISBN 9781609388195 (paperback) |
    ISBN 9781609388201 (ebook)
Subjects: LCSH: Jew, Jean Y.—Trials, litigation, etc. | University
    of Iowa—Trials, litigation, etc. | Sexual harassment in
    universities and colleges—Iowa. | Sexual harassment of
    women—Law and legislation—United States. |
    Sexual harassment—Investigation—United States. |
    Sex discrimination in employment—Law and legislation—
    United States. | Discrimination in higher education—Law
    and legislation—United States. | Roy J. and Lucille A. Carver
    College of Medicine.
Classification: LCC KF228.J49 C43 2022 (print) | LCC KF228.J49
    (ebook) | DDC 344.777/0798—dc23
LC record available at https://lccn.loc.gov/2021028953
LC ebook record available at https://lccn.loc.gov/2021028954

In loving memory of my sister, Jinny Chalmers,
a fierce advocate for education justice

Contents

Foreword

JEAN Y. JEW

There was a professor of anatomy
Whose colleagues all thought had a lobotomy.
Apartments he had to rent,
And his semen was all spent
On a colleague who did his microtomy.

I CRINGED WHEN shown a photo of this limerick, scrawled the afternoon of November 1, 1983, on the men's room wall in the department where I worked in the College of Medicine at the University of Iowa. It happened to be the same afternoon that senior faculty members were meeting to evaluate the performance of more junior faculty, to recommend promotions or advise about the progress needed for future promotion. It was the same afternoon that my performance for the past year was being discussed.

I wanted to do as I had always done for the past ten years in this department—lower my flushed face, pretend to believe that this was not how my "esteemed colleagues" regarded me, and retreat to my lab and classroom so I could continue to prove my worth. After all, this had been my modus operandi since I first arrived at Iowa and almost immediately found myself the target of sexual innuendoes and allegations. Nevertheless, my teaching and research efforts had flourished, and performance evaluations had led to my earning tenure and a promotion to associate professor. But sometimes the words hurt as much as "sticks and stones," eliciting not only discomfort and humiliation but also an awful sense of vulnerability. How could I pretend not to hear the professor who yelled as I walked down the hallway, "There goes that slut now!" How could I not feel shame when the dean of the medical school received an anonymous note stating Iowa taxpayers should not pay "for Chinese pussy!"

I could not hide my embarrassment on the occasions I sought help from college and university administrators. Their responses were always versions of the same: this is what women have to put up with in a male-dominated profession; if you file an official complaint, your career will suffer; you have been treated terribly, they may make life hell for you, but you have a good record and you'll continue to progress.

After ten years, I began to question the wisdom of this advice and even doubt the truth of their concern for my well-being and future. Skepticism had begun to chip away at my model minority acceptance of and submission to authority. Why should I have to put up with hell in my workplace? What could I do? Whom could I go to for help? Only one person responded, on condition of anonymity, to my appeal: "You have to find a lawyer. It has to be someone from out of state because the university has very long arms." I found Carolyn Chalmers.

Surgery was part of my training as a physician. Litigation insinuated itself into more than eight years of my life. Upon reflection after reading this book, I'm struck by how surgery and litigation are such remarkably apt analogies for each other. Both are harsh, even painful; however neatly resolved, both leave scars; both entail significant risks and uncertain outcomes. In their respective disciplines, surgery and litigation are considered options of last resort. Sometimes, one is fortunate enough to have a surgeon who is not only technically skilled but has the talent and personal qualities to give her patient the courage to believe that the risk is worthwhile. Sometimes, I believe more rarely, one is fortunate enough to have a lawyer whose expertise, commitment, tenacity, and genuine care convince her client that the last resort option is both endurable and worthwhile.

Jean Y. Jew, M.D.
Iowa City, Iowa
February 2021

Preface

BEFORE THE U.S. Supreme Court recognized a legal claim for hostile environment sexual harassment, years before the nation watched Anita Hill and Clarence Thomas give opposing accounts of his workplace conduct, decades before Harvey Weinstein's sexual misconduct inspired the #MeToo movement and Christine Blasey Ford and Brett Kavanaugh reenacted the Hill/Thomas drama, Professor Jean Y. Jew brought a lawsuit alleging a sexually hostile work environment in the College of Medicine at the University of Iowa. I was her lawyer.

When Jean arrived at Iowa's College of Medicine in 1973, women were just beginning to be admitted to male-dominated faculties. At the age of twenty-four, with her M.D., she was distinguished from other faculty in the Department of Anatomy by her gender, her youth, her ethnicity, and her medical degree. Some male professors, believing a Chinese American woman did not belong on their faculty, began disgracing Jean with sexual and ethnic slurs. Their insults were redolent with tropes about Chinese women being sexually exotic, manipulative, and submissive. For ten years, she lived with the shaming and the toll it took on her before she sought out legal help.

Employment laws that we now take for granted were in their infancy. Hostile environment sexual harassment was an area of law still under construction. A hostile environment sexual harassment decision against a university was unprecedented. Jean and I had to figure out for ourselves how to use the law to confront a sexist and racist smear campaign. To prevail, we would have to convince people that leering was as visceral a violation as a physical grope; that universities were no more welcoming to women than male-dominated factory floors; that equivalencies between academic freedom and hate speech were false; and that women, not just men, could launch risky litigation and see it through.

This book is a personal account of what it was like for two women to go up against a large medical school ensconced in a flagship land-grant university in the U.S. heartland at the dawn of sexual harassment litigation. It is also a story of how demeaning stereotypes about Chinese women were used by Jean's colleagues to discredit her academic accomplishments and how she ultimately took a stand and stopped them. Through one university hearing and two court trials, Jean and I were required to be very brave, very often. Our relationship of trust and mutual respect, and our complementary skills, shaped the litigation in ways large and small.

The power of the law and the courts to constrain an institution bent on avoiding justice is integral to our story. In the current moment, civil trials are an endangered species and the contested values they raise are frequently resolved in confidential arbitration and mediation, sheltered from the public eye. The civil trials recounted here were in the public eye and teach what trials can do. The judicial system has sufficient institutional weight to shift cultural paradigms, including misogyny, in a way that women's voices, even choruses of women's voices on social media, cannot accomplish alone.[1] By determining how law applies to the facts of individual lives, judges and juries shape societal values. The University of Iowa, an institutional powerhouse, had to come to terms with the injustice it fostered because an even more powerful institution, the judiciary, insisted on it.

In this memoir, I endeavor to tell what legal work is really like when representing a vulnerable client, on an issue of deep personal and social concern, against an institutional monolith, through an eight-year battle. Not an exposition of how to try a lawsuit or even an explanation of how this case was tried, this is an insider, subjective view of a lawyer's and a client's work together. Others may remember events differently. Dialogue is my best estimate, striving to be true to my memory, the speakers, and the context. I sometimes hypothesize what was in the minds of people, anchored to what I know of what they said and did.

I had an extensive archive to draw on. My former law firm, with Jean's consent, delivered to me the case files—all fifty-three banker's boxes. The pleadings, correspondence, attorney notes, depositions, and two transcripts—one of the faculty investigation panel hearing and one of the federal court trial—are sources of quotations. To ease reading, I have consolidated some statements from the same speaker without using ellipses.

Explicitly offensive language is included as it appeared in the 1970s and 1980s in Jean's work environment. This was necessary thirty years ago for judges and jurors to consider what speech is and is not prohibited sexual harassment and whether and how it injures. It is necessary for the reader today for the same reasons.

Litigation makes extraordinary demands on all involved. Many have said that a sexual harassment plaintiff loses even when she wins. This was not true for Jean Jew. The law brought grace to her life. It has been a kind of grace in my life to work with Jean again, years later, on this book. We shared our respective recollections of the litigation, our lives before we met, and our lives since the case ended. As violence in our country against Asian Americans mushroomed along with the coronavirus, preserving this history took on added significance. Although it has not always been easy to revisit difficult experiences, Jean and I have come to appreciate again how our determination and effort contributed to making the University of Iowa a better place for faculty and staff to work and for students to learn.

PART I

❖❖❖

A University Gets the Benefit of the Doubt

CHAPTER 1

Tipping Point

THE TILE ABOVE the urinal looked like a blank whiteboard. Tempting. Seizing an opportunity to continue a smear campaign, an anonymous someone took up a black marker and scrawled a demeaning limerick.

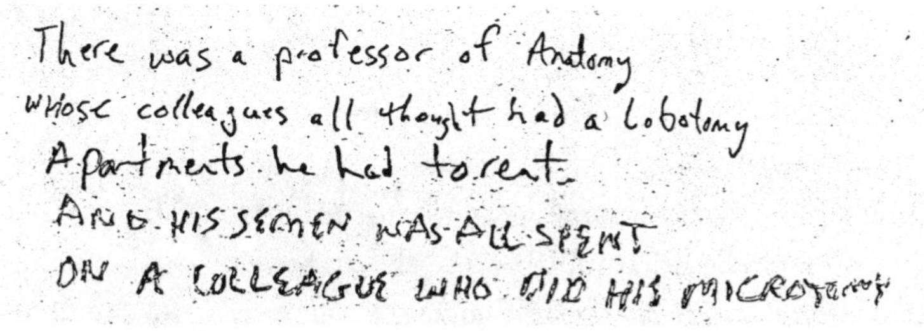

> There was a professor of Anatomy
> Whose colleagues all thought had a lobotomy
> Apartments he had to rent
> And his semen was all spent
> On a colleague who did his microtomy

Figure 1: Photograph of limerick that appeared November 1, 1983, in the Anatomy Department men's room.

The location of the limerick was strategic. Placed in the Anatomy Department's men's room just above the round, chrome flush, no one using the urinal could miss it.

Most of the tenured faculty in the Anatomy Department were men. Likely all of them read the limerick that day, perhaps more than once. None washed the black ink off the white wall. Most of the medical students were men. They also read the limerick on their way to attend class or lab. None of the women knew it was there. Jean went about her work that day, unaware.

The male faculty and male students who read the limerick knew that it referred to Professor Terence Williams, whose ten-year term as chair of the Anatomy Department had just ended, and his research

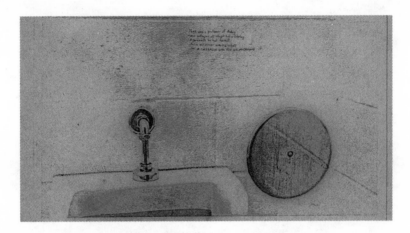

Figure 2: Photograph of the location of the limerick, above the urinal and the urinal flush in the Anatomy Department men's room.

colleague, Professor Jean Jew. Male faculty also knew that on the very day the limerick appeared, November 1, 1983, Jean was to be evaluated by male professors on her progress toward promotion to full professor.

Jean was vaguely troubled when she passed Williams in the hall that afternoon. He was clearly agitated and searching for the departmental photographer. Williams said that he had discovered something important about her that had to be photographed. Jean immediately responded, "Please don't. I'm sure you're overreacting." She was afraid him making a fuss over something that probably amounted to little more than the slights and indignities she encountered almost daily would only cause more embarrassment for her and needless antagonism from the senior faculty evaluating her that day.

It was not until a few days later, when Williams showed Jean a photo of the limerick, that she knew she had been wrong. Williams had not overreacted. The limerick was uniquely arresting for its timing, on the day of her review by senior faculty, the lewdness of its language, and the impunity of its location, where so many men would see it and no women could.

On the same occasion, Williams gave her a second photo of graffiti not previously shared with Jean. This second incident of graffiti had appeared in the same men's room, on the same wall, one year earlier

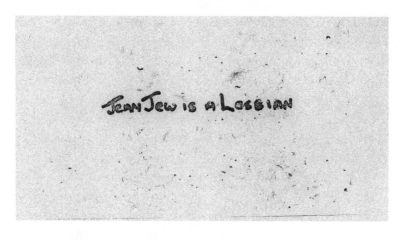

Figure 3: Photograph of graffiti that appeared in the Anatomy Department men's room January 4, 1982.

on the eve of faculty evaluations. While both slurs were manifestations of the flood of sexual innuendo that had circulated about her since she first arrived at the University of Iowa, the replication of timing, public placement, and sexual language in the two scrawls suggested a determined initiative to damage or end Jean's professional career.

As Jean examined the photos in her hand, in her mind's eye she scrolled through lewd incidents that marked the ten years she had been at the College of Medicine. In the summer of 1973, she was just twenty-four years old, with a newly minted M.D. degree and excited to begin her first academic job. Excitement dissipated as sexual slurs multiplied. What had looked so promising at the outset had soured over the years that followed.

⁘

On her very first day in the Anatomy Department, a male faculty member came into Jean's lab. What should have been a welcome greeting instead was off-color and off-putting. "What do you think of Indira Gandhi's requirement that men get vasectomies?" Jean demurred. She thought, *What is this?*

Sexualized cartoons, annotated with specific references to Jean, began to appear in the Department of Anatomy. Posted in the main hallway in the Anatomy Department was a cartoon that showed two voluptuous women wearing only G-strings and pasties. They were pictured gyrating on an elevated dance floor above a male audience. The original caption on the cartoon was obliterated. Instead, a handwritten caption in green ink read, "I'm his neuro-anatomist." Only one person in the Anatomy Department, or for that matter in the whole College of Medicine, was both a woman and a neuro-anatomist—Jean. Other sexual cartoons were posted in the hallway throughout her first few years at Iowa. One pictured a naked, paunchy man drinking at a bar, smoking a cigar, and confiding, again in a handwritten caption in green ink on the cartoon, "She's only my microtomist." Another showed a naked man, labeled in green ink as "Dr. Williams," and a naked woman prone on a couch, "Dr. Jew." One pictured a sexy woman, labeled "Jean" in green ink, at a bar talking with several men, saying, "Terry, bring me my slippers."

In her second year at Iowa, Jean earned a tenure-track appointment as an assistant professor and a warning about Professor Robert Tomanek. A junior male faculty member told her about a conversation he and his wife had with Tomanek while shopping at a nearby mall. "We happened to bump into him at Sycamore Mall. He said that Williams was screwing you. That's the word he used. He asked, since our place was across from yours, if we had seen Dr. Williams's car parked at your house overnight. And then he asked if we could see into your windows and catch any activities going on with Dr. Williams. We were shocked." Jean's quiet "Thank you for telling me" was born of her shame. Outrage would take years to mature.

Professor Tomanek was to take the lead in spreading sexual slurs about Jean in the years that followed. When I first met him years later, his close-cropped sandy hair and knotted string tie made him appear plain in a fussy way. He was Czech, or more precisely Bohemian, with reputedly pious values exhibited in moralistic judgments about others' perceived behavior. A young Chinese woman doctor arriving in his department in 1973 was as startling as the sudden appearance of a UFO. At that time no woman was in a tenure-track faculty position on the Department of Anatomy faculty. Jean became an object of attention. Seeing her working side by side in a lab with Williams, Tomanek presumed sexual relations rather than scientific research.

Jean must have ransacked her memory of her short tenure at Iowa to try to find a cause for Tomanek's animosity toward her. She would have been reluctant to assume that her gender, her Chinese ethnicity, her youth, and her unmarried status made her an unwanted stranger who did not belong. In time, this conclusion became inescapable. By just being who she was, Jean was an affront to the default portrait of a College of Medicine faculty member—male, white, and middle-aged. Over the next several years, Jean was aware of sexual rumors, but few people spoke about them to her face until an incident in January 1979, soon after departmental approval of her tenure and promotion to associate professor.

On that occasion, Professor William Kaelber slandered her publicly. In the course of a heated argument with a junior faculty member, Kaelber yelled out into the hall as Jean passed by, "There goes that bitch now. She shouldn't have been promoted to associate professor. She's a stupid slut. I don't care that she and Williams are having an affair. I knew from the beginning that she was a dumb bitch." That evening Jean called her colleague and asked, "What was that all about?" When he repeated Kaelber's slurs, Jean began to cry. She wrote a letter complaining of "personal vilification and sexual harassment" against Professor William Kaelber to the dean of the College of Medicine to no avail.

The graffiti in her hands in November 1983, when viewed against this decade-long backdrop splattered with slurs, presented an escalation of the sexual slander campaign. It had long blunted her energy and cheerfulness. Now she feared that it was strategically targeted at halting her career. She decided to discuss it with then vice president for academic affairs, Richard Remington. He counseled her, "No question you have been harassed. They will continue to make your life miserable, but you will continue to progress."

Why should they be permitted to make my life miserable? I have put up with this for ten years believing that I would not be hurt and my career would not be damaged. So what the administrators have been telling me all these years is not true. I am not going to be all right.

Jean had arrived at her tipping point.

⠿

On November 23, 1983, Jean reached me at my desk in my Minneapolis law firm. She said she was an associate professor in the Department of Anatomy at the College of Medicine at the University of Iowa.

"Do you take cases outside of Minnesota?" she asked.

"Rarely," I said.

I answered the phone with little intention of pausing in my work and no intention of taking on a new case. Every week, my law partner, Kathleen Graham, and I received calls from women seeking legal help to deal with the hostile work environments they were experiencing as they entered traditionally male workplaces in token numbers.[1] A powerful legal tool to challenge sex discrimination in the workplace, Title VII of the 1964 Civil Rights Act, was newly available to challenge hostile harassment. Graham was among the first lawyers in the Twin Cities known to take employment discrimination cases based on sex and race. I was her back-up in these groundbreaking cases, hence the frequent calls for help.

At the time of Jean's call, Graham and I were in trial in federal court representing about a thousand women in a sex discrimination class action against Jostens, the Minnesota maker of graduation and Super Bowl rings (among other things). Submerged in that fight, we were depleting our firm's coffers and our personal strength. That morning I did not want another plaintiff's employment case that would not bring in revenue until the end of the case, and then only if we won.

"I'm sorry, but I have a heavy caseload here in Minnesota. I prefer not to travel for work." (I was saying "no" kindly.) "I can check around for names of some employment attorneys in Iowa with experience and good reputations," I said. Holding the handset wedged between my head and shoulder, I continued reading the draft on my desk, the final due in court at the end of the day. "As a practical matter, it is difficult and expensive for a client and attorney to work effectively across a distance." In 1983, long-distance phone calls were costly and billed by the minute.

"I need a lawyer from outside Iowa," Jean said.

"Why?" I asked, being polite.

"My complaint is against the College of Medicine at the University of Iowa. I've been advised that most Iowa attorneys represent the university in one way or another, and those that don't are alums and donors and don't want to get involved." As an afterthought she added, "I was advised that I had to find a lawyer outside of Iowa because 'the university has very long arms.'" I could hear, in her low-pitched, clear voice a search for just the right words to convey her thought. She spoke in complete phrases, separating them with periodic rests. I heard the punctuation in her account, the rise and fall of emphasis, all with unhurried pacing. *I bet she is an effective teacher.*

"What is your issue?" I had not meant to ask that. The question slid out. I immediately regretted opening the door to a longer conversation.

"My annual evaluation by senior faculty in my department just a few weeks ago was so flawed that it could make it impossible for me to ever be promoted to full professor," Jean said.

Hmmm, I thought to myself. Promotion to the faculty rank of full professor is not an "up or out" decision, like tenure. A negative tenure decision means the faculty member has to leave the institution following a terminal year. A positive tenure decision brings lifetime job security and usually promotion to the rank of associate professor. Once tenure is secured, many productive associate professors never achieve the rank of full professor, choosing to be fine teachers rather than wellsprings of scholarly tracts. Tenure denial is worth a pitched battle; a disappointing evaluation for promotion to full professor, not so much.

Jean continued, "By flawed, I mean it coincided with graffiti about me, written in black marker, above the urinal in the men's bathroom."

"What was written?" I asked. As she read the limerick to me I made a note to myself: *She is averse to have these words sully her tongue.* After a pause, my response was noncommittal, "I'm not following this."

"Dr. Terry Williams is the professor of anatomy referred to. He has been chair of my department and was my mentor at Tulane Medical School. He has dabbled in real estate in Iowa City and has some rental property." Jean's answer came at a steady pace and with fully thought out sentences. She was making a good impression on me. *She would make a good witness.*

"I'm his research collaborator, and much of my research work is funded as a co-investigator on his grants. I'm the one referred to as the colleague doing his microtomy," Jean said. *Also the one referred to as the recipient of Williams's semen.*

Jean added, "In ten years here, I've been the object of slurs, and other faculty have been warned to stay away from me, but this is the first time I've felt that the harassment could ruin my career. For me to demonstrate the independent scholarship needed for promotion to full professor, I've been directed to change my research field and no longer collaborate with Dr. Williams. Effectively it means starting over. Maybe I will not be permitted to do collaborative work with anybody. And if permitted, who would be willing to collaborate with me given the salacious stories and warnings to stay away from me?"

I was attending to her now. In her calm voice, I heard a southern lilt. I permitted our conversation to gather momentum. She talked about salacious cartoons. She told of sexual innuendos about her, fueled by some senior male faculty. Below the surface much of the time, it emerged just three weeks ago as she was being evaluated on her progress toward promotion to full professor.

I understood that many might perceive university faculty as above crude disparagement of women, but not me. Representing women faculty in claims under the Rajender Consent Decree at the University of Minnesota taught me that male faculty could behave toward women newcomers like men in other male-dominated workplaces behaved. The Rajender Consent Decree was the outcome of litigation by Shyamala Rajender, an Asian Indian woman faculty member in the Chemistry Department. Women faculty used the complaint process established by the decree to pursue claims of sex discrimination at the University of Minnesota throughout the 1980s. With Kathleen Graham, I represented many of these claimants.[2]

My first Rajender client was an Argentinian woman challenging denial of tenure in the medical school. Her case took me into the byzantine world of academic medicine where women and minorities were not in evidence. I learned that loathsome behavior occurred in the male-dominated culture of medical school. Harassment was especially virulent against minority women because of the interplay of sex, race, and national origin discrimination. I witnessed the University of Minnesota's obduracy in the face of claims of sex discrimination, the male privilege embedded in its medical school, and the myriad misogynistic strategies enabling both.

When Jean said that a faculty member in another department had asked one of her colleagues, "Where's Terry and his Chink?" I was surprised. Without consciously thinking it, I had assumed she was a white woman. I added to my notes and underlined, "She is Chinese." Knowing Jean's ethnicity and race, I made sense of her detractors' choice of sexual slurs. *She is Chinese—suffering from sexualized tropes about Asian women. She is an anomaly within the College of Medicine—her ethnicity, her gender, her race, her youth, her unmarried status, and her success. She probably wears a white lab coat like those worn by senior male faculty, but it does not camouflage the many ways she is unlike white men faculty in her department. Her presence alone threatens. They don't want her there. And they are using the concubine stereotype to force her out.*

Jean was matter-of-fact. Apart from reading the limerick and repeating the epithets, she expressed little emotion. She listened closely to my questions, and her answers were to the point. She did not try to overwhelm me with a fire hydrant torrent that gave me no opportunity to close down the intake valve. I listened for her ability to tell her story, to sort out for the listener the important from the unimportant, to avoid hyperbole, to realize when she had lost me and to backtrack to pick me up. She did all of this without urgency. I trusted her responses. I liked her already.

"When did you get tenure and how did that go?" I asked, thinking, *Four years ago her research with Dr. Williams was positively reviewed and tenure granted. She must have a record of quality research and teaching that had gained support within the department and the college. Why now is her career so viciously undermined?*

"In 1979. The tenure process wasn't smooth," Jean said. She did not expand.

"Did you do anything about these smears?" I asked.

"I was very junior to everyone else in the department. I had no one to speak to about such personal things. No one to advise me. More recently I've spoken to Dr. Williams about it. He told me that he asked the departmental photographer to go in the men's room, photograph the limerick, and make prints of the photos. Dr. Williams also told me that a year before, in 1982 on the day the senior faculty were evaluating me, there was graffiti in the same place. Dr. Williams gave me copies of photos of the graffiti in the men's room. Dr. Williams was my professor and supervisor and now also my friend and colleague. But we don't talk about this easily. He is my senior."

"Did you report this to the university?" I asked.

"I reported an earlier incident in 1979 to Dean Eckstein and to Vice President for Academic Affairs May Brodbeck," Jean said. "In 1979, they said there was nothing they could do. Just a few weeks ago I reported the two graffiti incidents in the men's room to Vice President for Academic Affairs Richard Remington. He told me, 'They'll make your life hell, but you're going to continue to progress.'" *Really, after seeing her bear it for years, their advice to her is keep on doing what she is doing? No wonder she called me.*

Sensitized by my own experience with discrimination as a working woman and a woman lawyer, I was quick to bruise with the injustice of Jean's. My indignation on her behalf smoldered quietly.

"How have you managed?" I asked.

"I felt like all women entering the profession have to expect some of this. But it would be totally unrealistic of me not to realize that the little bit I was hearing was just the tip of the iceberg," Jean concluded. "I wonder how I can show that I deserve to be where I am."

In our phone conversations I had only Jean's voice, no visuals or contradictory information from the university's point of view. What little I learned in that first conversation was not enough to evaluate her case. Yet thirty-five years later, when I reviewed the case files, the first document spindled was the new case report dated November 23, 1983, the date of her phone call to me. My name is listed three times on the new case report—as the billing attorney, the originating attorney, and the responsible attorney. The fact that I opened a file on the day we first talked does not necessarily indicate an impulsive decision to take the case. Perhaps I opened the file for business reasons—to let my law partners know I had been consulted on a matter involving the University of Iowa, to permit a conflict of interest check with other work in the firm, or to allow me to keep a record of my attorney time on the file. But my memory is that I decided to take Jean's case in that first phone call. Snap decision. Denigration of women provoked my swift condemnation, not ambivalence.

On November 23, I did not tell Jean whether I would represent her. When we hung up, she did not know that my role as her advocate was almost a fait accompli. Instead, I asked her to send me a detailed chronology, which she did a few days later, along with her CV, photographs of the graffiti, and her November 1983 evaluation report. We talked again a week later. On this second call, I asked her for a brief sketch of each of the senior faculty in her department, all male, focusing on those she believed were biased against her from the very beginning—Tomanek and Kaelber. I dropped to the bottom line. "What do you want to happen?" I asked.

"I don't want there to be graffiti. I don't want it to be hidden. I don't want every person who comes into the department to be told that I'm sleeping with such and such, and that is the only reason I've gotten where I am. I don't want unreasonable demands in order to progress in this system. I want to be judged on my record," Jean said.

Not a hint of self-righteousness or entitlement, though she would be justified to feel that way.

My last question, "Why now?"

Jean said quietly, "Up to now these slurs didn't stop my progress in my career. This is the first time they were linked to a negative faculty evaluation. The slander isn't going away, and if anything, it is getting more destructive."

A few days later, I told Jean that I would represent her. "The behavior you've described is pretty egregious. I think the university would want to resolve this. It has a vested interest in appearing to do the right thing." I explained that my standard billing rate was $75 per hour and I asked her to pay a retainer to the firm of $750. This would cover about ten hours of my time, which I estimated would be about what was required. I expected we would begin by asking the university to investigate and take corrective action and that the university, when fully informed, would agree.

These expectations, in hindsight, seem so unfounded, yet they were based on my experience advocating for women faculty at the University of Minnesota. I was predisposed to empathize with and credit Jean's account when she called. I was predisposed to think the University of Iowa had gained some awareness of the obstacles women faculty faced, particularly in the sciences, and would be unlikely to shrug off Jean's complaint. Extrapolating from my Minnesota experience to the University of Iowa was a beginner's mistake. True, these two midwestern universities were beginning to come to terms with sex discrimination, but my assumption that they were at similar stages in this process started Jean and me down a path rutted with trouble.

⋮⋮⋮

Jean had been flummoxed about where to look for an attorney outside Iowa to advise her about the harassment she experienced in November 1983. A colleague referred her to an article in the *Chronicle for Higher Education* about the work Graham and I were doing under the Rajender Consent Decree.[3] Jean called three of the faculty women named in the article to ask about their experience pursuing their Rajender claims and for their feedback on Graham and me. They raved about Graham. "She can get anyone to say anything on the stand—things they never intended to admit to. She's great in the courtroom." About me, Jean was told, "Carolyn is a negotiator. She's great at it. Clamps on and won't let go."

"That's why I called you," Jean told me years later with a chuckle. "No way I could see going to court."

CHAPTER 2

Two Women

ONE IN-PERSON, brief meeting with Jean in those first months was sufficient. On her way back to Iowa from a neuroscience meeting in San Francisco in late 1983, Jean stopped for a few hours in Minneapolis to visit and, I presumed, size up the lawyer and the law firm she had hired. At thirty-seven years old, her face was framed by black hair in a page-boy cut that curved under her jaw line. Below black bangs, her eyes looked out with a self-possessed confidence. For a determined, successful research scientist and tenured associate professor, she cut a novel figure. Reassured by our visit that we could work well together, we carried on by telephone.

Jean was an expert at accurate observation of the finest details of life. As a scientist, she carved the tiniest slices of brain tissue, affixed them delicately to copper grids, and examined them through an electron microscope—a large instrument bolted to an immovable counter in a dedicated windowless room in the Anatomy Department, constructed on a solid substratum of rock. The work tolerated no tremors—of underground turbines or passing traffic. Steady hands and eyes were necessary to capture a revealing image. For hours at a time, she pored over subunits of cells and nerves that became visible only when magnified tens of thousands of times. She wanted to find ways to regenerate damaged nerve cells.

I brought an intuitive grasp of what makes a person tick, viewed in situ. I observed people, their emotions, the currents below the surface that brought them into relationships and broke them up. I matched these up with the potential benefits of judicial approbation and the dangers of being shredded on the barbs of the legal process. When Jean asked questions of me, she expected precise answers, correct spelling, and accurate details. I responded with myriad observations about the

15

humans involved and the law. Focused and laser-like, Jean's analysis was a far cry from the conch shell swirls of my mental process. Our different approaches were grounded in a core of shared values.

Jean and I came of age in the 1960s. Our high school and college years were accompanied by social upheaval reflected in the civil rights movement, Vietnam War, and women's rights movement. Resistance to injustice was the social milieu in which we became adults. Reverend Martin Luther King Jr. led the March on Washington in 1963. President John F. Kennedy was gunned down in Dallas in November 1963. In summer 1964, college students descended on southern states to register Black voters. Violence in 1968 mirrored the violence of 1963. Martin Luther King Jr. was assassinated in April 1968, and two months later Robert Kennedy met the same fate. The men graduating from college in that year were stripped of draft deferments for graduate school. Student protests against the Vietnam War disrupted campuses across the country.

As we entered adulthood, protective labor legislation restricting women from jobs requiring heavy lifting or night work were on the wane. Women were beginning to get positions as police officers, bill collectors, and bartenders. Classified ads seeking "men wanted" and "women wanted" were phasing out. While notable, changes in gender roles progressed at a glacial pace. Few women were breaking through barriers to professional schools. Those who did, once they matriculated, did not find careers open to them on university faculties or in elite law firms.

Against this cultural backdrop, Jean and I aimed to become a doctor and a lawyer. When Jean came to the University of Iowa in 1973, women in tenure-track faculty positions were anomalies and women of color in tenure-track positions were rarer still. When she was appointed assistant professor a year later, at age twenty-five, Jean became one of the few women in a tenure-track position in any of the basic science departments at the College of Medicine.

By the time we met in 1983, Jean and I were a few years short of forty. As women in male-dominated, postgraduate professional schools, later choosing occupations that had been off-limits to women, we had experiences in common. We both had been the only woman in the room, mistaken for support staff, and left out of important meetings. Our styles of managing in male-dominated environments were similar. We eschewed flamboyance in favor of reserve. We presented ourselves as polite and professional. Our business-like propriety concealed the granite undergirding each of us.

While Jean and I ran similar gauntlets in our respective professions, we came to them from very different childhoods. Jean was a first-generation Chinese American woman brought up in the deep South. I was a white middle-class woman brought up in several places, but never in the South.

⋄⋄⋄

My parents were white and well educated. I was schooled in upstate New York, Ohio, Wyoming, and Kansas. I did not know any Chinese American people growing up. My parents conformed to societal expectations for gender roles—my mother took care of the home and three children, and my father was a college professor.

When I graduated from Minnesota's Carleton College in 1968, I was unprepared for the limited professional careers open to me—secretary, nurse, or teacher. Male classmates were encouraged to plan for law school, medical school, or graduate programs. Their professional plans were put on hold in 1968 due to the Vietnam War, but not quashed.

For six years after graduation, I wandered around looking for doorways into the world. I was accepted into a master's program for aspiring teachers. Instead, I went to teach in India on a Fulbright Tutor Grant. When I returned to the United States, I settled in Cambridge, Massachusetts, and searched the classifieds. The "women wanted" ads listed subordinate and poorly paid women's jobs. Captive to gendered categories, I did not read the "men wanted" ads. I accepted that I was barred from better opportunities by my gender, no matter my qualifications.

A "women wanted" ad for a research assistant at Charles River Associates, a consulting firm in Cambridge, stood out as a uniquely challenging job. Why was it listed in the "women wanted" section? Once at Charles River Associates, the answer became apparent. Women were wanted in more ways than one. Before sexual harassment was named, I sensed it in my first full-time job.

Picture seven female research assistants, all white, at desks in an office suite converted from what were formerly bedrooms at the Commodore Hotel, just off Harvard Square. Most were new graduates of elite women's colleges. We were overqualified for the tasks of keying data onto punch cards and proofreading reports. Middle-aged, academic men, all white, moonlighting from their professor jobs at Harvard and MIT had us at their beck and call. Mobility was for the men, who approached and receded without warning, brushing against arms, breathing on our hair, flaunting crotches at eye level. The atmosphere nearly shimmered with sexual innuendo. We experienced these sex-based indignities in silence, our umbrage not manifested in action.

My relationship with Eric Janus developed during these years. After we were classmates at Carleton College, Eric went to Turkey with the Peace Corps while I taught in India. Eric returned to Massachusetts in 1970 to join me and enroll at Harvard Law School. Harvard Law, which had excluded women for most of its distinguished history, began admitting more than a few women in the early 1970s, fearing the loss of male law students due to the Vietnam War. Although I still could not picture myself as a lawyer, our women friends at Harvard helped me picture legal careers for women.

As an outgrowth of my experience in India, I enrolled in an anthropology Ph.D. program at Brandeis University. The few women faculty there were treated poorly. Gingerly trying to find a place for themselves, they were treated like economy-class travelers expected to disembark soon. I abandoned that path, concluding that at least for me, it likely was a dead end.

Eric and I married in 1971, and two years later, with his J.D. in hand and my M.A. in its final stages, we moved to Minneapolis with our toddler son, Seth. I decided to go to law school and focus on employment law. The University of Minnesota Law School was my third male-dominated institution in six years.

By the time I started, the number of women in law school had increased, but we had not yet made an impact on the sexism in the law school, as illustrated by a discussion in my first-year criminal law class. In the case under discussion, a wife killed her abusive husband in his sleep. When prosecuted for murder, she pled not guilty by reason of self-defense. The professor asked, "How could she plead self-defense when she murdered him in his sleep? She could have fled, or called the police, or taken all sorts of action short of murder." My hand shot up, before I had formulated my thought.

"Okay. Ms. Chalmers, go on."

Now what did I want to say? "I don't agree."

"Go on. . . . Tell us why."

"We are acting like she has the options of a middle-class man," I said. The professor frowned. Unusually quiet, he and the ninety other students waited. "Maybe she had no car, no parents nearby or money for a hotel. Or maybe she could not call the police—no phone, or no phone where he would not wake up and hear her or no trust that the police would not make things worse. Or maybe she knew that if she tried anything short of killing him, he would be enraged and murder her." My comment was met with silence. *Am I the only one to note the realities of a woman's life?*

My grades in law school reflected my interests. In a civil rights class, I earned a rare A+, and in a required property law class I barely passed with a D. I earned a J.D. in 1977. The placement office at the law school discouraged me from disclosing to prospective employers that I was particularly interested in employment discrimination litigation. I ignored the advice and was hired by the Dayton, Herman & Graham law firm,[1] which was looking for a junior attorney to support Kathleen Graham, a founding partner who already had a reputation in the emerging field of employment discrimination litigation.

Graham was a fearless guide through the uncharted turbulence of discrimination litigation, and I drafted close to her, sheltered from the worst. I learned how to do discovery, argue contested motions, and examine witnesses in the courtroom. Arming myself with a few practiced retorts to replace stunned silence, I learned to carry on in the face of rude behavior from opposing male attorneys.

Eric practiced civil poverty law at the Minneapolis Legal Aid Society, where alums of the civil rights movement had found community. Our daughter, Leah, was born in 1977. Eric and I routinized a flexible menu of shared responsibilities. At four years old, Seth's schedule was a mosaic of people and places—a babysitting co-op, a preschool where after three years he was practically a teacher's assistant, and a freelance "grandma" who toilet trained with Oreos. Seth and Leah ended up in one of our cars in the late afternoon headed home, rather than swept up in the arms of a child protection worker. We practiced give and take when one of us needed to be home with a sick child or prepare for trial at the expense of family responsibilities.

⁛

Jean's Chinese parents, newly married, immigrated to Greenwood, Mississippi, in the late 1940s. Greenwood is a town of about 15,000 people, the majority of whom are Black, lying fifty miles east of the Mississippi River on the edge of its delta. Like other Chinese immigrants, Jean's parents found an opportunity in the gap between white people and Black people mandated by segregation. They opened a grocery store primarily serving Black customers. They had five children, of whom Jean is the eldest. The family lived in the back of the grocery store. Cantonese was spoken at home. Their Chinese ethnicity shaped their values and conduct. They were one of a half-dozen Asian families in Greenwood.

The photograph in Figure 4, taken in 1951 on the opening of the grocery store, provides a glimpse into the culture in which Jean grew up. The three white male officials on the left include the mayor of Greenwood and the family's landlord. They wear barely perceptible smiles. Jean's parents, both with wide smiles, stand a bit to the right. They look almost buoyant. Opening their store is an achievement. They are at ease with their white male visitors, whom Jean remembers as very kind. These local dignitaries had helped her parents get the approvals necessary to open the store. Jean's father holds Jean's sister in his arms. Her head is craned to the side, staring up with a serious expression at the official closest to her. A bit off to the right in this tableau stand two Black young men, maybe boys, each in a butcher apron and looking directly at the camera without expression.

Growing up in Greenwood, Jean became practiced at being a minority. Greenwood's residents were stratified by skin color. "Everyone knew their place according to the color of their skin. So I was used to a society in which my family didn't really belong anywhere; we weren't

Figure 4: Jean's father, mother, and sister with Greenwood officials at the opening of the family grocery store, 1951. Courtesy of Jean Jew.

a part of Black society, but we weren't a part of white society, either. Without my sister and three brothers, I wouldn't have had anyone to interact with socially." Public schools, and other public amenities, were segregated. Mississippi provided school textbooks that were labeled inside the cover—W for white and N for Negro. The N books were not used in the white schools. Chinese children—seldom more than three or four at any one time in the whole school—were permitted to attend white public schools. Jean recalls frequently hearing "ching chong, ching chong" or "Chink" directed at her in school. She pretended not to hear.

Jean's parents instructed the children in survival skills: know your place, do not cause trouble, and work hard at your studies. Solving the problems right in front of them, rather than speaking up about insults or slights, was their focus. The children worked in the store on the weekends and during the summer. During the school year, homework was their priority. Her mother bragged that Jean was checking out groceries and making change at the age of eight, standing on a box to reach the counter.

Keenly aware of the racial hierarchy that placed Chinese people between Black people and white people, "my parents would always tell us that education was the key to everything—that it didn't matter if whites thought they were better, because education would make the difference." Jean was usually the only nonwhite student in her class, and although she did not feel ostracized, neither was there any camaraderie. Perhaps because they sensed the challenges Jean faced in spite of her abilities, her white teachers took the time and extra effort to encourage and advocate for her. Upon her graduation, they insisted she receive an award recognizing her academic achievements. Jean's parents sent all five children to college.

Although Greenwood was a hot spot in the civil rights movement, the family did not discuss racial politics or injustice. The lynching of Emmett Till in 1955 occurred just ten miles from Greenwood. Mississippi's White Citizen's Council, committed to resisting school integration after the Supreme Court's *Brown v. Board of Education* decision, was founded in Greenwood. Medgar Evers, a college graduate, a World War II veteran, and a NAACP civil rights activist, was assassinated 100 miles away in Jackson, Mississippi, in the summer of 1963 by a white supremacist from Greenwood. James Meredith, who was the first African American to attend the University of Mississippi in 1962, organized a "Freedom from Fear" voting rights march from Memphis to Jackson in 1966 through Greenwood. After Meredith was shot and hospitalized, Stokely Carmichael delivered his famous Black Power speech in the Greenwood Broad Street Park. Following the assassination of Martin Luther King Jr., demonstrations broke out in Greenwood. Jean's family sheltered inside as their store windows were shattered. Jean reflected, "Growing up in a system like that prepares you for discrimination. It makes you accept it more readily because you've put up with it all your life. But it does give you strength."

The family did not talk about sex, either. For all Jean knew, storks dropped babies down the chimneys. Her father instructed her that only Chinese were suitable marriage partners. Dating had to wait for the person you would marry. This was brought home to Jean the summer after her first year in college. She accepted an invitation to a movie from a Chinese boy. When she announced it at lunch, her father choked on his food and left the table. She was told to come straight home by

9 p.m. When she arrived, her parents had closed the store early and were sitting with her siblings waiting for her return. Jean decided dating was too much trouble.

As she was growing up, Jean recalled her father saying, "It will be wonderful if one of you would be a doctor and another a lawyer and you could take care of any problems that the family might have or we might have in our old age." With the encouragement of her parents and teachers, Jean aimed high—to become a doctor. She earned her undergraduate degree in three years at H. Sophie Newcomb Memorial College, Tulane University's coordinate women's college, in New Orleans. For those three years, Jean lived and studied among women. When she went on to Tulane's School of Medicine in 1969, she studied among men. In her medical school class of about 135, more than 125 were men and just 2 or 3 were Asian American.[2] Jean found friends among her male classmates while working in labs or over cadaver tables. She was not mocked with anti-Asian or sexist name calling, although more than one male professor pontificated that women did not belong in medicine. She did not perceive her race or ethnicity as a barrier. Her parents' maxim, that if she worked hard enough everything was possible, was proving true.

Jean met and worked with Professor Terence Williams while at Tulane's School of Medicine. Williams ran a well-funded laboratory with a large staff, including several medical students, of whom Jean was one. Williams was a white man, twenty years her senior, and married to Glenys Williams, M.D., who also worked in the lab. He and Glenys treated Jean like their daughter. Along with other staff and students in his lab, Jean worked with Williams into the evenings. Dinner was often sandwiches in the lab or a meal in a nearby restaurant before an evening of work. No one suggested that this was indicative of a sexual relationship. When she graduated with her M.D. in 1973, Jean aimed at an academic career and chose to become a research scientist rather than a clinical professor. At the time, the number of women research scientist faculty in medical school was infinitesimal.

In 1973, Williams was recruited for the position of chair of the University of Iowa's Anatomy Department, which he accepted. The department was riven with faculty disputes and had been without a chair for years. Williams's research program came with him. His wife accepted a clinical faculty position in the Family Practice Department in Iowa's College of Medicine. Williams invited three Tulane staff to come to Iowa—one man with a junior faculty appointment and two women, including Jean, as postdoctoral fellows.

Iowa City was a town of about 50,000 residents in 1973, nearly all white. Cathy Park Hong, a Korean woman, has written about her experience in 2002 as a graduate student at the University's Iowa Writers' Workshop.[3] She describes an "underhanded slow drip of racism" in Iowa City. A male classmate "ripped" on her first collection of poems in a social media post, suggested that minority poets be exterminated, and was not upbraided by a single comment on the post. Hong responded by scrubbing her poetry of Asian American ethnic markers. How much did Jean's race and ethnicity account for the harassment she experienced in the College of Medicine? She felt her gender was more of an irritant in the white male culture of the medical school than her race or ethnicity. Race was a factor, however. "Race put an edge on it—made it more tantalizing, juicy, lurid, visual."

At the University of Iowa, Jean worked in the lab with Williams as she had at Tulane. Sexual and racial slurs began where none had been evident at Tulane. She had no strategy for responding beyond what her parents had taught her—keep a stiff upper lip and go on about her business. She was in the lab most of the time, including evenings and weekends, which left no time for a social life. Had she had the time, there were few other women faculty and no Asian Americans to get to know.

As years went by, Jean built a successful academic career. In 1979, she was the only tenured woman in any of the basic science departments in the College of Medicine. She proved to be a fine teacher. She was the director of the Medical Neuroanatomy course, a required course for degree programs in the medical school. Over two hundred students were enrolled each year. As director, Jean gave lectures, recruited other faculty to give lectures, and supervised students in the laboratory.

Jean was voted Teacher of the Year six times by the first- and second-year medical students, and she was nominated twelve times. She served on the Anatomy Department's appointments committee, responsible

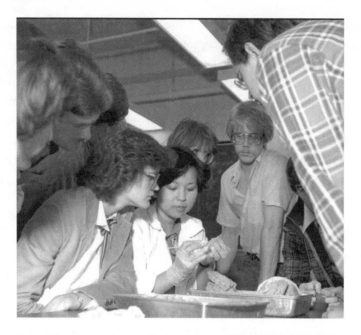

Figure 5: Jean Jew teaching medical students in a lab session of the Medical Neuroscience course, circa 1986. Courtesy of the Department of Anatomy, University of Iowa.

for recruiting and recommending new faculty candidates, and on collegiate committees reviewing clinical departments and medical school admissions.

⋄⋄⋄

We did not know all this about each other when I agreed to represent Jean. In the weeks that followed, we were disembodied voices over the phone, considering the pros and cons of different initiatives. We listened attentively, shared musings, and took the necessary time. Through the language we chose, our silences and our laughter, we came to know one another. Our discussion of options rotated and swiveled among several objectives, gyroscope-like, until we found our way forward.

I felt the stakes were too high to consider litigation. "Let's make an internal complaint of sexual harassment to the university." Jean questioned this suggestion. Since the university did not have a sexual harassment policy or investigation protocol, a faculty complaint would use the established grievance protocol. "It will be futile. Nothing has come of my complaints."

Jean's peremptory rejection of an internal complaint welled up from deep bruises left by previous rebuffs. Chief among these was the administration's response to her sexual harassment complaint after Kaelber shouted epithets at her in 1979. Making a complaint had been difficult for Jean, but she was convinced it was necessary. She thought that if anyone could stop the harassment, Dean Eckstein could. Eckstein's response: "These outrageous things said about you are being used as a device to get at Dr. Williams, not you. Iowa City is a small town, and it's a goldfish bowl, and a single woman has these sorts of problems when she's working in this environment."

Not mollified by Eckstein's response, Jean met with May Brodbeck, then vice president for academic affairs. A distinguished philosopher, scientist, and feminist whose academic career began in the late 1950s, Brodbeck would know how it felt to be the sole woman on a faculty—in Jean's case, the sole tenured woman in the basic science departments in the College of Medicine. Jean stated her problem to Brodbeck, "Whispering in the halls was bad enough, but what Dr. Kaelber did was worse. He gave voice to what I had been aware of but was not said out loud to my face. He was so blatant and public and so sure he could do this with impunity." Jean had expected Brodbeck to understand how damaging Kaelber's conduct was.

Brodbeck's advice was pragmatic. "Don't grieve this. I don't think we can do anything about this now that will not make matters worse for you." Incredulous, Jean said, "These sexual allegations are absolutely not true and are especially damaging for a woman. How can something like this be allowed?" Brodbeck was sympathetic but unyielding.

Jean concluded no one at the university would do anything to stop Kaelber and others. Four years later, based on this experience, she was not enthusiastic about my proposal to make another complaint directly to the university.

I pushed back. I argued to Jean that the university's refusal to respond to her earlier complaints in 1979 did not foretell how it would respond now that the 1980 Equal Employment Opportunity Commission guidelines on sexual harassment required employers to investigate complaints of sexual harassment and take corrective action when warranted. An internal complaint had a decent chance of being kept reasonably quiet, unlike a lawsuit. Court decisions prohibiting sexual cartoons and slurs, at least on construction sites, were emerging. My hope and expectation were that the university would conclude that it had a duty to stop the sexual harassment of a faculty member in its College of Medicine. I do not recall that we gave much thought at this point, as we would later, to whether Jean should complain of racial and national origin harassment as well as sex harassment.

"Let's give the university the benefit of the doubt," I urged.

Jean reluctantly agreed.

CHAPTER 3

A University Response

OUR FIRM'S STATIONERY was the color of green tea, distinguishing it from the cream-colored vellum used by many law firms. Dayton
Herman & Graham scrolled across the top in a green/gray font rather
than embossed black letters. Listed on the left side were the names of
the nine partners. Mine was the last name. Four associate attorneys were
listed on the right. Our stationery communicated: *we are a different kind
of law firm; we are informal; we work in the public interest; take notice.*

My January 1984 letter to Vice President for Academic Affairs Richard Remington, on Jean's behalf, demanded his attention, not just
because of the color of the stationery and letterhead, but because of
the letter's length: nine single-spaced pages reciting ten years of harassing incidents, citing sexual harassment law, and asking the university
to conduct an investigation and take corrective action. Beginning in
an accommodating tone, I went on to note that although Jean wished
"to facilitate a much-needed period of stability in her department,"
she could not continue to ignore the "extent of the sex bias . . . the sor-
didness of its manifestation and the University's failure to inquire into
it or correct it." An accommodating tone resurfaced at the end. "We
seek an informal resolution which proceeds with as much dignity and
propriety as possible under the circumstances."

The first response from the university was a message from Julia
Mears, assistant to the president of the university. The message slip
noted that she was "an attorney calling on behalf of V.P. Remington."
When we spoke, Mears informed me that the university did not have
a specific policy prohibiting sexual harassment. Instead, the University
Policy on Human Rights governed. Mears proposed following the university's grievance process for faculty—a panel of three faculty would
investigate, provide a report, and make recommendations to the vice

president for academic affairs. Mears's proposal was not objectionable, but it lacked details essential to ensuring a fair and competent panel process. Eight months of negotiations followed.

⁛

As predictable and tedious as a metronome, Mears and I went back and forth negotiating these details. With each exchange our relationship became increasingly contentious. Mears was hired at the university in 1981, one year out of law school. She worked in the president's office. I would come to believe she was attracted, moth-like, to the inner circle of university decision makers. She was fiercely protective of her superiors.

Mears worked closely with Mary Jo Small, a long-serving senior administrator, vice president for human resources, responsible for non-academic university personnel. Small was a no-nonsense, middle-aged, midwestern university administrator. She was a complex person—a sometimes advocate for women's rights and LGBTQ employees, she was personally conservative. She valued her place within the university decision-making circle, and she was also a fierce protector of the university's reputation.

I had much in common with these two women. Mears and Small had returned to law school and graduate school after some years in the working world. As ranking women in a man's world, they were trailblazers of a sort. They had advocated for women's issues. Despite having so much in common, our differences became predominant.

As if positioned at the end of a laundry chute, I pictured Mears and Small collecting the university's dirty linen—Jean's complaint was one—and supervising the cleaning process. Their influence with male superiors appeared dependent on being effective laundresses of nasty situations. They decided: no bleach on this one; gentle cycle and cold water for that; spin the hell out of those; hang that out to dry. Traditional women's work, this laundering fell to a tier of professional white women who were deeply invested in the way things were. Not surprisingly, they were allied with dominant, powerful men in their milieu and were at odds with women, like us, who complained about them.[1]

⁂

In negotiations with Mears, my top priority was selecting panelists who were competent, committed to a fair process, and recognized by their peers as opinion leaders of integrity. None could be dependent on the dean of the College of Medicine, John Eckstein, for departmental funding, professional status, or other endeavors. None could have prior opinions about the Anatomy Department, its faculty, or the history of rumors. All panelists needed to be familiar with the culture of the College of Medicine. Three faculty met these criteria, were mutually acceptable, and agreed to serve. From the College of Medicine, Professors Hansjoerg Kolder and Mark Stewart were joined by a tenured associate professor in the College of Business, Nancy Hauserman, who was an attorney and chaired the panel. Remington provided the panelists with a charge listing the questions for investigation. A court reporter was secured to send a daily transcript of the proceedings to the attorneys were not to attend.

The panel hearing was held on five days during August and September 1984. The atmosphere in the Anatomy Department crackled as faculty witnesses were taken away from pressing tasks and instructed to appear in the president's office. With only the sketchiest information about the subject matter of the inquiry, they walked from the College of Medicine across the Iowa River and up the hill to Jessup Hall. They waited in the vestibule of the president's office until they were called into the conference room, where they were sworn to tell the truth, and then asked to respond to the panelists' questions.

Jean followed her daily routine while the panel worked. As she had for years, she picked up Williams in her car, drove to work, parked, and walked into the College of Medicine, knowing that people were watching, but acting as if they were not. She taught medical students. She conducted experiments. She attended committee meetings. Faculty who passed her in the halls looked askance. She projected normalcy, all the while sensing disapproval, prurient curiosity, and perplexity.

Jean and I were traveling on parallel tracks—she through a fraught and dangerous time; I was invested in other efforts that distracted me from her vulnerability. We were collaborators on the journey, yet only Jean traveled on a ridge line of personal risk. During the hearing process, in spite of instructions from the panel to all witnesses not to discuss their testimony with others, Jean found herself the topic of a local evening TV newscast reporting that Williams and Jew were "close academically, financially, and, sources say, personally . . . his [Williams's] star has fallen and now hers [Jew's] has, too."[2] Jean was told that the newscaster, Jim Lyons, had called Tomanek's lab a few days prior and spoken with him behind a closed door. The head shot of Jean that accompanied the news story was available, to Jean's knowledge, in departmental files that only faculty could access. We suspected Tomanek was the source of the story but were never able to confirm it.

I did not have a speaking part—no need to prepare for direct or cross-examination of witnesses. Thick envelopes containing transcripts of the testimony arrived periodically on my desk—755 pages in all. Absent from the transcripts was the firmness that must have resonated in the timbre of Jean's voice, the sly intimations and fierceness in her adversaries' voices, the abject and angry tones of university administrators, and the panelists' occasional exasperated sighs.

The transcripts were my first introductions to the anatomy faculty and the university administrators. Witnesses testified forthrightly. Few had met with attorneys to polish their statements. Artful rhetoric had not yet been substituted for unique voices. Emotions were closer to the surface; credibility easier to discern. Lies were not well cloaked. Although I had never met them, by reading the transcript I learned about each of these men—their vocabulary, where they placed emphasis in their narratives, and the excuses they brought to bear.

⁞⁞⁞

Jean was the first witness on Wednesday, August 29, 1984. She explained that she filed the complaint because of a pattern of sexual harassment almost from her first day at the university and "attempts that I've made to do anything about it through administrative channels have really not been carried out, to my satisfaction." She noted that it was a hard decision to file a formal complaint and recognized it could do more harm than good. "But after ten years of it, I think that I want to take the chance and see. And that's really all I have to say about why I'm doing this."[3] Jean invited the panelists' questions. The subsequent exchange covers fifty pages of transcript.

Tomanek was questioned on the second day of the hearing. He denied that he made statements about a sexual relationship between Jean and Williams. Instead, he said everyone else was talking about it. "The rumor of a sexual relationship is constantly being brought up by numerous people, it was so popular it was a general thing, a joke after a while. Over the years the amount of information from a whole variety of sources that seems to support this whole thing was so overwhelming, that it just kept popping up."[4] While denying his role in keeping sexual slurs fresh, Tomanek acknowledged he asked suggestive questions of colleagues—"Did you overhear them checking into the same room?" "Were they holding hands at the restaurant?" He spread rumors others started—"I didn't see it, but I heard they were observed holding hands in a restaurant." "I wasn't there but somebody who was said they had adjoining hotel rooms." By these means—sibilant whispers, sotto voce—he had kept sexual rumors fresh in Jean's workplace.

When questioned by the panel, Kaelber went on the offensive. He purported to have relied on "reasonably good evidence" of a sexual relationship between Jean and Williams. He stressed his vituperative dislike for Jean, "[a] hell of a lot of people dislike Dr. Jew. But I am not talking about sex. I am talking about abilities, function, actions, teaching, et cetera." Kaelber singled her out for his animus because she received "a salary raise that made practically half of us look like a bunch of fools."[5]

Terence Williams was also questioned. He had been forced to resign as chair of the department a year before, following a diagnosis of multiple sclerosis. Williams thought the harassment resulted from a combination of several factors—Jean's association with him, his unpopularity with faculty, her very good performance, her M.D. that other faculty did not have, and her independent nature. Jean was "outspoken and she's not meant to be outspoken. The associate dean spoke to me quite firmly and quietly that I should control her, speaking as though she was a little bit of fluff." Asked about Jean's contribution to their common research program, Williams said, "Into all hours of the night she is delving into the literature and handling all kinds of things. When I'm too busy to do it. Indeed, very often I was the person who wasn't able to contribute all that much, and out of her kindness, she had done more than half of the work." Finally, about whether he had a sexual relationship with Jean, Williams denied it with a flourish, "Dr. Jew is as clean in her behavior and ethics and habits as Caesar's wife was said to be." Later, when asked again, he abandoned the flourish and denied it with one syllable, "No."[6]

The transcript reveals the panelists struggling to understand and find the right words to describe the relationship between Jean and Williams. "People still puzzle . . . still seem to want a label for what is between us," wrote Hope Jahren, a woman scientist and professor, about her collaboration with a male scientist. She observed that none of the available words—chums, soulmates, comrades, accomplices—adequately captures a close scientific collaboration between a man and a woman infused with creative energy and devoid of erotic chemistry. Jahren concluded, "I do us because us is what I know how to do."[7] Jean could have said the same about her work with Williams.

Dean Eckstein was short-tempered with the panelists' questions. In the fourteen years he had served as dean, John Eckstein was known as the final decision maker on all matters in the College of Medicine, and, some said, in the university. University presidents were reputed to serve at Eckstein's pleasure. He had outlasted several. Seeing Eckstein crossing campus, one could easily mistake him for an ordinary administrator going about an ordinary university job. A home-grown Iowan, he had a square face, with jowls covering heavy bones and a direct, pugnacious stare. He was built like a hard-working farmer. Despite appearances, Eckstein was no ordinary Iowan. Under his leadership, the College of Medicine expanded its national reputation and its powerful position in the university. He had an abiding commitment to the school, a poker face, and a willingness to wield power, even if harsh. He was much admired for his ability to find ways to achieve growth and change in a truculent medical school culture.

Eckstein acknowledged knowing about what he called "the gossip" about Jean, deploring it and yet taking no action to stop it. He was questioned closely about his inaction following Kaelber's tirade in 1979. His excuse: he was at a loss about what to do. "Well, most of the information that had to do with Dr. Jew was in the nature of gossip. . . . Now, I had no basis for going to people in the department."[8]

Panelists pressed him. "So all throughout those years, you have been aware of allegations within the department of sexual harassment, you talked it over with the appropriate administrative officer, but you didn't have a need to go personally to talk to individual members within the department?"

Eckstein responded, "I was not aware of sexual harassment in the department. I don't know what sexual harassment really is. After all this business came up, I found myself being rather confused." Eckstein's firm grasp on the tiller at the College of Medicine for over a decade made it difficult for the panelists to credit his self-portrait as Gulliver-like, immobilized by myriad, university-based grounding lines.

Panelists pressed him again. "But creating an environment so difficult for her that it stunted her growth. I wonder what you see as a remedial action against those? To avoid the continuation of the harassing behavior by some of her colleagues in anatomy against her. What action do you see?"

Eckstein provided a litany of increasingly testy excuses. "I don't know the extent—I don't know what they really have done. I have no firsthand knowledge except the documents that I have seen and the gossip that I have heard. I don't know what Dr. Tomanek really did." And: "I don't think there is any physical harm that has been claimed by her." And: "What about harassment of other members of the department, what about harassment of the dean, what about harassment of the vice president for academic affairs?" And: Williams "did not ask for help in dealing with this." And: the vice president for academic affairs "said no when I asked her was I expected to do something?" And: Jean "has not appealed to me."

Toward the end of his testimony, Eckstein sensed the panelists were not with him. "Your questions are coming at me in a context that I didn't expect, somewhat. Perhaps I haven't been as helpful as I could." His excuses were not working.

⁰⁰⁰

There was only one witness who surprised us. When asked by the panel if he had heard rumors, Rex Montgomery, associate dean of the medical school and newly appointed acting chair of the Anatomy Department, said he had been told that a "graduate student who had left the Department of Anatomy is reported to have seen such an act [sex between Jean and Williams]. I did not look into it."⁹ While acting chair of the sinking ship of the Anatomy Department, charged with righting it, Montgomery fled the wheelhouse rather than steer through the smut.

Unlike Montgomery, the panelists were not of a mind to let this pass. By the next morning, they had identified the graduate student who was the source of this story—Jane McCutcheon—and had her on a speaker phone. She said that one night in 1979 or 1980 she was working as a technician in Tomanek's lab as an undergraduate student at the age of nineteen or twenty. She opened the door to the Anatomy Department library and saw a man from behind, who turned. She believed he was Williams, standing in front of a library table. Two legs were visible on either side of the man. "They were in a position where they could have been making love."¹⁰ McCutcheon did not see intercourse. "Everybody knew that those two were together," Jean just "jumped into my mind, and the legs essentially didn't contradict that. She's a very small woman and she's Oriental, and the length of the legs and the skin color were not such that it popped into my mind that, 'Oh, that couldn't be Jean Jew,' but I couldn't say for sure it was." Reading the transcript of her testimony, I thought McCutcheon might be about to say the legs were yellow, but she stopped just short. She followed Tomanek's lead. "Dr. Tomanek has very strong views on extramarital relationships. He really disapproved of Dr. Williams personally," McCutcheon said.

The day after I read McCutcheon's testimony, I called Jean. Had she known about McCutcheon? What was McCutcheon referring to? What do you make of it? Her response, "she's lying," was a declaration that brooked no follow-up. I did not press Jean further.

At the end of the hearing, the panel invited Jean to return and comment on the testimony. She used the occasion to answer a question the panel had not asked her. No, she had not had a sexual relationship with Williams, not in the past or now. There was never any evidence for it and there couldn't be any because it wasn't true. Jean went on to point out the fault lines in McCutcheon's narrative. Jean and McCutcheon had never met. The library was in the main corridor across from the main office. It was usually unlocked, but if locked, virtually every faculty member and graduate student had a key to the three doors. The janitors used the library for their evening breaks.

At the end of the hearing, Jean's anger at her colleagues resonates on the transcript page. "What I find so appalling is so many people have accepted it as true."

CHAPTER 4

Opportunity Lost

TUESDAY AFTER THANKSGIVING, November 27, 1984, a year after Jean first called me, she and I received the report of the faculty panel's investigation.[1] In seven single-spaced pages, they unanimously answered the questions posed to them in Remington's original charge. All answers were in Jean's favor.

The panel concluded that vilifying comments and scurrilous sketches of Jean were common knowledge. "Virtually every witness save one admitted to having heard, if not participated in, conversations about the alleged relationship." The report did not spare professors Tomanek and Kaelber. Tomanek "was evasive but the panel has reason to think that he has been the initiator or one of the initiators of the defamation of Dr. Jew." And "Clearly Dr. Kaelber publicly defamed Dr. Jew." Kaelber's tone was "bitter and hostile." There was nothing in Jane McCutcheon's testimony "suggesting veracity." The panel declared that the alleged sexual relationship between Jean and Williams was not substantiated.

Turning to the university administration's response, the panel did not mince words. All of the key administrators were aware of the harassment at least by January 1979. None of the administrators "took any steps to improve the situation for Dr. Jew," with two possible exceptions— replacing Williams as chair and convening the panel's investigation. The panel found that administrators did not attempt to determine the author(s) of the graffiti or the anonymous letters. They failed to "investigate actively the harassing behavior."

The report detailed the information that led the panel to conclude that Jean's treatment was related to her sex. No male faculty member, including those who came to the department with Williams, received comparable adverse treatment. Faculty views that Jean's research findings were dependent on Williams were based on assumptions that women's accomplishments were dependent on the insights of men. Using accusations of an extramarital sexual relationship to discredit harms a woman disproportionately. The harassment also related to Jean's ethnicity, national origin, and race. No male faculty were of color. The incidents tainted Jean's work environment. Harassment had a destructive effect on Jean's "professional and personal reputations, both locally and nationally." It also probably affected "her productivity and the quality of her teaching."

The panel's recommendations to Remington were designed to give Jean's reputation a deep cleaning, which was what she most wanted. The president should "immediately" issue a statement condemning sexual harassment and committing to a work environment free from it. More specifically, the administration should issue a statement, with a mutu-ally agreed-on text, that "exonerates Dr. Jew." To the Anatomy Depart-ment, the administration should make clear that no further harassment will be tolerated. Faculty, staff, and graduate students should have an opportunity to learn of the panel's findings and expectations for reso-lution. Immediate efforts should be made to ascertain the author(s) of the anonymous letters and graffiti. A customized promotion process with written standards, subject to the strictest oversight by adminis-trators, should be implemented for Jean. Tomanek and Kaelber should have "individual conferences" with administrators and told "to cease and desist any harassment and defamation of Dr. Jew" and "the con-sequences of persisting."

These factual findings and recommendations by objective senior faculty members with a deep understanding of the culture of the Col-lege of Medicine settled on us like spring sunshine—fading hurtful stains and nurturing new beginnings. I was pleased. So far, things were going as I had hoped. The panel report provided a solid foundation for university corrective action.

Jean's reaction to the panel report was relief. She had feared that faculty might view the sexual slurs the way the administration had—as the sort of conduct a young, single woman, working with a senior male, had to expect. Faculty panelists could have been persuaded by witnesses who argued that Williams and Jew had brought this on themselves. Throughout the panel process, Jean was worried about the outcome.

"I'm just so relieved." Jean said to me. Her voice sounded sober, not celebratory. "I don't know if any other faculty members would have had the courage to come out and say it was outrageous."

⋮⋮⋮

Bolstering the panel report, the transcript provided a unique opportunity for university administrators to listen in as panelists discussed their reactions to what they were learning. Not only the quality of the panel's questions and the witnesses' responses, but the quality of the panelist discussions among themselves is captured in the transcript. No panelist was silenced; no panelist was showboating; no one was rushing to the finish line; each one listened to each other and the witnesses and asked probing questions. The panel process was transparent and accountable.[2]

With the panel report in hand and the transcript documenting their process, I expected the university to act on the recommendations. Not so. The university was silent. Tensions escalated as silence continued. Faculty in the Department of Anatomy were waiting. Jean and I were waiting. People who gave testimony to the panel were waiting. Panelists were waiting. Silence was not neutral. It did not foster a stable status quo—just the opposite. Slurs gathered momentum in the hiatus. A colleague reported that on a recent evening a philosophy professor asked, "What happened to that professor in the department who was having an affair with a Chinese girl?" A few weeks after we received the panel report, Jean wrote to me, "I arrived this morning to find that the nameplate on my lab door has been partially ripped away . . . vicious and telling!" Faculty adversaries spread rumors that the panel's purpose had been to investigate Jean for wrongdoing, not to investigate wrongdoing against her.

In early spring 1985 Jean wrote me, "Have you heard anything from the university regarding the progress towards or plans for resolving our complaint? Do they need nudging?" Yes, and apparently so did I. I was embarrassed. I began making periodic calls to Julia Mears for updates. She offered excuses for inaction—they were awaiting the conclusion of a hand-writing expert, Remington was with his dying mother, and other faculty disputes were taking up their time. I responded, "The university's inaction has worsened the harassment."

Jean and I were not alone in our frustration. Five months after the panel report, one faculty panelist wrote to Remington. Describing the panel process as difficult and emotionally draining, he asked, "I write now to ask if you could tell us something of what has resulted. It is a strange experience to work hard on such an assignment and not to know what the outcome of the various issues was." He indicated all three panelists would be grateful to know the outcome, "at least in general terms."[3] I do not know if he received a response.

In May, Mears wrote to me: "I am sorry I have been unable to respond to your recent letter. The demonstrators have left the offices, and the carpets have all been cleaned. I will be in touch with you soon." I did not know what she referred to when she mentioned "demonstrators." I just knew that prioritizing other concerns, at the expense of Jean's, followed a well-established pattern. I wrote to Mears again in August 1985. "Nearly nine months have passed since the panel issued its findings. . . . I can only reiterate that the University needs to take seriously the necessity of a meaningful proposal regarding the relief to which Dr. Jew is entitled." If I received a response, it was nothing substantive.

Mears and Small called in mid-October. Could I come to Iowa City to see if we could settle Jean's case? Of course. To negotiate a special promotion process for Jean, they proposed that she and Eckstein have a one-to-one meeting without attorneys present. I urged her to do so. It did not go well. Eckstein pounded his fist in a thinly veiled attempt at intimidation and declared, "I'm not going to be told how to run my medical school!" Jean's comment to me afterward, "You don't realize how much you ask of me."

The university made three unyielding demands at that point and repeatedly in the years that followed. The most significant was that Jean sign a general release of all claims in advance of knowing the details of the proposed promotion process or its outcome. The university also demanded that Jean sign a confidentiality agreement not to discuss her case or the settlement. Finally, all relief to Jean was contingent on waiver of our attorney's fees, which were about $15,000 at that point. This last, an attempt to trade Jean's interests off against my firm's interests, was an unsuccessful tactic. Despite repeatedly hammering on this wedge, the university found no purchase between Jean and me, then or later.

We had to let go of our hopes for university action on the panel recommendations. The reality was that administrators were firmly committed to inaction. The status quo could not be dislodged by a push from us or a shove from a panel. No matter that the university designed and chose the panel; no matter that university leaders could see how thoroughly the panel worked; no matter how carefully the panel considered the information; and no matter how emphatic its final recommendations—none of it moved them to action.

The panel report gave administrators something they could use to help Jean. When they did not, she concluded it wasn't that they could not help her, but that they *would* not help her. Jean had anticipated this outcome, yet held out hope that the university really cared about her. Now we had circled back to where Jean had started. Our hopes notwithstanding, Jean's intuitions had been correct. A complaint process within the university was futile.

PART II

❖❖❖

Recourse to the Courts

CHAPTER 5

Hard Decisions

STEPPING INTO ANY litigation is like beginning a slog across a wetland. The ground may or may not provide sufficient support to cover the distance. Resources are needed for the journey, though one cannot know at the outset how much or for how long. The vagaries of the terrain remain to be discovered. Consequences bubble up when least expected. Threats may emerge from wild creatures en route. Before beginning, there are several preparations to make—analyzing the applicable law, investigating pertinent facts, locating human and financial resources, and choosing among judicial forums. Not glamorous or dramatic, this work is essential. If not done thoroughly, it spells the difference between success and failure.

When I took Jean on as a client, I anticipated helping her through an internal investigation process that would likely result in corrective action by the university. I thought ten hours of my time would just about do it. When I read the faculty panel's report, I was confident an informal resolution was achievable. In October 1985, I was convinced otherwise.

I was stunned by how significantly I had underestimated the university's resistance. Ironically, my miscalculation, erroneous as it was, may have been ultimately productive. Minimizing future impediments helps us engage in daunting projects, economist A. O. Hirschman, argued. "The only way in which we can bring our creative resources fully into play is by misjudging the nature of the task, by presenting it to ourselves as more routine, simple, undemanding of genuine creativity than it will turn out to be."[1] Not knowing what lay ahead, we had begun. Had we known, we might have abandoned the effort at the outset.

The consequences of having taken that first step were now apparent. We had to decide whether to file a lawsuit without clear legal precedent. Courts had not addressed whether spreading sexual slurs in

47

the workplace behind a woman's back was analogous to demands for sexual favors, unwelcome gropes, or nude calendars in the lunchroom. It would be up to us to make the case that Title VII prohibited the full range of misogynistic behaviors, including sexual name-calling, intended to keep a woman out of a workplace where she was not wanted.

Nearly two years had passed since the limerick appeared in the men's room. We did not have evidence that Tomanek was responsible for the limerick, but we wanted to preserve Jean's right to prove it in state court under state law if evidence emerged. The Iowa statute of limitations for a defamation claim was two years. A lawsuit against Tomanek had to be filed by October 31, 1985, to include the limerick.

⁂

I don't recall that I talked with Jean about the historical underpinnings of Title VII, the federal statute prohibiting discrimination in employment, although I taught its history to undergraduates in the 1970s. At the request of a feminist historian, Sara Evans, a few feminist law students joined together to teach a course, "Women and the Law," at the University of Minnesota's College of Liberal Arts. We began the course with the 1873 U.S. Supreme Court decision in Myra Bradwell's case, holding that Illinois could reasonably conclude that a woman was unfit to be a lawyer. A concurring opinion went so far as to say this was foreordained by God. "The paramount destiny and mission of woman are to fulfill the noble and benign offices of wife and mother. This is the law of the Creator."[2]

A century later, a new law prohibited excluding women from most occupations. Shepherded through Congress by Lyndon Johnson following John F. Kennedy's assassination, as initially proposed, Title VII of the 1964 Civil Rights Act prohibited employment discrimination based on race, color, religion, and national origin, but not sex. During debate on the floor of the House of Representatives, an amendment was offered to add sex to the classes protected from discrimination by Title VII. Sometimes described as a last-ditch amendment to defeat the Civil Rights Act, in fact, the amendment to add sex was preceded by persistent lobbying from women and civil rights advocates. An unlikely coalition in the House of Representatives passed the bill. After one of the longest Senate debates in history, the 1964 Civil Rights Act, including a prohibition on sex discrimination at work, was signed into law by President Johnson and became effective in August 1965.[3]

As initially passed, Title VII exempted all "educational institutions with respect to the employment of individuals to perform work connected with the educational activities of such institutions."[4] This amendment codified a tradition of judicial deference to personnel decisions made by higher education institutions and religious schools. The exemption was nullified eight years later when Congress passed Title IX of the Equal Employment Opportunity Act of 1972.[5] The House committee report explained the need to end sex discrimination in higher education employment. "In the field of higher education ... in the area of sex discrimination, women have long been invited to participate as students in the academic process, but without the prospect of gaining employment as serious scholars."[6] One year after Title IX was enacted and less than a decade after Title VII had passed, Jean began working at the University of Iowa.

People of color entered white, male-dominated workplaces in the 1970s and faced race-based hostility. In time the courts recognized race-based harassment at work as violative of Title VII's prohibitions on race and color discrimination. Judicial recognition of sex-based harassment lagged behind, despite its prevalence. Even feminist women law students teaching courses on women and the law in the mid-1970s (of whom I was one) did not name sexual harassment or teach that it was prohibited in the workplace by Title VII.

The term "sexual harassment" is thought to have originated in the summer of 1975 when Lin Farley was planning a speak-out at Cornell University to address what she was learning was a common experience for working women.[7] Women organizers debated what words would capture the offensive conduct to be discussed. Sexual abuse, sexual coercion, and sexual intimidation had some currency, but were geared to blatant behaviors. The women settled on "sexual harassment" as inclusive of the range of gender-based hostility.

A 1975 New York Times article reported on the speak-out and on sexual harassment.[8] Government officials were quoted, legal initiatives were documented, and women's stories of harassment were told. The

Figure 6: Sexual harassment speak-out poster 1975. Courtesy of
K. C. Wagner.

article made the case that sexual harassment was widespread in the
workplace. Among its many readers was Jean Jew.

The first lawsuits alleging sexual harassment as a form of sex discrimination under Title VII were dismissed outright—tossed on a scrap
heap of failed cases.[9] Trial judges, analyzing sexual demands imposed by
supervisors on women subordinates, accepted the rationale that sexual
propositions were personal misconduct, not caused by employers, so
employers could not be held to account under Title VII. Such sexual
demands were "nothing more than a personal proclivity, peculiarity,
or mannerism . . . satisfying a personal urge . . . with no relationship
to the nature of the employment."[10] Requiring employers to officiate
biological urges would swamp both employers and the courts. "The

only sure way an employer could avoid such charges would be to have employees who were asexual."[11]

Six leading early cases were all appealed. By the late 1970s, four U.S. Circuit Courts of Appeals had held that sexual harassment at work was a cognizable claim under Title VII.[12] The Circuit Court opinions did not rule on whether a particular plaintiff had proved that she was subjected to sexual harassment in her workplace—just that she had a right to try to prove it. The prohibited behavior came to be labeled quid pro quo sexual harassment, understood as "this" (job benefits) for "that" (sex) or the threat of "this" (firing) for "that" (refusing sex).[13] None of these cases arose in educational workplaces.

The women who brought these groundbreaking sexual harassment cases were frequently women of color. Black women were burdened with a legacy of sexual exploitation and stereotypes about sexual availability, making them particularly vulnerable to sexual harassment at work. Civil rights activism in the 1960s gave them some confidence in the courts and the strength to complain. Black women were plaintiffs in three of the six cases that went up on appeal—Paula Barnes, Diane Williams, and Margaret Miller.[14] The claim of a Black woman employed at Cornell University, Carmita Wood, was an impetus for the speakout at Cornell in 1975. The plaintiff in the important 1981 case of *Bundy v. Jackson* was a Black woman.[15] Michelle Vinson, the plaintiff who brought the first sexual harassment case decided by the U.S. Supreme Court in 1986, was also Black.[16] Black women suffered grievously from sexual harassment and took to the courts courageously. But the judicial decisions that affirmed the rights of these women made no mention (in rare cases only one or two mentions) of the plaintiff's race.

Two influential women, one white and one Black, stand out at the end of the 1970s for pushing the law of sexual harassment forward. Catharine MacKinnon's 1979 treatise *Sexual Harassment of Working Women*,[17] was the first thorough legal analysis of quid pro quo sexual harassment in the workplace. MacKinnon called on the courts to see sexual harassment as a social and economic phenomenon, not a biological urge. In 1980, the EEOC, under the leadership of a Black woman, Eleanor Holmes Norton, announced that sex-based hostile speech and conduct, not just physical touching or demands for physical sex, also wronged women workers. The 1980 EEOC Guidelines on Sexual Harassment prohibited two types of sexual harassment—quid pro quo harassment and sexually hostile work environment harassment.[18] In 1981, the D.C. Circuit Court followed the EEOC Guidelines in holding that sexually hostile work environment harassment, even when it did not lead to loss of tangible job benefits, was prohibited by Title VII.[19]

⁂

The EEOC Guidelines provided the legal framework for Jean's complaint of a sexually hostile work environment, but whether she could prove a case of hostile work environment sexual harassment given her facts—a sophisticated workplace, no sexual propositioning or touching, and institutional norms of academic freedom—were cutting-edge questions. Proving a Title VII case against sexist slurs by faculty members at a university would be particularly difficult. In a university, words are the coin of the realm and are protected by the unique policies of tenure and academic freedom. These norms had led the courts and Congress initially to defer to university academic employment decisions.[20]

Even if Jean could prove a Title VII claim, would there be a tangible remedy for her? She was still employed as a tenured associate professor, still salaried, still teaching and researching. We could not prove she lost pay as a consequence of sexual harassment unless we convinced a judge to order her promotion, which would be very unlikely due to judicial deference. Even if promotion were ordered, Jean's back pay damages would be limited to the increment between an associate professor and a full professor's salary. Damages for emotional distress, which subsequently became the source of large financial awards in sexual harassment suits, were not available under Title VII at that time.[21]

Legal shoals were compounded by extralegal problems. Jean's goal, to silence the sexual slurs, was at odds with a legal process that required her to repeat, in public documents and in a courtroom, the awful things that had been said about her. A lawsuit could amplify the slurs by handing defendants a megaphone to repeat them, ostensibly in self-defense. Media would cover the dispute. Public criticism decrying Jean's assault on colleagues could emerge. As the legal process took its own sweet time (another predictable feature), it would be Jean's word against that of her opponents. An authoritative decision by a judge or jury debunking the slurs could come too late to resurrect her reputation.

Reputational damage from the stigma that sticks to a plaintiff suing a major institution was also likely. Cast as a troublemaker in the University of Iowa, disparagement beyond its walls would follow. Rumors that an academic woman makes trouble travel among universities like electricity on a wire. So far, Jean had received her share of national grants, achieved publishable results, and was an accomplished teacher. Filing a lawsuit could change that.

If we lost her case, her pain and shame would balloon and her remaining reputation would be eviscerated. Deciding to sue meant committing to win, yet that result would be beyond our control. A lawsuit was a bad option, but it was the only option we could see. Jean could not start a lawsuit, or finish it, without me. I could not help her do that without my law firm's agreement to provide resources for what I now recognized was sure to be a battle, if not a war.

◊◊◊

A massive steel door stood ajar with a pie-sized brass dial mounted in the center. Painted glossy black and embellished with scrolling tendrils in gold, the door was a remnant of the days when the business of the Lumber Exchange Building was buying and selling lumber. Cash and goods had been stored in the room behind this door. My law firm used the space as a conference room, to the mild consternation of those who entered, ducking their heads so as not to bruise them on the steel jamb.

My nine partners were seated around the conference table on October 17, 1985. Debris from box lunches was scattered about. I had asked for this meeting. A lawsuit requires substantial resources. Against a behemoth like the University of Iowa, it would take a deeper pocket than Jean's. Jean had a good faculty salary, but it was nowhere near enough to pay our law firm bills if her case went the distance. I needed my partners' agreement to begin the lawsuit.

Title VII of the 1964 Civil Rights Act has a fee shifting provision that makes it possible to limit a client's financial obligation to her attorney during litigation. The client pays for out-of-pocket costs as they are incurred, but attorney bills are deferred until the end of the case. If a plaintiff wins, Title VII provides that the losing employer shall pay the plaintiff's reasonable attorney's fees and reimburse her for costs. If the client loses, the attorney and the client are out of luck. Commonly referred to as a type of contingent fee arrangement, it is a risky proposition.

Arriving early, I unfurled twenty-five feet of brown butcher paper along the walls. Rosemary McClain, a paralegal helping us, had drawn a timeline of Jean's professional life at Iowa's College of Medicine from 1973 to 1985. The piece was unwieldy but persuasive. Along the horizontal axis were the harassing incidents that Jean experienced. Below the line were the university responses—or more accurately, lack thereof. Tacked up with pushpins, the timeline extended across two walls of the conference room.

Like a banker considering a big loan, my partners' approval depended on their confidence in the asset that secured the loan—Jean's case. The likelihood of a win had to substantially outweigh the probability of a loss. The wager had to be made, and the loan advanced, without knowing the total sum at stake. "Jean has paid $6,000 toward our bills. She has been billed for my attorney time at my standard hourly rate of $75 an hour and costs." I reminded them that we didn't like to abandon a client who has paid some of our bills. "Since June of this year we have spent substantial additional legal time in preparation for filing a lawsuit. Unreimbursed attorney time is now about $9,000. Even out-of-pocket costs will be considerable, especially for court reporters at depositions and for travel expenses."

My partners asked questions. Didn't most of the slurs occur outside the statute of limitations for defamation? Have you checked whether the university is immune from a damage suit? Will you be bringing the case in state or federal court? If state court, what do you know about the jury pool in Iowa City? Other questions focused on sexual harassment law. Are there good precedents in similar cases? What remedies have been ordered in sexual harassment cases? Lots of questions were about the size of Jean's damage claim. Did she lose pay? Did she lose other job opportunities? Did she suffer a physical injury? If you seek emotional pain and suffering under state law, is Jean all right with having her medical records disclosed?

Chuck Dayton and John Herman, founders of the firm, were environmental lawyers and had little experience in employment law. Their brows furrowed as they listened to the back and forth. Kathleen Graham, also a founder, was solidly in my court. "I figure it will cost about $30,000 in fees and expenses based on two weeks of discovery, one-week trial prep, a two-week trial, and one-week post-trial," Chuck offered. I readily agreed, thinking this was an underestimate. "If you approve this, it will be my only contingent fee case until it is over," I said. Closing the meeting, Chuck said, "Please prepare a budget."

A week before the October 31 deadline for filing a lawsuit, I sent a budget to the firm estimating attorney's fees at $47,000 over two years, 1986 and 1987. Documented in my notes, I estimated Jean's case had a 90 percent chance of success on the merits. In hindsight, this looks like another overly optimistic assessment. But while my earlier prediction that the university would want to do the right thing in her case had not proved true, the panel's report and the university's refusal to act on it had tilted the legal odds in our favor. Recent legal developments also strengthened Jean's case. Just months before my meeting with the law partners, the U.S. Supreme Court had decided a sex discrimination promotion case, *Hishon v. King & Spaulding*.[22] Although it was not a sexual harassment case, it bolstered Jean's promotion discrimination claim. The Supreme Court held that promotion to partnership in a law firm was an employment decision covered by Title VII, rather than a constitutionally protected right to freedom of association. If law partnership promotions were covered by Title VII, it was very likely that faculty promotions were, too. I thought it possible that the university would come around once we filed suit and showed how determined Jean was. I told Jean that most lawsuits settle and never get to trial.

Probably because I simply would not be denied, my partners agreed to take Jean's case on a contingent fee basis with the hope that it would require little time and fees would be reimbursed. I was grateful for the law firm's support. I was firmly committed to seeing that its risk was rewarded. But the paramount emotion I felt was relief. I could not say then, or adequately capture now, what a make-or-break decision it was for Jean and me. With the firm's resources behind us, Jean had a chance.

∴

The toxicity of the slander against Jean derived from the combination of her sex, race, and Chinese national origin. Sexual denigration of Jean was the solvent in which race and national origin slurs floated. Offensive epithets like "Chink" and "Chinese pussy" demeaned her national origin. When six Asian American women were murdered in spa and massage parlors in Atlanta in 2021 for the sexual "temptation" they presented,[23] the web of ethnic, racial, and sexual assumptions trapping Asian American women, fixing them as sexually erotic and immigrant, was publicly exposed.

While Jean's sex, race, and ethnicity were inextricably enmeshed in the harassment she experienced, Title VII was thought at that time to require identification of one precipitating cause for discrimination, not several. The few Title VII cases that considered whether a plaintiff could combine protected class characteristics in a single case expressed concern that multiple discriminatory claims would muddle proof of causation or give a plaintiff two bites at the apple. Cases alleging more than one cause of discrimination, when originally filed, were winnowed to state a single discriminatory cause by the time of trial.[24] I had seen this in my cases. Shyamala Rajender was Asian Indian. In her complaint in 1973, she alleged sex, race, and national origin discrimination against the University of Minnesota. As the litigation went on, only her claim of sex discrimination was certified as a class in 1978 and settled by the 1980 Rajender Consent Decree. My first client pursuant to the Rajender Consent Decree, Sylvia Azar, an Argentinian, could not add a claim of national origin discrimination to her sex discrimination claim. As one trial court held, Black women could state a "cause of action for race discrimination, sex discrimination, or alternatively either, but not a combination of both."[25]

Kimberlé Crenshaw critiqued the rigidity of single-axis discrimination jurisprudence in a pioneering 1989 article.[26] Crenshaw recognized that requiring just one legal cause of discrimination distorted and flattened the reality of intersecting identities in peoples' lives, particularly in the lives of Black women. Instead, she argued for a jurisprudence that reflected the authentic intersection of race, sex, age, and other biases. By the 1990s, some courts noted that requiring a single discriminatory animus distorted life experience. Maivin Lam, an Asian American academic, sued the University of Hawaii for sex, race, and national origin discrimination in hiring. Reversing the district court, the 9th Circuit Court of Appeals noted in 1996, "the attempt to bisect a person's identity at the intersection of race and gender often distorts or ignores the particular nature of their experiences.... Asian women are subject to a set of stereotypes and assumptions shared neither by Asian men nor by white women." Lam could prove a Title VII case by showing "the employer discriminates on the basis of that *combination* of factors, not just whether it discriminates against people of the same race or of the same sex."[27]

Had the Lam decision come earlier, we could have presented Jean's injuries as resulting from an inseparable mix of immutable characteristics—race, national origin, and sex. Whether we would have done so depended on whether we could solve the proof problem. To show that the harassment was caused by a combination of Jean's Chinese national origin, race, and sex, we would have needed to know how other Chinese men and women faculty were treated in the College of Medicine and more widely in the university, a subject on which we had no information. The numbers of Chinese American women faculty were vanishingly small.

A cohort of all women faculty in the College of Medicine would still be small, but numerous enough to support some statistical analysis. Because we believed women faculty of all races and national origins were subjected to sex discrimination in the College of Medicine, and because Title VII law at that time favored a single-axis claim, we decided to allege sex discrimination. We compressed Jean's multidimensional humanity into a single dimension.[28] The law as we understood it forced us to work with only a portion of the reality of Jean's experience.

∶∷∶

Essential pieces were falling into place. Hope for an early settlement was waning. Financial and other support from my law firm had been secured. The next step was to line up another attorney to work with me. Bob Zeglovitch had just joined our firm after a judicial clerkship with a federal district court judge. He was a promising rookie, having graduated with high honors from Rutgers Law School. He was available—not yet swamped with assignments from other lawyers. I was confident of his values. He would embrace Jean's fight against sexual harassment. He would not have any problem working well with a woman in the role of lead counsel on the case. He began by preparing Jean's legal complaint, which named two defendants. Against the University of Iowa, she claimed sexual harassment pursuant the Iowa Civil Rights Act and breach of her employment contract. Against Tomanek, she alleged defamation and invasion of privacy.[29]

We decided to file the complaint in state court under state law, not federal court under Title VII. The Iowa Civil Rights Act closely mirrored Title VII, but certain key provisions were better for Jean. The Iowa statute permitted damages for emotional pain and suffering, which were not available under Title VII at that time. The Iowa Civil Rights Act also permitted trial by a jury, which Title VII did not. Since many Iowa judges graduated from the University of Iowa Law School and were active alums, we speculated that we might prefer a jury drawn from residents in Johnson County. The defamation claim against Tomanek was a state law claim. To pursue both claims against the defendants in one lawsuit with minimum procedural complications, we needed to be in state court.

Jean's complaint, filed in Johnson County Court on October 30, 1985, narrated an understated story. Specific, false statements were made, some since October 1983, claiming that a sexual relationship existed between Jean and Williams. The false statements were spread widely in the workplace. They damaged Jean in her employment. The university knew of the harassment. Jean complained to the university in 1979, 1982, 1983, and 1984. A faculty panel investigated, found that Jean was harassed due to her sex, and recommended corrective action. The university did not implement the panel's recommendations.

The complaint concluded with a declaration of harm: "As a direct and proximate result of the University's wrongful acts, plaintiff has suffered damage to her personal and professional reputation, her job opportunities and great mental anguish."

CHAPTER 6

Kicked Out

THE JOHNSON COUNTY Courthouse is affixed to a slight rise on the edge of downtown Iowa City. Well past its centennial, the stone bastion flaunts its antiquity via two turrets on each side of the entrance and a tower set back and rising from the center high point of the building. A few months after Jean's complaint was filed, on a frosty afternoon in January 1986, I entered the courthouse for the first time. Jean and I were to meet Judge William R. Eads in his chambers at 1 p.m. with the university lawyers. At stake was whether, at the university's urging, the judge would kick Jean's claims out of court. We had overlooked a home-grown statute, the Iowa Administrative Procedure Act, which arguably blocked Jean from taking her civil rights claim directly to state court.

Now that a lawsuit had begun, the University of Iowa turned to the Iowa Attorney General's Office for legal representation. Attorney Julia Mears, the university's assistant to the president, gave way to attorneys from the attorney general's office in Des Moines. Merle Wilna Fleming, an assistant attorney general in the administrative law division, was the first lawyer from that office assigned to represent the university. Fleming was the third middle-aged woman responding to Jean's complaint. Mears, Small, and Fleming were a foreboding female phalanx protecting male university leaders from people who could do them harm, like Jean and me. A surreal tableau—women pitted against women on an issue of concern to women—while the men in power over them were given a pass and spared getting their hands dirty. University leaders deleted Jean's case from their task list and gave subordinate women free rein.

Merle Fleming was immune to my efforts to establish a working relationship. Our interactions were testy in the extreme. I tried to lance the boil. I wrote, "Neither of our clients is well served by this impasse. Can we agree to minimize this unpleasantness?" No answer.

I was the recipient of Fleming's hostility, and like a lightning rod I grounded most of it. She was dismissive. "Your client's case is marginal, without merit," she said. "Dr. Jew and Dr. Williams's relationship is all-encompassing. They invited the gossip. There is no jury in Iowa that will believe that a man and woman who work together like Dr. Jew and Dr. Williams wouldn't expect there to be talk like this. There is no jury that's going to find sexual harassment in this case." Jean and I held on to our belief that if Merle was right, it wasn't fair and it shouldn't be legal.

⁛

The university's motion to dismiss Jean's complaint was based on Iowa's Administrative Procedure Act, which they asserted required state employees to bring discrimination complaints to the employer, not to court. Recourse to the courts for state employees was limited to judicial review of their employer's adherence to administrative procedures. I was stunned. *Who knew this statute was lying in the weeds in Iowa?* The Administrative Procedure Act was a unique creature, drawn up by a law professor at the university. I argued that the Iowa Civil Rights Act permitted all employees, state employees as well as private-sector employees, to bring civil rights claims directly to state court. The question for the judge was which Iowa statute governed Jean's claims against the university.

Judge Eads did not get up from behind his desk as we arrayed ourselves on sturdy library chairs facing him. After greeting Mears and Fleming by first name, he said, "And you are Ms. Chalmers, come all the way from Minneapolis to join us." It must have been important to him to emphasize my outsider status, as it was the only thing he said. He had no questions for us. Immobile as a mannequin, he could hardly keep his eyes open.

Fleming was a specialist in Iowa's Administrative Procedure Act, and she was triumphant about catching us in this state law trap. She argued that by not bringing claims to the university under the act, Jean had forfeited her discrimination claim under the Civil Rights Act. I responded that Iowa's Civil Rights Act was not subordinate to Iowa's Administrative Procedure Act, and even if it were, Jean had exhausted administrative procedures by submitting an internal complaint to the university and participating in a faculty panel hearing. I made my argument all the while thinking, *This judge is going to put us out on our ear and will be happy doing it.* Judge Eads adjourned us with "I'll take it under advisement," which I doubted very much.

A few months later, Judge Eads adopted Fleming's reasoning and dismissed Jean's claim against the university, holding that a person aggrieved by agency action must bring her claim in accord with the Iowa Administrative Procedure Act unless expressly exempted. I was chagrinned. *Minnesota lawyer brought in to fill a gap left by locals, trips over Iowa state law.* "Judge Eads dismissed the claims against the university," I told Jean when we got his decision. "He let the state law claims against Tomanek remain." Scarcely out of the gate, we were pulled off the track. It was an ignominious beginning. "I'm sorry. No, embarrassed—to be caught in procedural snares. An Iowa attorney might have known."

Jean consoled me. "We've expected this ever since the argument." She reminded me that we had local Iowa lawyers working with us. In those wild days in late October 1985, we had asked Jim Hayes, of the Meardon, Sueppel, Downer & Hayes law firm in Iowa City, to join us as local counsel. Iowa state court rules required out-of-state attorneys to associate with Iowa counsel to argue in Iowa courts. Hayes's firm had a fine reputation and had represented clients adverse to the university—a serendipitous skill set for our needs and a unique one in Iowa City. Lucky for us, Hayes agreed and assigned a junior, and very capable, associate, Paul McAndrew, to assist us in navigating the local mores of the court.

"It really gripes me for the university to get the upper hand at the very outset," I added to Jean. "We'll refile against the university in federal court where I know what I'm doing. We will certainly do that, but not just that." I added, "We can appeal Judge Eads's decision to the Iowa Supreme Court—ask them to decide if his decision is good law in Iowa." Jean was listening intently. I continued, "What about amending the Iowa Civil Rights Act to explicitly provide that state employees can sue under the Iowa Civil Rights Act despite the Administrative Procedure Act? My environmental law partners lobby the Minnesota legislature all the time." Talking to each other about what we could do restored our resolve. We joined battle on three fronts.

Jean got on the phone to various state legislators, those representing her district and others. Together they drafted an amendment to the Iowa Civil Rights Act, even though most bills were already in the funnel at that late stage in the session. Making cold calls to legislators would not be the only new endeavor Jean would undertake or skill she would master. The amendment Jean lobbied for became law August 1, 1986.

This provision [the Iowa Civil Rights Act] also applies to persons claiming to be aggrieved by an unfair or discriminatory practice committed by the state or an agency or political subdivision of the state, notwithstanding the terms of the Iowa Administrative Procedure Act.[1]

We opened a second front by appealing Eads's decision. I argued that the Iowa Administrative Procedure Act, properly understood, did not preempt state employees from suing under the Iowa Civil Rights Act. Although we had no intention of proceeding in state court after what we had experienced, we did not want to leave Eads's decision unchallenged. I presented to five judges on Iowa's Supreme Court, keenly aware of being an inexperienced outsider. One year after that fateful afternoon in Eads's chambers, the Iowa Supreme Court validated our legal theory:

We detect that the lines of exclusivity are not as rigidly drawn as defendants' argument suggests or as the district court found. We agree with plaintiff's assertion that where, as in the present case, the action challenged bears scant relation to the agency's statutory mandate or supposed area of expertise, agency employees should enjoy the same right to pursue matured statutory causes of action as other employees.[2]

Prior to the Iowa Supreme Court's ruling, we filed Jean's Title VII sex discrimination complaint against the university in the U.S. District Court for the Southern District of Iowa. The federal court complaint stated one cause of action against the university and its board of regents for failing to take corrective action in the face of a long-standing pattern of sexual harassment, as required by Title VII of the 1964 Civil Rights

Act. The defamation claim against Tomanek was a state law claim and remained open in state court, as there were procedural difficulties for federal court jurisdiction over that claim.

We had coughed up the lump Fleming and Eads had stuck in our craw. Filing the federal suit, lobbying the legislature, and appealing to the Iowa Supreme Court replenished our resolve, raised our spirits, bound our wounds, and gave fair warning to the university—danger ahead.

CHAPTER 7

Misogyny on Offense

AS THE SEA IS captured in a tide pool, the information necessary to prove Jean's claim was in plain view in the report of the faculty investigation panel and in its record. Yet five more years of grueling effort—years filled with emotional highs and lows—preceded trial. Throughout 1985, we waited in vain for the university's answer to the panel's investigative report. In October, we filed suit and spent 1986 recovering from Judge Eads's dismissal of our claim against the university. Three more years were taken up with preparing for and participating in two trials. Through it all, attorneys offended. Judicial setbacks surprised. Jean's career slowed. Economic pressures built. Not uncommon, yet all of it was unnecessary and some was painful.

Energy was squandered in a legal process called discovery where several tools are used to force information from an adversary while shielding one's damaging information from disclosure. Discovery proceeds via depositions of witnesses under oath, written questions or interrogatories, requests for documents, and motions seeking the court's help to compel adversaries to cooperate, permit amendment, quash subpoenas, and dismiss claims. As it begins, discovery is like starting a jigsaw puzzle—turning pieces right side up, searching for corners, and assembling the outside edges. By the time discovery closes, all the pieces should fit. In between the beginning and the close, conflicts among attorneys are layered on top of client conflicts, resources gush like geysers, and pieces go missing.

Filling in the puzzle in Jean's case involved multiple conferences with Merle Fleming and then appearances before magistrate judges in Des Moines requesting orders to compel adequate answers to discovery requests. All told, it took over a year to get basic personnel information on Jean and comparable faculty. We sat through dozens of depositions and spent hours in windowless rooms reviewing documents.

In fall 1988, Fleming resigned from the attorney general's office. Frayed as our relationship had been, it was better than my relationships with the male attorneys who replaced her, Dean Lerner and Scott Galenbeck. Lerner was a relatively new attorney in the Consumer Protection Division. He was soon joined by Galenbeck from the Administrative Law Division, who added experience to the team. They were approximately my age and had comparable legal experience. Beyond that we seemed to have little in common.

In his first call to me, after introducing himself, Lerner gave fair warning of what I could expect from him. "I've been doing a lot of talking with Julia Mears and Mary Jo Small . . . I'm laying down the ground rules," he said, as if Fleming had not already wielded this cudgel. "All I see here is Williams giving preferential treatment to Jew and discriminatory treatment to others." I envisioned his chest puffed out, chair tilted way back, feet resting on his desk. "I tried the facts out with females in the office and it was a no go. This case does an injustice to women bringing real cases of sexual harassment."

No matter the reasonableness of our requests, Lerner and Galenbeck refused them. Would they label the documents they produced to inform us which of our requests they pertained to; or at least number them in consecutive serial order to avoid confusion? No. "We do not intend to number the documents, attempt to identify the documents and delete documents that appear in more than one file." Would they let Jean review documents when I was not available to join her? No. Would they notify me if they contacted the court to change a hearing scheduled by conference call, into one requiring personal appearance? No. Contested motions and tiresome interactions piled up as we neared trial in November 1989.

Lerner and Galenbeck resurrected sexual smears about Jean. When interviewing potential witnesses, they repeated the slurs and then asked if the witness observed conduct suggesting that the slurs were true. They requested Jean's medical records, including gynecological records. They argued that Jean's use of birth control pills in the 1970s suggested a sexual relationship between her and Williams, despite medical records confirming they were prescribed to control heavy menstrual bleeding. They sought approval for an adverse physical examination to presumably include a gynecological evaluation. The defense was steeped in misogyny, impervious to how their strategy contravened the university's stated values of promoting gender equity and condemning racism.

By permitting the attorneys to slut-shame Jean, the university added institutional weight to Tomanek's hostility. Tomanek's conduct was horrid, but he was one individual in cahoots with a few others. He could not have done such damage but for the university's initial refusal to attend to Jean's complaints and later its sexist defense strategies. Instead of reining in their lawyers, university administrators let them attack Jean and later me. Empathy for Jean's concerns, which had been expressed in response to her 1979, 1982, and 1983 complaints, evaporated when she filed suit.

What accounts for the university's misguided effort to prove a sexual relationship? Perhaps university administrators and their lawyers believed cultural stereotypes of Chinese women as sexual playthings or as deceitful and powerful dragon ladies. They did not know Jean personally. Lewd rumors may have shaped their perceptions in the absence of face-to-face contact with her. Their "misogynistic backlash... under the mantle of moralism, as well as under the cover of anonymity"[1] may have simply been a knee-jerk response. For Jean, defense tactics caused a painful injury, secondary to the primary injury she had experienced. For me, defense strategies were distracting and depleting.

The attorneys from the attorney general's office seemed to think, mistakenly, that if true, a sexual relationship would be an iron-clad defense. Had they proved a sexual relationship, we would have argued that spreading sexual slurs with a discriminatory motive to damage Jean's university career, even if a sexual relationship existed, violated Title VII. There was no suggestion that sex, even if true, had been imposed on Jean by Williams without her consent. Williams had not dispensed unmerited benefits to Jean in exchange for sex. Faculty could have registered concerns about an apparent conflict of interest on Williams's part, as Jean's supervisor—but only if raised via appropriate channels. Using a woman's private life decisions, even if true, to tarnish her reputation, damage her career, and perhaps force her out of the workplace arguably violated Title VII.

In hindsight, the university attorneys' focus on proving a sexual relationship obscured more substantive defense arguments available to them. The tenure code protected Tomanek and Kaelber, both tenured professors, from most discipline, especially discipline for speech. It also assigned them a responsibility to evaluate junior faculty in the department, including Jean. The protections of the tenure code were bolstered by academic freedom and its special place in First Amendment free speech jurisprudence. While these defense themes would not have ensured university success, they would have raised legitimate arguments over regulating speech in the academy that are debated by faculty today. The Iowa Attorney General's Office mentioned free speech and tenure in passing, but were drawn, as if by an intangible magnet pull, back to the sex theme.

❖❖❖

At work, Jean experienced setbacks. Some of her departmental responsibilities were withdrawn. In spring 1987, her assignment as director of the neuroanatomy course—the course where she met with all first-year medical students—ended. Her teaching role in neuroanatomy was reduced to just a quarter of the lectures she had given previously and no review classes. Her time overseeing students in the laboratory was cut in half. She was no longer included in meetings for the course. About the same time, she was removed from the departmental appointments committee. Jean wrote me, "I've lost the opportunity to participate on this committee, which not only isolates me, but will have an impact on my annual evaluation and my pay."

Having been admonished by senior faculty in the 1983 performance evaluation to demonstrate independence in her research, Jean tried to strike up new collaborations. Preliminary conversations with potential collaborators went nowhere. "People are being warned. They are careful not to appear to impede or seem hostile, but I'm a pariah." Scientific productivity was dependent on having graduate students in one's lab. By late spring 1988, few graduate students were coming by Jean's lab to explore opportunities. "They've heard I'm trouble," Jean said, "and they know that their progress is dependent on the good will of multiple faculty in the department."

Pressure from my law firm mounted. Our small firm had merged with the much larger Minneapolis law firm, Leonard, Street & Deinard, in April 1988. I had fifty-five new partners and a new managing partner. Jean's case had about $200,000 in unreimbursed time and months of work anticipated in the future. The economic burden of the case was now borne by colleagues who did not know me and were not committed to advancing women's rights. The new law firm's appetite for continuing to finance Jean's case was not a foregone conclusion.

George Reilly, the managing partner of Leonard, Street & Deinard, was a tall, lanky Irishman of few words. Ongoing resources for Jean's case depended on his approval. Reilly walked into my office one morning in fall 1988. "How much more attorney time do you expect on this University of Iowa case?" he asked. I paused. Maybe George was carrying water for other skeptical partners, or maybe these were his own worries as a diligent managing partner. It was bad enough to have the University of Iowa against us. *Please, not the law firm, too.*

"George, sit down and let me tell you about this case before I answer your question." I still had at hand the twenty-five-foot timeline of brown butcher paper. I unrolled it, walked along the timeline, and essentially gave a closing argument about why we would prevail in the case. I told him our chances had improved with the recent U.S. Supreme Court's first Title VII sexual harassment decision in *Meritor Bank v. Vinson.*[2] Vinson, a young female bank teller, gave in to her male supervisor's demands for sex for three years before filing a Title VII lawsuit in 1978. She was promptly fired. Reasoning that her acquiescence made her relationship with her supervisor voluntary, the district court judge ruled against her. The Supreme Court reversed unanimously, reasoning hostile environment harassment that "is sufficiently severe and pervasive to create an abusive environment" and is unwelcome is prohibited by Title VII.

I credit Reilly for appreciating just how far out on a limb Jean and I were, and that I could not abandon her there. While we were hemorrhaging resources in the case, I had other work for corporate clients paying my bills. That helped. And Reilly helped. He had my back for now, should any law partners urge the firm to drop the lawsuit.

⁞⁞⁞

In summer 1989, with federal trial on the horizon, Jim Hayes, our Iowa local counsel, Jean, and I were strategizing about settlement. We bemoaned that among the several obstacles to settlement were Galenbeck and Lerner's disapproving views on Jean and me.[3] Hayes described it as a psychosis among the attorneys in the attorney general's office. We suspected that university leaders were cocooned with reassurances about the merits of the case, infuriated by stories of our unreasonableness, and advised to leave everything up to their lawyers.

Because the thorny problem presented by Jean's case was not pleasant, university administrators delegated it to the lawyers to worry about. They may have agreed with Vartan Gregorian, who said that of all of his tasks as president of Brown University, "adjudicating sexual mores" continued to confound him. "How do you deal with that? Why are you bringing this to me?"[4] As Jean's case neared trial, we believed administrators were hiding behind their lawyers to avoid the case.

Hayes, Jean, and I decided on a strategy to address this. Jean and I would present her case on a videotape. We would give two copies to the Iowa attorney general and ask that one copy be forwarded to the university leaders. They could watch us and judge us for themselves. Ethical rules prohibit attorneys from contacting an opposing party directly, but a videotape given to their lawyers to share with university leaders was within the rules.

When watching the thirty-year-old videotape, I see a much younger me standing in one of the law firm's conference rooms with a semi-professional camera operator. I introduce myself and lean toward the camera. I begin in a calm, conversational voice. "We have made this video for the purpose of settlement. It is directed to Iowa Attorney General Thomas Miller. It is confidential and should not be viewed without his express permission. Its purpose is to provide information about this case and to urge the university to explore settling it."

For twenty minutes I took the arguments the university's attorneys promoted, turned them into questions, and answered them. Was it sex harassment? Yes, because. . . . Were the statements about Jean protected academic speech? No, because. . . . Were the rumors about a sexual relationship true? No. Even Eckstein had said, "No, I never believed it."

Jean was filmed in her office in the Anatomy Department, Iowa College of Medicine, sitting at her bench, back against windowless white cinderblock walls, white lab coat on. At her side is an ultramicrotome, where she sectioned tissues. She spoke in complete phrases and sentences, pausing to construct her thoughts, with no script in hand. "I made a big investment when I chose a research career. I have lost time, productivity, stature, and achievement that I will never get back. I don't want to lose any more of it—that's why I hope it can be resolved." The screen goes black. These quietly spoken words hang in the air. The end of the video is not declared. A few seconds pass before the viewer senses it.

A hail Mary pass three months before the federal trial started, the video was intended to get our message directly to university leaders and circumvent the roadblock we believed the attorneys patrolled. Hayes had political connections in Iowa, knew Attorney General Tom Miller personally, and met with him in Des Moines to deliver the video.

Not until the trial was over were we told that university decision makers had not received or viewed the video.

⁂

A deluge of legal activity hit in the last few months before trial began. Nearly every week Bob Zeglovitch and I drafted, revised, finalized and filed a pleading or memorandum with the federal court. The university moved for summary judgment dismissing Jean's case, describing Jean as "a plaintiff without a conscience."[5] Motion denied. Lerner and Galenbeck tried to make me a witness in the case and thus ineligible to continue as Jean's attorney. Attack deflected. Two weeks before the trial, a judge wrote, "While I find the plaintiff's counsel's proposal to be reasonable, defendants' counsel has labeled the motion as 'extraordinary' and 'preposterous.'"

He sees through their hyperbole. Will Judge Vietor?

CHAPTER 8

Trial Day by Day

TRIAL OF JEAN'S claim against the university was set to begin in the federal courthouse in Des Moines on November 13, 1989, six years almost to the day from Jean's first call to me. Before leaving the Twin Cities for Des Moines a few days prior, I stopped for Eric to take a photo in our driveway. Our minivan is packed full of banker's boxes. I look younger than my forty-three years. Squinting at the camera, I look resigned.

The four-hour drive is straight south, not a turn the whole way. Since taking Jean's case, I had become familiar with this drive and its effect on me. Crossing from Minnesota into Iowa, I tensed up. I was persona non grata in Iowa.

A roller derby of an experience lay ahead—racing for dominance in a limited space, making myriad decisions in split seconds, suffering the consequences immediately, and striving not to be body slammed or tripped. Our team convening in Des Moines that Saturday was Bob Zeglovitch, Sheila Canard, Jean Jew, and me. It was not a deep bench, but it was sturdy. Bob and I divided the witnesses between us, preparing for direct or cross-examination of those in our respective columns.

Sheila had been secretary, legal assistant, and booster during the run-up to the trial. We wanted her with us in Des Moines, and she agreed to come. We needed her to find exhibits during testimony; to type, copy, distribute, and file memoranda on issues that would arise but could not be prepared for in advance; to contact and schedule witnesses; and to find lunches for us, among other things. As it turned out, no hour was too early or late for her to step up and take care of a need. She cooked breakfast for one of our expert witnesses who liked a hot meal in the morning. She was our eyes and ears, watching everything going on in the courtroom while Bob and I were at the podium. In her quiet way, Sheila owned the struggle every bit as much as the rest of us.

The Savery Hotel in downtown Des Moines was our home for nineteen days in November—twelve trial days, one Thanksgiving, and three weekends. Not yet renovated into the boutique hotel it is today, it was on the National Register of Historic Places even then. Its good bones were perceptible through worn carpets and chipped baseboards. We had five rooms reserved at one end of the floor—one each for Jean, Bob, Sheila, me, and a work room. During the trial, we circulated among the rooms, doors open, conversations spilling into the hall. We became regulars.

Jean met us at the Savery on Saturday. Now that we were face to face, I talked with her about something that troubled me. We had been given precious little information about several of the university's witnesses. The university lawyers withheld their names until the last minute—despite rules requiring them to provide this information to us in advance. What little information we had scared us. We were told they would tell the true tale of a sexual relationship between Jean and Williams. They would tell how Jean, like Tomanek, spread ugly rumors about other colleagues. These witnesses, some of whom we had never heard of, reportedly would bring Jean down.

"Jean, who are these people? Why haven't you told us about them?" I pressed. She and I were on a bracing walk along the river. My fast walk was her jog. "Lawyers have to know the bad as well as the good. If you know what they are talking about, tell me now." My impatience at nonstop surprises from the university's trial lawyers was now directed at her. I was intense. My instruction to her: come clean, now, here.

"I don't know why they would say such things." Jean said, trying to catch her breath. "They are lying. They could not have seen sex or heard what they say they heard, because it didn't happen."

"Why would these accomplished people lie?"

Jean repeated, "I don't know. But that is what they are doing." Dead end. Believing her, we still were not any further along in knowing what to do.

Day 1, November 13

On Monday morning, amid blustery winds and a low-hanging sky, we hauled boxes through the hotel lobby and out to the curb, packed the minivan, and drove the several blocks to the U.S. District Court-house—a historic building. Completed just before the stock market crash in 1929, its classical revival, limestone facade faced a nondescript city street on the edge of downtown instead of the Des Moines River flowing at its side.

As we hauled a dolly up to the main courtroom on the second floor, random thoughts flitted through my mind. *Don't break a sweat. Strive for crisp and poised. Why are Galenbeck and Lerner here ahead of us? Why did they choose the counsel table on the right side of the courtroom? Does it give them an advantage? Where will Sheila park the minivan? Does she have change to feed the meter?* I heaved a sigh of relief when we were in Judge Vietor's courtroom. Skittery, alert, and all business.

Harold Vietor, chief judge of the U.S. District Court for the Southern District of Iowa, had overseen the restoration of the main courtroom where Jean's trial took place. Behind a railing, pews of buffed walnut filled the back half of the room. The front was dominated by the judge's "bench"—a misnomer, since it was a long, imposing table, not a bench. It was raised on a platform of Tennessee marble. On the judge's right, a few feet below him, were the witness's table and a chair. Directly below and in front of the bench were desks occupied by the courtroom deputy and the court reporter. The judge's law clerk had a desk at the side of the bench. Between the bench and the railing in front of the public seating was a large open space occupied by two massive oak tables, separated by a lectern in the center. Both faced the judge. We sat at the one on the left.

Precisely at 9:00 a.m. the judge's law clerk, Helen C. Adams, stepped into the courtroom from a door to the right of the bench. A pleasant change from the young men typically hired as law clerks for federal judges, Adams was a young woman newly graduated from the University of Iowa Law School. "The judge would like to see you in chambers. Follow me, please," she said. Because Title VII did not permit jury trials, Jean's case would be tried by a federal judge. We were about to meet him. All our years of effort came to this terrifying question: What would Judge Vietor think of Jean's claims? His empathy for a Chinese American woman tarnished with sexual slurs was not a given.

In our favor: Judge Vietor was appointed to the federal bench by President Jimmy Carter in 1979 after fourteen years serving as a state court judge. He was married with two daughters and a son. Local lawyers thought highly of him as smart and hard-working. Not in our favor: he was in his early sixties. He went to the University of Iowa for his B.A. and law degrees when the law school was nearly all male. He served in the all-male navy in the Korean War. He was known to be hard on attorneys. "Eat your Wheaties every morning," one Des Moines lawyer advised. Our research into Vietor's prior cases was a deep dive that yielded no results. We found no decision on sexual harassment or sex discrimination.

In his chambers, Judge Vietor was not elevated, not robed, not suited, not far off, just a tall, big-boned man across a desk, his white shirt sleeves rolled up. A table extended into the room from the judge's desk. Attorneys and their clients sat on either side of it. He greeted us and began by ruling on several evidentiary motions each side had filed.[1]

Plaintiff's motions to exclude testimony of former university President Freedman—denied; to exclude expert testimony of psychologist—denied; to exclude unsubstantiated allegations of plaintiff's misconduct—denied. This last came with a sobering embellishment from the judge. "I'm tentatively of the opinion that any testimony concerning any alleged misconduct on the part of the plaintiff is admissible."

The university's motions to exclude a report by the U.S. Office of Federal Contract Compliance—denied; to exclude testimony of Professor Ursella Dellworth regarding the university's record on diversity—denied; to exclude testimony of our statistical expert—denied; to impose a gag order on attorneys and parties—denied; to close the courtroom to the public—denied; to exclude psychological evidence—denied; to exclude the faculty investigative report—denied. Another sobering comment: "At the time the panel report is offered, I'm going to want to have plaintiff articulate clearly what disputed facts—or what relevant facts she seeks to prove by the panel report; and I will also at that time have to thoroughly hear counsel on this issue of whether the panel report constitutes settlement negotiations."

Judge Vietor interrupted the cadence of requests and denials only once—when considering our motion for an order protecting a witness from intimidation. At the deposition of one of our expert witnesses, Carl Davis, university attorneys had threatened criminal prosecution if he testified in support of Jean. The threat was documented in the transcript of Davis's deposition. We brought it to the judge's attention in a motion for a protective order.

THE COURT: I want to get some information on that. I'm concerned...

GALENBECK: I did not intend to threaten him, Judge.

THE COURT: Well certainly it's an implied threat. I can't read your remarks to him at the deposition any differently than that. I would like to know what you meant by saying, "Hey, we might go after you criminally if you testify as a witness for the plaintiff in this case."

GALENBECK: I'm not a prosecutor. I work in the commercial law division of the attorney general's office.

THE COURT: Whether you personally prosecute cases or not is beside the point. You are an assistant attorney general of Iowa, and you made remarks to him that certainly were reasonably interpreted to be a threat that if he testified, he might be criminally prosecuted.

GALENBECK: But if you're asking whether I intend to do anything or whether I think that a prosecutor somewhere would prosecute this man, certainly not.

THE COURT: Counsel are ordered to refrain from impliedly or directly suggesting further to the witness, Dr. Davis, that he might be criminally prosecuted if he testifies as a plaintiff's witness in this case. Counsel for defendant promptly confirm by writing to Dr. Davis and his attorney that subsequent investigation has determined that no action would be taken under that statute if he testifies as a witness for the plaintiff. Get that letter out within a day or two.

GALENBECK: Yes, Judge.

THE COURT: [Consulting his watch] Put the kind of effort into stipulating to uncontested facts that you've put into fighting each other, and you can shorten this trial by half or more, and with that gentle admonition, let's go into the courtroom and try this case. Be in the courtroom promptly at a quarter to 10. That's about nine minutes from now."

Judge Vietor's mien was opaque, but his message was clear. Nothing would derail him. He was determined to decide Jean's case on the merits. Nine minutes later, we were at our places in the courtroom. Galenbeck and I gave opening statements outlining the witnesses we planned to call and the documentary evidence we would introduce. After opening statements, Bob and I planned to spend about a week calling our witnesses and introducing exhibits to prove the legal elements of Jean's Title VII claim. We would question our witnesses on direct examination. The university attorneys would cross-examine them; if necessary, we could ask them additional questions on redirect to follow-up on the points brought out on cross-examination. Then the university would have about a week to call witnesses. They would conduct direct examination, we would cross-examine, and they could redirect. Both sides could present narrowly tailored, rebuttal witnesses. We expected the trial to take two weeks.

We began our case with the testimony of two university administrators who had the authority and responsibility to correct Jean's work environment and had not done so. We knew it was a risky way to begin. They were adverse to us and motivated to defend the university. They would try to wriggle out from under our questions—heading anywhere but on the course we set. We could have begun with Jean telling her story and been sure to stay on course, or called lab techs and staff who would testify firsthand to Tomanek's initiatives to spread slanderous statements. We did both later. But to begin the trial, we decided to put the spotlight on the university's decision to let the harassment continue unabated. The institutional failure had been the most crushing for Jean and was at the heart of her lawsuit.

⁘

Bob questioned Vice President for Academic Affairs Richard Remington.[2]

> ZEGLOVITCH: Prior to the time that Jean actually came to see you, you were aware of the innuendo that she and Dr. Williams were having a sexual relationship, were you not?
> REMINGTON: I had heard gossip to that effect.
> ZEGLOVITCH: And at the time that you heard that, you felt very concerned for Dr. Jew personally, didn't you?
> REMINGTON: I felt concerned.
> ZEGLOVITCH: And it seemed to you at that time that perhaps Dr. Jew was being asked to bear a burden that was inappropriate; isn't that so?
> REMINGTON: Yes.
> ZEGLOVITCH: And it was your feeling at the time that if these innuendos were actually being made regarding Dr. Jew's sexual relationship, that this was not something that you would really expect a human being to put up with; is that correct?
> REMINGTON: Yes.

Although he was concerned about the burden placed on Jean, Remington clarified that he viewed her as "a detail." He blamed Williams for catalyzing faculty hostility and doing nothing to stop it. Remington's principle concern "was Williams and his role, that was the major issue in the department." Bob presented him with anonymous, scurrilous letters sent to Eckstein. He showed Remington photographs of graffiti. Remington conceded that, bundled together, the rumors, gossip, slurs, and graffiti needed investigation, and he appointed a faculty panel to do this.

> ZEGLOVITCH: You thought the report of the panel reflected a thorough job on their part?
> REMINGTON: I thought the investigative work they did was thorough.
> ZEGLOVITCH: You thought the report was an interesting report and, in general, a competent report, correct?
> REMINGTON: That's correct.

ZEGLOVITCH: And the faculty panel you appointed made several recommendations to you to correct Dr. Jew's environment.
REMINGTON: That's correct.

When asked if he agreed with the recommendations of the panel, Remington's answers skittered away. He had said at his deposition in 1988 that he found the faculty panel's recommendations "were a pretty good summary of what needed to be done."[3] A year later Bob's questions had become "too broad to answer," and Bob's paraphrases of Remington's testimony were "not what I intended to say."

Questions about specific actions he could have taken and didn't gave him less room to equivocate. Did you determine one way or the other whether the conduct violated the sexual harassment policy? No. Call in Dr. Tomanek or Dr. Kaelber to admonish them? No. Call in Dr. Jew? No. Meet with the dean of the College of Medicine to discuss implementing the recommendations? No. Meet with department faculty to set expectations for future conduct? No. Offer Dr. Jew a process that excluded Tomanek and Kaelber from voting on her promotion? No. Remington's response to the panel report was to hire a handwriting expert who tried, unsuccessfully, to identify the author of the graffiti and anonymous notes.

Asked why he had not acted on the faculty panel's recommendations, Remington said that the panel report failed to show "sexual harassment to my satisfaction"; presented no "evidence that could lead to [the] conclusion" that the harassment had a destructive effect on Jean's reputation; and provided no basis for disciplinary action against Tomanek or Kaelber. "None whatsoever."[4] He cycled through rationales, hoping to land on one that would bridge the gap between his responsibility to determine whether facts violated university policy and his abandonment of that responsibility in Jean's case.

⁂

Remington's refusal to respond to the faculty panel report is still confounding. The 1980 EEOC Guidelines on Sexual Harassment charged employers with a duty to investigate sexual harassment complaints and take prompt corrective action. The university had designed a format for the investigation, selected faculty for panelists, instructed the panel, and initially approved of the final report. Presented with a transparent investigation conducted by respected academic leaders in accord with university legal responsibilities and procedure, administrators had a firm foundation to take action, but they did not.

I wish I could ask Remington and Eckstein why they did not respond to the report. This question was key to our legal case decades ago and stays with me. Their answers in depositions and in trial were carefully groomed to fit the university attorneys' narrative and not intended to reveal their real thoughts. In what must have been lengthy discussions in Jessup Hall, I picture an echo chamber in which those present affirmed the well-polished tale—Williams was to blame for mismanaging the department, alienating faculty, and injuring Jean—supported by input from their lawyers advising that the conduct Jean complained of did not constitute sexual harassment. There was no advocate in that inner circle for the wise and obvious decisions that would have saved much expense and pain.

As the University of Iowa was tabling corrective action for Jean, the University of Pennsylvania was tabling corrective action for an Asian American woman on its faculty. These university responses were nearly mirror images of each other. Rosalie Tung, an associate professor at Penn, filed an EEOC complaint challenging the university's denial of her tenure in 1985. She alleged national origin, race, and sex discrimination. Like Jean, she first made a complaint to the university. Like Jean, the faculty grievance panel concluded in her favor, finding that "certain procedural irregularities" had occurred that "taken collectively result in a flawed review of Dr. Tung's qualifications." Like the University of Iowa, Penn did not act on the faculty panel's findings and thwarted the EEOC's subsequent litigation with procedural obstacles that the U.S. Supreme Court ultimately rejected.[5] Soon thereafter, the case settled. Tung continued a distinguished academic career elsewhere.

Iowa's and Penn's rejections of faculty panel reports and persistent arrogant responses to complaints by women of color defy rational explanation. These institutions fought opportunities to support talented Asian American women faculty at a time when they touted their commitment to diversity. Reactive assault on these women, while contrary to purported university values and interests, was consistent with protecting their territory from unwanted newcomers.

⁑

Court adjourned sharply at 5 p.m. That night at the Savery, we convened in my room. Preparation for the next day was held in abeyance while we debriefed together. We queried Sheila: When we speak, what is the judge's body language? Poker faced. Is he attentive? Yes. How about with opposing counsel? He is attending to them, too. How did Judge Vietor react when Remington had to answer that string of no's? Poker faced. Which of Remington's points registered with the judge? Don't know. With the law clerk? Don't know. Did we score any points? Don't know.

Remington ultimately conceded the facts we needed for our case, but it was a messy job. The questions and answers lacked rhythm or a narrative arc. Bob doggedly pinned him down, cut him off, circled back, and confronted him with prior sworn testimony. We concluded that the first day's testimony was workmanlike but boring. Because this trial was to an experienced and attentive judge, we were not as concerned about the absence of drama as we would have been if we were trying to persuade an audience of novice jurors. On the other hand, we did not want to try the judge's patience. Everyone likes a story and is more likely to remember a clear narrative. We needed to pick up the pace and gain some momentum.

We went back to preparing for the next day—crafting questions, linking them to exhibits or deposition transcripts, anticipating questions from the defense, and consulting. This was the rhythm of every evening—relax, debrief together, supper in our room or the hotel restaurant, gear up for tomorrow, call home and then try to sleep.

Day 2, November 14

Remington was still in the witness chair. In response to Galenbeck's questions, Remington picked out a melody that would become the university's refrain: Williams was to blame. Williams's mismanagement of the department justifiably enraged faculty. Their hostility was caused by Williams and directed at Williams. Because the harassment was intended to humiliate Williams (a man), it was not sex harassment against Jean. Remington regretted that Jean was within the orbit of their anger. But she was in the wings, not on center stage. She was never the center of attention. Williams was. Williams's malfeasance was an earworm in Remington's mind.

Bob could not stop Remington from retreading this theme.

ZEGLOVITCH: I'd like you to look at the reference in the middle paragraph to, "Basic science chairman paying for Chinese pussy." You don't deny the reference to Chinese pussy was a sexually derogatory reference to Dr. Jew, do you?

REMINGTON: I don't deny.

ZEGLOVITCH: You would agree that the clear suggestion in that note is that Dr. Jew was giving sexual favors in return for advantages, wouldn't you?

REMINGTON: The burden of that document, I think, is quite different from that. It is really talking about the basic science chairman. I think I've testified several times that I was unable to conclude that what we had was a situation involving sexual harassment.

Brush ourselves off. No weeping wounds. Still standing. Get ready for Dean John Eckstein, our next witness.

⁂

We needed lunch, but where could we eat the box lunches Sheila found? It wasn't appropriate to eat in the courtroom, and it was too cold to eat outside on a park bench. While we were beginning to feel comfortable in the courtroom, we were not comfortable elsewhere in the courthouse—a warren of insiders. Courthouse staff we passed in the halls or saw in the restrooms were strangers to us, unlike the staff in Judge Vietor's courtroom, who had begun to feel familiar.

When a notorious trial is proceeding—and ours had that cachet in the Des Moines courthouse—it captures the attention of the insiders. They are curious. *What is happening in there now?* The ultimate reality show, a trial has potential for startling developments without warning. A presiding judge is circumspect. But he converses in chambers with his law clerk, within earshot of his secretary and court reporter, who in turn share new developments with counterparts working for other judges. Staff insiders keep lips zipped vis-à-vis outsiders, but inside courthouse offices, chatter happens.

Judges must consider only the evidence presented in the courtroom—but they are curious about the personalities of the people before them. Chitchat can soothe judicial isolation. If the judge's staff—secretary, law clerk, bailiff—feel friendly toward the plaintiff's team, and the judge feels friendly toward his staff, chitchat gives the judge a little more information about personalities—indirectly and not inappropriately. Likability is a close cousin to credibility and persuasion.

"There is a lunchroom in the basement," Sheila said. Bob, Jean, Sheila, and I went down, not knowing what we would find. Filling all but one of the five or six tables in a small basement room sat a dozen people, amid vending machines and cigarette smoke lit up by overhead florescent tubes. Conversation quieted when we entered, but after we sat down at the open table, pulled out our sandwiches, plugged the vending machine for drinks, and began to eat, the buzz resumed.

"Did you catch the Nebraska game last Saturday?"

"The judge hands me edits at 4:30 and then I'm late to pick up at day care. Any ideas?"

"Sally is pregnant. Take note everybody, I'm taking three weeks off next summer even if she is out on maternity leave."

"Can you spare a cigarette? Still, I'm cutting down."

And so on. We listened to them, and we talked among ourselves. Surprised when we first joined them, the regulars got used to us coming down daily. Self-consciousness dissipated. I'm pretty sure we were the only courtroom lawyers to eat bag lunches in that room, maybe ever. We never saw a judge or a law clerk there. Our suits stood out among the beige uniforms on the courtroom deputies and the sweater/skirt sets on the secretaries. Our presence disrupted expectations about snooty out-of-town lawyers from the big city. We debriefed the morning's work and noodled about the afternoon witnesses even though we were within earshot of others. We were careful and yet, on subjects that accredited us, willing to be overheard. Anticipating our direct examination that afternoon of John Eckstein, we kept our voices down.

After lunch, Eckstein gave us the same story Remington had. Williams was the culprit. Jean was collateral damage. Eckstein and Remington's hands were tied. What happened to Jean was Williams's doing and his to correct. Time and again Eckstein acknowledged doing nothing to address the slurs and innuendo about Jean, believing the response was in Williams's, Brodbeck's, or the lawyers' hands. Besides, it was such nasty stuff, such a mess.[6]

CHALMERS: What was your reaction when you heard faculty members refer to Dr. Jew as a "hatchet woman"?

ECKSTEIN: I don't think I interpreted it as derogatory to Dr. Jew. I interpreted it as being a derogatory statement about Dr. Williams. I was thinking about Dr. Williams every time I heard the word "hatchet woman."

CHALMERS: You understood Jean's January 15, 1979 complaint about Professor Kaelber as a formal complaint of sexual harassment, correct?

ECKSTEIN: Yes, I did.

CHALMERS: You did not do any investigation about Dr. Jew's complaint of sexual harassment following this January 15, 1979 letter, did you?

ECKSTEIN: Investigate the complaint only in the sense that I turned it over to Vice President Brodbeck. I was expecting Dr. Williams to investigate these matters and do something about them. She [Brodbeck] asked me to talk with Dr. Williams, to explain to Dr. Williams that Iowa City was a small community. If he were going to work late at night with a young woman in his laboratory, that he should leave the door open, and explain to him what this sort of behavior on his part was doing to her. I told him he should avoid the appearance of what seemed to be making things very bad for her.

CHALMERS: You did not talk with Dr. Tomanek at this time, did you?

ECKSTEIN: No, because I think it was Dr. Williams who was causing all the trouble.

Later, I showed Eckstein two anonymous letters he had received in February 1982, prior to the "Jean Jew is a lesbian" graffiti on the men's room wall. One asked, "If Williams doesn't fuck Jew, why does Harry Tongue see his car at her house every night when he gets home?" I inquired specifically about the other.

CHALMERS: Now, did you understand this reference to, quote, "pay for Chinese pussy," to be a reference to Dr. Jew?
ECKSTEIN: I don't think I understood it at all. It was kind of a repulsive thing. I think I just thought of it as more of a mess.

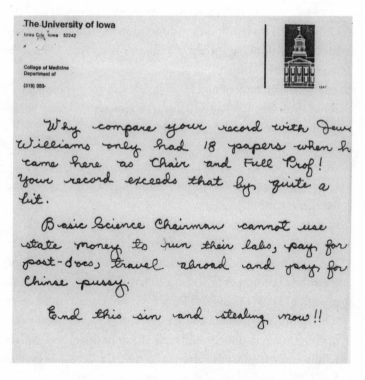

Figure 7: Anonymous letter put into a faculty mailbox February 5, 1982. Copy provided to Dean Eckstein contemporaneously.

⋆⋆⋆

When Jean made her first complaint in 1979, Eckstein and Brodbeck's responses were in keeping with the times, but so unwise.

Early 1979 was a particularly divisive time in the Department of Anatomy. Two tenure decisions and one promotion decision riled faculty factions and catalyzed criticism of Williams. Williams opposed tenure for a professor, Dr. Oaks, at year end 1977. Oaks filed a grievance in summer 1978 alleging bias on Williams's part. As Oaks's grievance was being prepared for a committee review and a grievance hearing, Williams supported Jean's tenure and promotion to associate professor and Paul Heidger's promotion to full professor. University approval of Jean's tenure made her the closest comparable for Oaks. He combed through Jean's record looking for weaknesses. Oaks's supporters made scurrilous claims about Jean's relationship with Williams. In this environment, Brodbeck's and Eckstein's perspectives were understandable.

The damage to women when sexuality is tossed around at work was still under the radar in 1979. Even the term "sexual harassment" was new to the lexicon. Most administrative actions, including discipline or convening a grievance panel, did contain the risk, as they pointed out, of further injuring Jean. True then, it remains true for a complainant today. In 1979 arguably they were not legally required to act. They could decline to act and avoid the risks. This is what they did.

As to actions they advised Jean to take, stereotypes misguided Brodbeck and Eckstein about the person before them. This young, single, Chinese American woman was ignoring the social conventions. She was defying socially mandated boundaries between a junior woman working with a senior man by working late into the night, eating with him, and carpooling. Eckstein and Brodbeck did not see it as their job to stop gossip, which they saw as a fact of life. Unless Jean conformed her behavior to Iowa City's social norms, they assumed she was fair game for the "seductress" stereotype—a common image imposed on token women in male-dominated workplaces.[7]

They counseled Jean that she should accept burdens not shouldered by similarly situated male junior faculty. Stop carpooling with Williams. Stop going to dinner together. Stop working in the lab at night—even though these changes would impose significant impediments to her research; even though they did not ask this of young male academics working with senior mentors; even though her research career could not succeed without the money, staff, and coaching of the only senior neuroanatomist on the faculty.

Had they listened deeply enough to hear Jean's pain, Brodbeck and Eckstein could have done so much to support her—simple things like checking in with her periodically, attending a departmental faculty meeting to review expectations of faculty behavior, meeting with offending faculty individually to communicate expectations, and consulting with feminist leaders for problem-solving ideas. Perhaps a formal complaint would make things worse for Jean, but that was not their only option. They had the means to address her concerns by implementing low-key interventions short of a formal complaint.

Jean was not a receptive audience for their advice. Her behavior mirrored the conduct of junior male academics. A productive research program with a senior scientist, all of whom were male, was necessary for her academic success. She would continue the working relationship with Williams in public view, even if others looked on with warped gazes.

Jean's rejection of their advice to conform to social mores bespeaks her sureness about who she was, regardless of what others expected of her. Her immunity to ambient norms about women's roles had roots in her childhood. She had rejected Mississippi's segregated and biased expectations for her. To thrive, she had navigated the nearly all-male, mostly white Tulane Medical School. By the time she was counseled to defer to Iowa City's social conventions, ignoring society's messages had been essential to Jean's success.

§§§

After the long, frustrating afternoon, we commiserated in my hotel room. Sheila's reaction was florid. "He said that Dr. Jew and Dr. Williams … I made a note, quote 'were creating the problem, had created the problem, caused the trouble.' He really said that!" Sheila tried to cheer us up by suggesting that we had succeeded in revealing Eckstein's ineptitude. We weren't buying it. In presenting his perspective, Eckstein was blunt. He was without artifice. He was believable. The judge was unreadable.

We second-guessed our decision to begin our case with senior university administrators. While they had little room to maneuver since we had their testimony on the record in depositions, it was cumbersome to use their prior testimony to corral them. We had thought that more important than exposing the jerks who were harassing Jean was exposing the leaders who did nothing to stop the jerks. But the delivery was too choppy to engage a listener. We had our fill of trying to make our case from the mouths of university administrators.

A strategic pivot was called for. Eckstein would be questioned by Galenbeck in the morning, and then I would have a last chance. We decided that when Eckstein stepped down, we would not call more adverse witnesses. From now on we would call ordinary people who were sympathetic to Jean. The faculty panel had largely limited interviews to faculty during their investigation. Staff members and graduate students would provide new information not provided to the faculty panel.

Day 3, November 15

Questioned by Galenbeck, Eckstein blamed Williams for the hateful conduct of some male faculty. If a woman faculty was caught in crossfire, it was unfortunate for her, but not an action item for the dean. He had forced Williams to resign the chair position in 1983 because Williams had not achieved Eckstein's goals for the department. It had nothing to do with improving the environment for Jean.

When Galenbeck finished, I went a second round with Eckstein.

CHALMERS: Dean Eckstein, you've previously testified that you were well aware in the seventies and into the eighties of a pattern of gossip and rumor and innuendo about Dr. Jew and Dr. Williams; correct?
ECKSTEIN: Yes.
CHALMERS: And you received anonymous letters and you were aware of graffiti that was posted and you had personal knowledge of some of these incidents; correct?
ECKSTEIN: Yes.
CHALMERS: And these incidents, even though they explicitly

referred to Dr. Jew and her sexuality, you took as really directed
at Dr. Williams and his administration; correct?

ECKSTEIN: That's true. . . . It was part of a broad attack on Dr.
Williams.

CHALMERS: And you thought it was being used as a tool to force
Dr. Williams out; correct?

ECKSTEIN: Yes.

CHALMERS: And in fact in the summer of 1983 you did force Dr.
Williams out, did you not?

ECKSTEIN: I asked him to resign.

CHALMERS: But you never disciplined or reprimanded Dr.
Tomanek, did you?

ECKSTEIN: No.

CHALMERS: You never disciplined Dr. Kaelber, did you?

ECKSTEIN: No, I didn't discipline Dr. Kaelber.

This man had led the College of Medicine deftly for seventeen years,
managing men who made up the tenured medical school faculty. He
was skilled in dealing with the many conflicts among male faculty in a
male culture. Were his skills transferrable to a woman faculty members'
grievances? All we know is that they did not transfer. Faculty criticisms
of Williams obscured his comprehension of Jean's injury.

Our strategic pivot began with the next witness. Linda Dawes was
a graduate student in the Anatomy Department from 1982 to 1986. In
a medical school, research faculty, as distinguished from clinical faculty, depend on graduate students to help in their labs. When deciding
which lab to join, graduate students are influenced by rumors about
research faculty. They learn from each other which faculty have a record
of publications in peer-reviewed journals, a history of success placing
students in academic jobs, continuous grant funding, and generosity in
giving credit to graduate student discoveries. Graduate students tend
to avoid faculty embroiled in political infighting.

Dawes testified that the sexual slurs about Jean circulated "almost
continually" among graduate students. At a picnic that Williams hosted
for the graduate students, Dawes described coming into the backyard
with another graduate student, Steve, and seeing Jean at the grill:

DAWES: [Steve] said something along the lines of, "I can't believe that she is actually here at their house in front of all of us. Can you believe it?" He said something about didn't they worry about appearances at all, that this was just broadcasting their affair. And then he made some rather crude remarks when they were preparing the shish kebabs. "Well, you know, that's not the only kind of poking she did."

ZEGLOVITCH: Do you recall Dr. Tomanek ever making any statement regarding a purported sexual relationship between Dr. Jew and Dr. Williams?

DAWES: Yes, he called her a slut to me. It took place in the spring of 1983. It occurred in his office, and I had met him in the hallway and had asked him about some references for a seminar and we were talking about those references, and then suddenly to me out of the blue he started talking about the way things were in the department. He suddenly says that "Well, the only way you can get ahead here is apparently to be involved with Williams in a real estate deal, to do business with him or to be sleeping with him like that"—and he called Jean Jew a slut, "like that slut Jean Jew."[8]

Next up was Tena Perry. Her testimony about Tomanek mirrored Dawes's but from Perry's perspective as a clerk typist in the Anatomy Department main office. She described an incident that occurred soon after she started in that job in 1979 or 1980.

PERRY: I was in the break room area in the department. And the coffee pot is there, and Tomanek came in for a cup of coffee, got his cup of coffee and he was chatting, and he started telling me about Dr. Jew and Dr. Williams having an affair, and kind of wanted to know what I thought about it. He was explaining to me what was going on and had been, he said, for quite some time.

CHALMERS: Who initiated the conversation?

PERRY: He did.

CHALMERS: Was there an innuendo in his statement?

PERRY: Yeah, I think so.

CHALMERS: What was it?

PERRY: That if it hadn't been for Dr. Jew having an affair with Dr. Williams, that she wouldn't be—have gotten where she was without the relationship.

CHALMERS: What was your reaction to his statement?

PERRY: I didn't really say anything either way. I was kind of surprised that he would take the time to explain it to me. We really didn't have any involvement in any of that. I thought it was a rotten thing when he could not say he had actually seen anything himself. It was just gossip spreading and I didn't think it was very nice actually.[9]

Judge Vietor was paying close attention. He took notes on two yellow pads—one for our witnesses and one for theirs. On each sheet he drew a line down the center. He recorded his notes on the direct examination on one side and his notes on the cross-examination on the other. When one of us objected that a question misstated prior testimony, he referred back to his notes and set us all straight. It seemed that he was listening very closely to these women—unassuming, plain spoken, and strong—taking risks with their work relationships and with their jobs.

⁘

Back at the Savery, in sweatpants, leaning back against the bedstead or worn upholstery on a sturdy armchair, we were content with the way Wednesday had gone. One more day of short witnesses, and then Friday we would close out the week with Jean's testimony and, depending on how that went, perhaps close our case-in-chief. To do that we had to be confident we presented evidence adequate to prove the elements of the Title VII sexual harassment claim—that the hostile conduct was based on gender, the conduct was severe or pervasive enough to be both objectively and subjectively offensive, and the employer had notice of the conduct and failed to correct it. The university would have their chance to call witnesses to disprove or rebut our evidence. We would have a chance to call rebuttal witnesses after that.

I called Eric when the day was over. "Finally, we had a really good day."

"Good, very good, excellent. I'm so glad to hear it," Eric said, relieved by the relief in my voice. "Do you think you will be able to get back for Thanksgiving?" An indirect way of asking, how much longer this was going to go on. Thanksgiving holiday was a week away.

"Don't know." I mused out loud. "At the end of today the judge said solicitously to Jean, 'Dr. Jew, that lectern is not obstructing your view of the witness, is it?' I think he wanted to hear her voice in his courtroom. Today all she said was 'No, it is not.' That will have to hold him 'til Friday."

"Stay strong. All is well here." We talked about how the kids were holding up. My attention wandered back to my work, and I said goodnight.

Day 4, November 16

We needed to push back on the terrible things being said about Terry Williams. But we did not want to call him as our witness. We did not like the optics of presenting Williams as Jean's defender. It did not comport with presenting Jean as an independent scholar deserving promotion to full professor. Another problem was Williams himself. He was maligned by the university—in his career and in the trial. To be a good witness for Jean, he had to subordinate his resentment about his own treatment and camouflage his anger. We were not confident he could do that. If he strayed off message and began describing his, rather than Jean's, injuries, he would exhibit the flaws that the university attributed to him.

The safer option was to call Williams's wife, Glenys Williams. Married in England thirty-three years before, they now had grown children. Glenys was composed and attractive. Her gray hair was full around her face and collected into a bun in back. Her eyes were strong, her gaze direct, and her walk confident as she took the witness stand. For several years, Glenys had worked in her husband's lab at Tulane, for a few of those with Jean. At the time of the trial, Glenys was a clinical faculty member in the College of Medicine. She testified that Jean was a close friend of hers and of her husband's who often joined them socially. She said there was no sexual relationship between Jean and Williams.[10]

We called Pat Palmer, a research assistant who had worked in Tomanek's lab for five years.[11] In that job she was his captive audience.

CHALMERS: Do you recall any occasion when Dr. Tomanek talked with you about Dr. Jew?

PALMER: Yes, I do. I believe it was five or six weeks after I was employed. He came into the laboratory and was quite upset about something and started talking and moving around the room and talking rather loudly about being screwed over by the university or the department. And he said that it was no wonder he was being screwed over because he wasn't doing what she was doing.

CHALMERS: Who was he referring to?

PALMER: Dr. Jew.

CHALMERS: Did he say anything further about Dr. Jew in this conversation?

PALMER: Yes. He referred to an incident—a rumor about she and Dr. Williams being found on the sofa in his office having intercourse.

CHALMERS: Would you tell us, as best you can recall, the precise words that he said?

PALMER: Sometimes he would say that Jean and Terry were caught screwing on the sofa. Sometimes he would say that they were caught fucking on the sofa. And it depended, again, on how upset he was. There were times he was very upset.

CHALMERS: Did you learn from anyone else of comments about Dr. Jew and Dr. Williams having a sexual relationship?

PALMER: Yes, I did. At one point a person who was employed in our laboratory came out of his office and said to me that she was told by Tomanek the sofa story, that Dr. Jew and Dr. Williams were on the sofa. Another person later employed by Dr. Tomanek also said the same thing; that, you know, that he referred to that incident.

Pat Palmer's testimony was a high point. It was immediately followed by a low point.

At two o'clock our next witness, Dr. Paul Heidger, a professor in the department sympathetic to Jean, had not arrived. Judge Vietor was antsy. This week and the next, Thanksgiving week, were set aside for our trial. He had a criminal case scheduled to start the Monday after Thanksgiving. We were not making enough progress.

THE COURT: Well, what about your client? Can we get her testimony started?

CHALMERS: Pardon?

THE COURT: Can we get your client's testimony started? I take it she's going to testify?

CHALMERS: She's going to testify, yes.

But please, not now. Not until tomorrow. Five years to prepare for this moment, and I'm not ready!

Shaping Jean's chronology and facts into a persuasive story deserving of remedy was the most critical challenge of the case. My questions— open-ended and crafted to elicit the information the judge was puzzling over—and Jean's answers ideally would alternate in an easy rhythm. This should be structured in a narrative arc with a beginning, middle, and end, revealing Jean's values, effort, outcomes, obstacles, injuries, and hopes. Through her testimony, Judge Vietor would get to know her, like her, and credit her account. Choreographing the narrative was a creative act, with the one witness with whom I was in complete sync. It was my responsibility. I knew all this but was chagrined that I had not yet done it.

Trial requires successful pivots. A hole opens up in the defense— lunge. Opposing counsel slings rotten tomatoes—duck. A witness does not appear when scheduled—temporize.

THE COURT: I would rather keep busy.

CHALMERS: Very good, your honor. We call the plaintiff, Jean Jew.[12]

We just had time for a short exchange about Jean's childhood and education at Tulane before the judge cut us a break. Our other witness finally arrived, and the judge allowed us to substitute Professor Heidger for Jean. He related his knowledge of the slurs together with his respect for Jean's skills. When he stepped down, the judge did not cut us any more slack. He recalled Jean to the stand for the last twenty minutes of the day. At 5:03, that very long afternoon ended. Turning to counsel table, before Jean could step down from the witness box, Judge Vietor addressed her directly.

> THE COURT: Doctor, what is the correct pronunciation of your
>   name?
> JEAN: Jew.
> THE COURT: Jew, not "Chu"?
> JEAN: It sounds the same to me when you're saying it.[13]

I was touched. Although he had heard her name pronounced several times by witnesses and attorneys, he reached out to learn if he should pronounce her name more like "Chu" or "Shu" or "Xu." His question showed deep respect for her ethnicity. Perhaps her family pronounced it differently than the white people in his courtroom. Her response revealed her personal reserve. Her name was pronounced as it appeared, "Jew." Nearly fifty years ago her family exchanged a name signaling their ethnicity for one that signaled an ethnicity to which they did not belong. What was done, was done. Jean preferred Judge Vietor to focus on what could be undone.

⁞ ⁞ ⁞

Returning to the Savery, I knew, Jean knew, and I knew she knew, that I was not prepared for what happened that afternoon. She, who never stood up before a class without a carefully polished lecture, had put her career in the hands of a lawyer who had not met this standard in shaping her life's story. I did not speak to her about my fear that I did not have the energy that night to do good work. She did not speak to me about her own fears. She waited quietly through our debrief for the time when we would go back to work. After supper, Jean and I retreated into my room, where we crushed ten years of slurs, shock, self-help responses, and pain into a narrative. By midnight we had done what we could to create a script of the conversation we would have in the courtroom. We were ready to tell her story, in her words, her way—by that I mean precisely, carefully, and without exaggeration.

Day 5, November 17

Friday morning, I considered what to wear.

A courtroom is a stage where costume communicates, especially for women attorneys. To be the only woman at the lectern in a courtroom was normal—not comfortable, but customary—for me. Everyone else taking a turn standing there in those years was a white male in a dark suit. In those days, women were encouraged to wear suits that echoed those worn by men—a gray or navy suit, white blouse, and subdued string tie or neck scarf. For women, a skirt completed the outfit— pantsuits on women in the courtroom were verboten. A few women permitted the fit of their clothing to have a sexy edge or would wear noticeable make-up. Most of us in the first wave of women practicing law did neither. We chose not to draw attention to our bodies or com- municate any sexual nuance. My clothes were reserved, though not so reserved as to be masculine. On Friday morning I chose a charcoal pinstriped skirt with a cropped plum and teal jacket. It was a sturdy choice. It would not wilt.

I have no memory of what Jean wore. In the witness chair she was small, calm, and sure. She made steady eye contact with me and occa- sionally turned to make eye contact with the judge. Her diction was precise and her voice clear. One of her friends made the two-hour drive to Des Moines to sit in the courtroom and keep company most days. The only other semi-regular attendees were a reporter from the *Des Moines Register* and Tom Diehl, Tomanek's personal attorney. Some days a few witnesses came in advance of their appointed time to observe. Important business before the courts is open to the public, but the public seldom attends.

THE COURT: Good morning, everybody. Dr. Jew, would you resume the witness stand, please?

Jean and I began with the incidents in the early period—between 1973, when she came to Iowa, and 1984, the year her formal complaint was submitted to the university. As we went along, I tried to elicit her emotions—how she felt.

CHALMERS: As a result of your conversations with Dr. Black, did you feel any concern for your professional development?

JEAN: It concerned me a lot that before people would have met me at all and been able to form their own opinion based on my performance or whatever, that the first thing they would have heard about me was that I was sleeping with the chairman. I think it had the effect of isolating me. I certainly was very reluctant to take initiatives myself to work with other people simply because that sort of allegation had been so distasteful, and it's something that no one can condone.

I turned to her communications with Brodbeck and Eckstein in 1979.

CHALMERS: What did Dean Eckstein say to you in response to your letter?

JEAN: He said, "But, you know, Iowa City is a small town, and it's a goldfish bowl, and a single woman has these sorts of problems when she's working in this environment. My pursuing such a complaint would only make things worse for me."

In 1982 and 1983 she went to see Vice President Remington.

CHALMERS: What motivated you to go see him [Remington]?

JEAN: It wasn't just the promotion, but my entire future at the University of Iowa was in jeopardy with this sort of thing going on. He said, "You've got a good CV. They'll make your life hell, but you're going to continue to progress."

In the courtroom, Jean described the hostility that followed the submission of her 1984 complaint letter and the panel hearing. Tomanek told a faculty colleague that Jean and Williams had been seen holding hands in a restaurant. A philosophy professor asked an anatomy professor, "Is the Chinese girl still having an affair with that professor in Anatomy?" Jean's nameplate outside her office was wrenched from the wall, left hanging. A professor in her department reported being told that Williams and Jean were seen having sex on a library table. The evening TV news reported that Jean was close to Williams, "His star is falling, and now hers is, too."

So far, while sitting at counsel table or on the witness stand as intimate details of her life were being exposed, Jean's demeanor was self-possessed. To successfully convey the impact of the university's refusal to stop the slurs, she had to reveal her pain. She loathed doing this. Nonetheless, she came as close as she could to the truth of her injury.

CHALMERS: Did your awareness of these incidents affect your own self-confidence?

JEAN: I think that when you go through years and years of knowing that people are being told that you have gotten where you are solely because you've been sleeping with the chairman, that no matter what you do, you question, "Well, is this going to be good enough to convince them that I deserve this, that I'm competent enough to do this work?"

CHALMERS: You learned about some of the specific incidents indirectly and after the fact. How did [that] affect you?

JEAN: Whether or not I knew about all of the incidents, I knew enough that it would have been totally unrealistic of me not to realize that the little bit that I was hearing was just the tip of the iceberg.

CHALMERS: Dr. Jew, have you had any physical effects?

JEAN: From about 1980, '81 to the present time, I've had a chronic eczematous condition.

CHALMERS: Have you had psychological symptoms related to the working environment you've described here?

JEAN: It's only been since, I guess, over the past year or two that the depression rose to the level that might be determined a clinical depression, where I have had to take medication, and I'm still on that.

Judge Vietor's pen flew over the pages on the legal pad he had designated for our side. He leaned toward Jean to catch every word. At one point, he stopped us, "Wait a minute. I'm not a fast note-taker." Getting the sense of it, close-enough approximations, surmising— none were good enough for him. He wanted every word. Painful, ugly, demeaning, shaming, stunningly personal yet simultaneously public, the sexually denigrating words were at the heart of Jean's decision to come forward and my decision to take and pursue the case. If details were clumped into like bundles, and each sharp point dulled to fit a more palatable, generalized description, then Jean's lawsuit would defy comprehension. The naked purpose to malign her, the wounds, both tangible and intangible, and the administrators' decision to sacrifice her—all were sequestered in the details. One simple question ended the swale of smut.

CHALMERS: Did you ever have sex with Dr. Williams?
JEAN: No.
CHALMERS: Dr. Jew, I would like to change the subject now and talk about promotion.
JEAN: Good.

We moved on with relief. After discussing the criteria for promotion to full professor, the facts that showed Jean's credentials met the criteria, the prejudicial impact of Tomanek and Kaelber's votes in 1983, and the impossibility of a fair vote in the future if they participated, we ended her direct examination by contrasting Jean's expectations of the university when she came sixteen years ago with her feelings now.

CHALMERS: How did you expect the university to treat you as an individual?
JEAN: I thought if I proved myself to be competent, to be an asset to the university, that the university would regard me as such and, you know, do everything in its power that's reasonable to keep me and to value me as a faculty member.
CHALMERS: How do you feel now?
JEAN: I feel that I am a value and an asset to the university. I don't

think that the university recognizes that, nor do I think that they particularly care, especially right now. I think it would be much more convenient for them if I were to leave.

⁝⁝⁝

Jean decided to stay, speak up, and fight for change. University attorneys used Jean's decision to discredit her. They argued that she was not seriously injured since she never attempted to find employment elsewhere. They appeared to urge her exit, perhaps because the university's interests lay in silencing her. Jean's response, when questioned about why she did not leave, was that she did not want senior male faculty to succeed in their goal of driving her out. It made no sense to her that she should be burdened with starting from scratch to build a research program since she had done nothing wrong. She was skeptical that the grass would be greener in a different university. Faced with injustice, as her close friend remarked, "Jean is like granite—immovable."

Women scientists facing institutional sexism not infrequently elect to move on to work in a different university. In her memoir *Lab Girl*, Hope Jahren, a geochemist and geobiologist, describes butting up against sexist barriers. She moved from Georgia Tech, to Johns Hopkins, to the University of Hawaii, to the University of Oslo.[14] Exit served both her scientific career and university interests in quieting her voice.

Jean's and Jahren's contrasting responses had strikingly different consequences. Jahren found better opportunities to develop her scientific career with each move. Jean, deciding to voice her concerns from within the institution, had to shortchange her scientific research work to pursue her complaint and fend off university backlash. Women scientists facing sex discrimination may be better served by leaving the offending institution. The offending university, and the women in it, may be better served when one of their own stays and fights.

⁝⁝⁝

After lunch on Friday, Galenbeck began his cross-examination. Jean's precision with language, both as a listener and speaker, blocked every line of attack. My intuition that she would be an excellent witness, an intuition I had in our first phone call, was spot on. She approached each question like the scientist she was—what is really being asked here and what is my true answer? During cross-examination, Jean's answers were firm. Knowing her well, I knew that anger lay underneath some of her blunt responses, although it never showed.

Jean parried Galenbeck's attempts to establish that the slurs were not sex-based since they were also directed at Williams.

GALENBECK: Isn't it fair to say that these are comments about both you and Dr. Williams?

JEAN: Not in every case. I don't think that Dr. Williams was called a slut or a whore.

GALENBECK: You wouldn't dispute that those [anonymous] letters were about Dr. Williams, in addition to whatever else they might have been about?

JEAN: I think the references to me were much more derogatory than they were about Dr. Williams.

Her answers communicated that her expectations of appropriate university action were reasonable, not extreme.

GALENBECK: Are you saying that you did not oppose those investigations of your conduct and your relationship with Williams?

JEAN: I'm saying that if there was a basis for believing that relationship existed, then they had a right to question me about it, and they should have pursued it, as well; and once they found that there was no basis for it, then something should have been done to provide me with relief, and nothing ever was.

At the end of Friday Judge Vietor posed his questions to her.

THE COURT: I have a matter I want to ask before I forget it, a couple of questions. You indicated earlier on your cross-examination that you never went to the people who were spreading rumors to tell them what they were saying was false and to ask them to stop saying it. Did you ever suggest to Dr. Williams that he go to those people and tell them that what they were saying was false and to stop saying it?

JEAN: No, I did not.

THE COURT: One more question. Why did you not do that yourself, or why did you not go to Dr. Williams and suggest that he do it?

JEAN: I went to the person that I thought would be most effective in doing something about it, and in my mind even now that is clearly Dean Eckstein. I just did not think that Dr. Williams would be able to do anything about it.

On that note we adjourned for the weekend. Overall, we had had a good first week. Galenbeck's cross-examination of Jean would continue on Monday, and then we would rest our case and the university would begin to call its witnesses. The plan was to present all of the fact witnesses to Judge Vietor in these two weeks. Judge Vietor intended to postpone expert witnesses until May 1990, when his schedule had some open days. Jean's case would not be submitted for his decision until the expert witness testimony was completed.

⁝⁝⁝

The next week the university would control the narrative, and the testimony from its witnesses would be hard to bear. Bob and I turned our attention to preparing for them. We could not contact senior university administrators directly because they were, in some sense, the university—a party to the litigation and represented by counsel. But we could contact nonmanagement university employees to learn what they intended to say. We reached only a few. Sometimes the phone numbers were wrong, or they did not answer their phones. Others declined to talk with us when we identified ourselves. If witnesses didn't want to talk with us, they didn't have to. We didn't know which of these witnesses would be called on any particular day the following week.

I doubt we did anything fun in Des Moines that weekend. I did not resent working because being prepared was the best antidote for anxiety. In twelve years of law practice, I had been lead counsel in many lawsuits, but few had gone to trial. As I reread the transcript, I see signs of my inexperience.

I didn't miss my family. I would have been just as unavailable to them had I been home. My grim visage at the dinner table would not have strengthened family bonds. My retreat behind a closed door the rest of the time could be accomplished better in Des Moines. It made things simpler by not trying to reenter family life with a sixteen-year-old son and a twelve-year-old daughter. All I needed was to be told they were doing well in my absence.

"What will we do about Thanksgiving?" Eric asked again that Friday night. He had talked with Jane Young, Bob Zeglovitch's wife. "Jane and I can come down with Leah and Seth on Wednesday. She and I can figure out something for Thursday and maybe go to observe court?"

"What will we do for Thanksgiving dinner? It would be hard on the kids, and probably a big bore for them," I said.

"I don't know what we'll do for dinner . . . something. The kids are interested to see what's going on. It's not a long drive and the weather looks clear so far. Jane is up for it so we will have two drivers." Jane was a very outgoing, lively librarian with a laugh that filled a room and cheered all present, always.

"OK," I said.

Day 6, November 20

Monday morning opened with Judge Vietor's decision that trial would continue on the Friday after Thanksgiving. For Jean's third round that morning, the themes of Galenbeck's cross nested like Russian dolls. One was painted as a dissembling sexual paramour. If that did not convince, twist it apart and reveal a doll painted as a desiccated spinster. The innermost, painted as a lesbian perhaps? Take your pick.

GALENBECK: Do you consider Williams as your best friend?
JEAN: No.
GALENBECK: Is there any individual with whom you spend more time than you spend with Dr. Williams?
JEAN: Not if you consider work time as well, no.
GALENBECK: Is there any person with whom you spend more time socializing than you do with Dr. Williams?
JEAN: Perhaps.

GALENBECK: In fact, since you moved to Iowa City, have you spent another evening socializing with a single man, other than Dr. Williams?

JEAN: Dr. Williams is not a single man.

GALENBECK: Have you had a date since you came to Iowa City in 1973?

CHALMERS: Objection, relevance.

THE COURT: Well, I guess we'll receive it—the answer subject to the objection. I've got a problem—

GALENBECK: I'm just exploring the—obviously the appearance that the two of them spend so much time together, Your Honor.

THE COURT: Go ahead and answer.

GALENBECK: Let me ask this a different way then: Have you had any—a romantic relationship with any man since you came to Iowa City in 1973?

JEAN: No, I have not.

Nothing was too private or personal in the hunt for circumstantial evidence of a sexual relationship. Galenbeck asked Jean about using birth control pills from 1973 to 1978. Did she contemplate a sexual relationship with Williams during this period? Innuendo was effectively conveyed by Galenbeck's question, never mind Jean's negative answer.

Before Jean was excused, I had a chance to question her. I reprised Judge Vietor's question to her at the end of the day on Friday and asked her to explain why she did not go to Tomanek directly and ask him to stop.

JEAN: Well, first of all, the nature of the allegations was just very humiliating. . . . You know, I was ashamed. Secondly, it was not in my background or experience to have a confrontational—to confront someone. It had always been ingrained in me that you go through channels, you go to the person in authority if you have a complaint. Also, I was very vulnerable. I was, you know, a relatively junior-level faculty member compared to Dr. Tomanek . . . and I think most of all it would have been very difficult because the way that the allegations were made in such a cowardly way. I was never confronted with anything directly. . . . There was no way for me to fight it directly.

The courtroom was quiet while Jean walked back to her chair at counsel table. She did not expel a deep sigh of relief for a job well done or share a smile with me.

THE COURT: Call your next witness.
CHALMERS: Your Honor, plaintiff rests.
THE COURT: You rest?
CHALMERS: Yes.
THE COURT: That is correct?
CHALMERS: That's correct.
THE COURT: Very well.

We did not know what to make of the surprise in his voice.

⁝⁝⁝

Concerned as we were about the university attorneys' plan to embellish the salacious themes beyond what Tomanek had dared, we were immensely gratified to learn that they had so little to work with. Proving Jean was a liar was an impossibly high bar to clear—irrational to even attempt—as they only had innuendo and circumstantial presumptions to undermine the credibility we were gaining from Jean's consistent, clear, reserved denials. A standard question to their witnesses was, "Did you form an opinion as to whether Dr. Jew and Dr. Williams were having a sexual relationship?" Judge Vietor allowed many questions like this that were objectionable under the rules of evidence. Because the judge, instead of a jury, would be deciding contested facts, he could disregard improper questions and answers. Excluding testimony was riskier on appeal than including it. Some of their witnesses answered this question yes, they had an opinion, but when cross-examined, could not show any factual basis for their opinion. Ignoring the lengthening odds, university attorneys tread and retread the sex track, refusing to distinguish suspicions from facts.

Judge Vietor was not taking detailed notes of their repetitive testimony. He looked over at our table from time to time and made eye contact with us. Bob noticed this pattern, and we discussed it during our debriefs. Was Judge Vietor foreshadowing that he wasn't buying what the university attorneys were selling?

The university's first witness was George McHenry, the longtime administrator of the Anatomy Department.[15] According to the university lawyers, his testimony would verify a sexual relationship between Williams and Jean.

ZEGLOVITCH: Have you ever heard Robert Tomanek make a statement on the subject that Dr. Jew and Dr. Williams were having a sexual relationship?

MCHENRY: He made a statement to me once in the hall that he thought they were; that he believed in God and he didn't have proof that there was a God, but he was sure that they were having a sexual relationship.

ZEGLOVITCH: Do you have any reason to believe that Dr. Jew and Dr. Williams have had a sexual relationship at any time?

MCHENRY: No.

The second witness traveled from the University of Cincinnati Medical College to say that he saw Jean rub Williams's upper back and neck briefly while Williams sat in his desk chair in his office. He never saw any other touching. From the National Institutes of Health in Washington, DC, a scientist traveled to tell us that Jean asked for adjoining hotel rooms with Williams at a scientific conference and helped Williams host a reception for academics in his room. Monday ended with testimony from a former undergraduate student who worked as a custodian in the Anatomy Department. University lawyers had described his testimony as confirming that Jean and Williams embraced in Williams's office. At the trial, he said he saw nothing of the sort. No embrace. He had walked into Williams's office in the evening. Surprised, because he had not knocked, Jean and Williams stood up from the sofa where they had been reviewing papers.

Professor Coulter, the chair of the Department of Anatomy who arrived in Iowa after the lawsuit was under way, was one of those who answered yes, he had concluded there was an inappropriate sexual relationship. His conclusion was not based on any firsthand knowledge but on materials he had been shown by university administrators. Professor James West, who was in his lab with Kaelber in 1979 when Kaelber shouted out slurs about Jean, answered, "I didn't [conclude they had a sexual relationship] until now. Because if it weren't true, there would be no need to complain about it and cause all this fuss. So maybe it's true." Jean's decision to speak out was the basis for his conclusion.

Bob and I prepared for cross-examination, but did little of it, as their witnesses did us little harm.

Day 7, November 21

Six additional witnesses testified against Jean. Five faculty—four at the University of Iowa College of Medicine and one from Chicago. Their testimony described Tomanek as their friend, criticized Jean as a friend of Williams, and criticized Williams for playing favorites. Without knowing any of the terms and conditions of others' employment, they opined that the College of Medicine did not discriminate against women. Without reviewing Jean's promotion file, they opined that she had not shown the requisite independence for promotion. Mixed in were supportive comments, noting that Jean was an award-winning teacher and researcher. She had served ably on College of Medicine committees. Ricocheting back to the sex theme, the sixth witness was a former research assistant for one of the faculty witnesses adverse to Jean. Now a police officer, he said he saw Williams come to Jean's door at 10:30 in the evening with a magazine that he handed to her, full stop. No blood drawn.

Some testimony the university put on damaged its case. Complaining that Williams denied his request for a refrigerator in his lab, one professor told us his proposed solution with pride, not irony. "I suggested openly in the faculty meeting that the refrigerator be placed in the men's room. We all frequent the men's room at one time or another during the day and we could use the common refrigerator."[16] Another defended his comment during the senior faculty's evaluation of Jean's progress toward promotion in 1983 as a perfectly acceptable diversity joke: "The Anatomy Department has a black, a woman, two Jews, and a cripple, and our Jews are also Chinks."[17]

Day 8, November 22

On the third day the university called nearly a dozen witnesses. One by one, people Jean had previously considered neutral testified for the university. Jean never altered her attentive gaze or added an inadvertent shake of her head or furrow to her brow. I imagine she wondered: *Why would he say that knowing it was false? I know he is not my friend—but to lie?* Unobtrusively, she passed me notes: *Remind her I took over her class during her maternity leave. Ask him to compare his publication record when he was promoted with mine. I could not have attended that meeting with Williams: I was still a med student preparing for final exams in New Orleans.*

The university's first witness on this morning before Thanksgiving was Jane McCutcheon.[18] Despite the faculty panel's determination that she was not credible, university attorneys continued to give McCutcheon billing as their star witness. Today I have no picture of her no matter how I search my memory, although I spent a day taking her deposition and cross-examined her twice. I cannot conjure up hair, height, dress, face, glasses, facial expression—nothing. She has vanished from my mind—the only place I could accomplish this.

GALENBECK: Now, could you tell the court what you saw?
MCCUTCHEON: I opened the door; and I didn't get very far into the room, and there was a man. And his back was towards me, and there were a woman's legs facing me. And he sort of half turned, and I saw that it was Terry Williams, and then I took off as fast as I could.
GALENBECK: Now, did you see someone else?
MCCUTCHEON: I didn't see a whole person. I saw legs.
GALENBECK: And could you describe the legs that you saw?
MCCUTCHEON: Well, they were short. They weren't—They were darker than Caucasian legs, and they were kind of stubby.
GALENBECK: Who did you think this other person was?

MCCUTCHEON: Dr. Jew.

GALENBECK: Why did you believe this to be . . . Dr. Jew?

MCCUTCHEON: Part of it was the assumption, because I had heard a lot of gossip that they were having an affair; and part of it was because the legs were consistent with what I would have expected to see of Dr. Jew's legs.

My cross-examination focused on inconsistencies in her three recitations. In Judge Vietor's courtroom, she couldn't recall the man's face, couldn't say now why she identified him as Williams, couldn't be certain who he was, and never identified Jean. She "wouldn't trust the accuracy of her memory at all on that incident." Galenbeck's only comeback to these inconsistencies was that I had intimidated McCutcheon by my questions in her depositions in 1986 and again in trial. Despite this, he asserted she had resolutely done her "very best to tell the truth."

Judge Vietor's skepticism was evident when, for the first time with a witness, he interposed his own questions to McCutcheon. He asked her about the details—what time of year (don't know), what time of day (best as she could remember, evening), lighting in the room (fluorescent), and what was the distance from the door to the table (not more than me to the end of this table)?

When the judge let us go two hours early on Wednesday afternoon for the Thanksgiving holiday, he mused out loud: "It's curiouser and curiouser that nobody is calling Dr. Williams." *Hmm. He wants to see and hear Williams. Damn! We've got to call him.* With that he adjourned. "We'll see you all Friday morning at 8:45. Have a good Thanksgiving."

Thanksgiving, November 23

Our families arrived Wednesday night. The kids were mostly watchful, supportive, and patient. Seth was a junior in high school, and Leah was on the cusp of her teenage years. They may have helped cook the next day in the Savery's party room. Bob and I were still toiling in the trenches even on the holiday. I spent much of Thursday in my room preparing to cross-examine Tomanek, who would be the lead-off witness on Friday.

Our small group gathered in the party room mid-afternoon. We echoed in the big space. Banquet tables had been pushed to the outer walls, and chairs were stacked six high. Our families had pulled a few tables to the center and added flowers, a tablecloth, and paper plates.

I have to assume rotisserie chickens and take-out Thanksgiving meals were not available in those days in Des Moines. Instead, our chicken emerged from a can legs first. White, all mushed together, and covered in quivering aspic, it was unappetizing. Eric and Jane swaddled, dried, stuffed, seasoned, baked, and carved it. They also cooked salmon steaks (much more appetizing). I remember the scrawny bird as the center-piece of our Thanksgiving meal, supplemented with tinned cranber-ries, refrigerated crescent rolls, frozen vegetables, and pie. Best efforts were made at happy chatter despite the gray day and vacant downtown streets. Promptly after the meal, Bob and I exited and went back to work.

I talked with the kids about what to expect the next day. "Jean and I will leave about 8:00. You guys will come later with Dad and Jane. Wide awake and breakfasted, please," I said. When Seth was hungry, there was little advance notice and hell to pay. "You'll sit in the audience section and will be quiet no matter what happens. No gasps or whispers to each other. There will be other observers, perhaps a dozen, some with us and some against us—and you won't know who is who. There will be a bathroom break mid-morning. There are only two bathrooms on the floor. No talk in the bathrooms, even with me or Dad. You might be overheard. Take a snack for mid-morning." I stopped short of telling them what to wear. Whatever Eric had packed would do.

"Tomorrow we expect Dr. Tomanek to be the main witness. We think he is responsible for many of the bad things that happened to Jean. After the university lawyers question him, I will have a turn. Anything could happen. Keep your poker faces on."

Day 9, November 24

Assembling in the courtroom Friday morning, I thought that Judge Vietor would be pleased to see our families and know they had joined us for Thanksgiving. We were not the extreme ideologues that university lawyers continued to sketch.

As I listened to Lerner's questions and Tomanek's replies, anger supplanted nervousness. Tomanek's physical appearance—a goatee and a rumpled, down-home sport coat—was designed to convey that he wouldn't hurt a flea. He frequently turned to the judge when speaking. I thought his smile was unctuous. He detailed his complaints against Williams for denying him raises and resources he felt he deserved, while squandering them on Jean instead. Tomanek defended his judgment that Williams and Jean had a sexual relationship, basing it on his "perception," their "appearance," and persistent "talk." He concluded by saying that he was critical of Williams for the perceived sexual relationship, but not of Jean because she "was not germane."[19]

Let's see how this works out for him, I thought as I stood up.

CHALMERS: Between 1973 and the present you've had practically no opportunity to work with Dr. Jew?

TOMANEK: That is correct.

CHALMERS: You have not talked with her?

TOMANEK: Correct.

CHALMERS: And you have not done research with her?

TOMANEK: Correct.

CHALMERS: Or shared laboratory space, served on panels with her, walked by her office or laboratory regularly, or observed Williams treating Jean differently in faculty meetings?

TOMANEK: Correct.

CHALMERS: And on occasions when you saw them outside of work, they were no more frequent than perhaps once a year?

TOMANEK: Correct.

CHALMERS: And you never saw firsthand any evidence of any intimate physical conduct between them?

TOMANEK: Not to my recollection, no. That's correct.

⁛

Jean sought only the same privileges junior male faculty enjoyed, but these were at odds with society's expectations of the appropriate role for a young, single woman faculty member. Her salary reflected her M.D. degree, which neither Tomanek nor Kaelber had. If earned by a male M.D., her salary would have been an indication of worth. But when received by a woman, Tomanek and Kaelber were apoplectic. Jean's precocious skills, her gumption in the face of their criticism, and her disregard of their well-understood social conventions appeared to infuriate these men. Cultural tropes of Chinese women—as comfort women and concubines—resulted.

While Tomanek's obsession with Jean's sexuality was personal, it was rooted in societal misogyny. Hating women who do not conform to society's views of their appropriate role was and is a social phenomenon.[20] For what they viewed as her astounding impertinence, these men used their cultural stereotypes of the sexuality of an unmarried Chinese woman to disdain, insult, and erase her accomplishments. Maligning Jean was her punishment for aspiring to a place in a white man's world.

Jean searched for reasons for Tomanek's obsession with her sexuality. She went about her work without any insignia of sexual availability—no revealing clothing, chitchat about sex, coy glances, or casual touches. "Business-like" and "pleasant" were the words others used to describe Jean. She would have been reluctant to conclude that her unalterable attributes—her national origin, gender, race, youth, and marital status—were what goaded him. That by just being who she was, she was an affront.

$$\diamond\diamond\diamond$$

Although identified by most witnesses as the ringleader of the rumors, Tomanek had no recollection of ever being admonished to stop the sex talk.

CHALMERS: Now, before Dr. Jew's complaint was filed on October 31, 1985, did anyone ever tell you—any university official, that they believed you were making statements about a sexual relationship between Dr. Jew and Williams, and you had to stop doing that?

TOMANEK: No.

CHALMERS: No university official ever said anything like that to you, did they?

TOMANEK: That is correct.

Each line of questions was pointed, in sharp contrast to Tomanek's *aw shucks* manner. We established that Dean Eckstein had authorized a special promotion process for consideration of Tomanek's promotion to full professor in 1981 and excluded Williams from the process; Tomanek was allowed to name external reviewers; and Tomanek was not required to sign a release of claims or a confidentiality agreement, all of which distinguished his process from the proposal Eckstein made to Jean on the eve of filing suit.

I was in control of the pace, tone, and subject matter. I wanted to reveal Tomanek as the cad I believed him to be. I also wanted to prove that the university knew all this about him and yet sided with him. The university was paying for one of the lawyers representing Tomanek in Jean's state court defamation case, Tom Diehl, to sit in the federal courtroom and observe. No public resources were spared to coordinate Tomanek's and the university's defenses. Tom Diehl was present on Friday for Tomanek's testimony, giving me an opening for this line of questions.

CHALMERS: Is one of your attorneys present in this courtroom?
TOMANEK: Yes.
CHALMERS: Would you point him out, please?
TOMANEK: Thomas Diehl sitting there.
CHALMERS: How is your lawyer being compensated?

Lerner was on his feet, outraged.

LERNER: Objection, Your Honor. This is attorney work product
    —I mean attorney-client privilege.
THE COURT: It's not your [Lerner's] privilege to assert anyway.
    It's the witness's privilege. Now, his lawyer is here, and I can
    hear him on this subject. Can we have your [Diehl's] assurance
    that if the ruling is that the question is to be answered, you can
    provide the answer?
DIEHL: Certainly.
CHALMERS: Dr. Tomanek, have you had any conversation with
    any university official regarding whether or not your attorney's
    fees will be paid by the university?

DIEHL: I do not assert any objection to that question.

CHALMERS: With whom?

TOMANEK: Julia Mears.

CHALMERS: And what did she tell you?

LERNER: Objection; hearsay, Your Honor.

THE COURT: You may answer.

LERNER: And relevance.

TOMANEK: She said, "I would like you to go over and see one of my colleagues to represent you," and that's when I went to the law firm that is now representing me.

CHALMERS: And was it your understanding from that conversation that the university would be paying your fees?

LERNER: Objection; calls for speculation.

THE COURT: You may answer.

LERNER: And relevance.

THE COURT: Answer.

Judge Vietor seldom used this commanding tone to a witness. It indicated to me his impatience with Lerner, his skepticism about Tomanek, and his reservation of judgment on whether I could get this right.

DIEHL: You can answer.

TOMANEK: Yes.

Tomanek's understanding was later verified by Julia Mears's testimony under oath in the state trial acknowledging that the state would be paying Tomanek's attorney's fees and expenses while contributing nothing "at all" to Jean's.

The kids were watching—attentive and still. Seth leaned forward with his elbows on the back of the bench in front and with his chin in his hands, watching. Leah arched back against the bench back, as if being hit with Tomanek's words. Most everyone in the courtroom was caught up in the tension—one side resisting, the other pressing, the judge directing.

Without looking back at him, I knew Eric was watching intensely. I knew how much he hoped that my questions that morning would unmask Tomanek. At the break, Eric said, "You nailed him."

"Really? Do you really think so?" *Repeat that again, slowly, please.* I couldn't get enough of it.

Our family's visit buoyed us up. I took pleasure in the serendipity of having a dramatic moment on a morning when they were in the audience. My sorrow to see them leave on Saturday was modulated by the fact that we only had a few more days to go.

Day 10, November 27

Thirteen witnesses, some the university's and some ours, testified in the final three days of trial. Judge Vietor was impatient with this parade of repetitive accounts.

> THE COURT: I have a heavy docket. This case has gone on for more days than it should already, and I'm going to start cracking down. There is no purpose in just bringing out that a witness knew about, heard about all these different things. It's already well established in the record that these things went on.

We seized opportunities. We showed that close collaborations between men—full professors and junior faculty—raised no comparable presumptions of inappropriate relationship or scrutiny of research independence. When a woman professor testified that she had not been harassed although her academic achievements resulted from a close collaboration with a male professor, we brought out that her senior male collaborator was also her husband, a fact omitted in the direct examination.

> CHALMERS: You wouldn't contend, would you, that a woman has to marry a man in order to collaborate scientifically with him?[21]

Since we were on the last lap, the judge began asking a few of his own questions about how gender affected university decision making. He was eliciting information that sometimes helped us and sometimes hurt us. In response to his questions, Julia Mears testified that it was imprudent of Williams and Jean to travel together to conferences.[22]

THE COURT: Would that have been true if both were of the same sex, if Dr. Jew, for instance, were a male?

MEARS: When people travel always together, vacation together, it raises a fair question about the neutrality in which the department is administered. I think it would have raised the same question if they were both men.

THE COURT: If the university had had clear proof that there was a sexual relationship, would the university's response to this situation been any different?

MEARS: Well, it partly would depend upon when we would have had such knowledge, but yes.

THE COURT: Well, at the conclusion—let me say at the conclusion of the panel report.

MEARS: If we knew that, Professor Williams would not have been able to consider Professor Jew for promotion to full professor, for one thing.

THE COURT: If at the time of the panel report it had been clearly proved and the university clearly knew that there was not a sexual relationship, would the reaction of the university be any different from what it was?

MEARS: I don't think so. If there were a sexual relationship, we would take that as a sort of complete finding that these people could not deal with each other in an arm's length way. If there is not a sexual relationship, that does not mean the absolute opposite, that does not mean there cannot be some sort of personal relationship that, despite not being sexual, may nonetheless make it difficult for the people to deal with each other properly. It wouldn't have changed things.

Sexual relationship?—tagged. No sexual relationship?—tagged. Research collaboration with a male mentor?—tagged. Friendship with the chair?—tagged. Suspicions and rumors inevitably flourished. Even if unfounded and injurious, the university thought there was nothing to be done about them.

Day 11, November 28

Responding to Judge Vietor's not-so-subtle request, we called Williams as a rebuttal witness, despite our fears that he could come across as irascible. For several years we had hewn to the principle that Jean's case was about Jean, not about Williams. If he adopted a defensive or accusatory tone, he would not convince. We considered these risks over the weekend as we prepared.

Williams's beginning was inauspicious. He walked to the witness chair slowly. With his rumpled gray hair falling onto aviator glasses, he looked the part of an academic. Oddly for November and especially in a courtroom, his feet were bare and in sandals. The first thing he did on the stand was to tell the judge he was taking off his jacket and he hoped the judge did not mind. His declaration intimated a lack of deference to the court. On the surface the judge was nonplussed, "If you're more comfortable, go ahead."

ZEGLOVITCH: Do you have any medical conditions that make it difficult for you to give your testimony here today?

WILLIAMS: I have a medical condition; but if I don't get over- heated or I don't get too tired, I should be okay.[23]

ZEGLOVITCH: What is that medical condition?

WILLIAMS: Multiple sclerosis.

Judge Vietor's tone changed.

THE COURT: Doctor, if you feel fatigued, or anything, you just let us know. We can take a break and pick up when you're able to. Understand?

WILLIAMS: Appreciate that. Thank you.

After establishing Williams's professional credentials and his thirty- three-year marriage to Glenys, Bob asked Williams if he had had a sexual, or a physically intimate, relationship with Jean.

WILLIAMS: No.

ZEGLOVITCH: Why didn't you make a conscious effort to spend

less time with Dr. Jew in order to minimize any appearances of impropriety?

WILLIAMS: The amount of work that two electron microscopists have to do together and require—it would have been a tremendous impediment in our research work if we had to cut it down in some way. In addition, we had nothing to hide. It would have just been to present a different appearance that we would have been doing that. Certainly would have been an impediment.

ZEGLOVITCH: Did you ever do anything with respect to Dr. Tomanek?

WILLIAMS: I really believe that if—unless I had the full support of the dean on this matter, if I had raised the matter of sex with Dr. Tomanek, it would have raised additional talk. Additional problems might have arisen. So I addressed, in 1977, his—he was disruptive, and I believe I said malicious behavior. I confronted him with this, and I told him to shape up.

THE COURT: You told that to Dr. Tomanek?

WILLIAMS: That's what I told him.

THE COURT: Dr. Tomanek?

WILLIAMS: That's correct.

THE COURT: May I have a clarification? What was it—when you spoke to Dr. Tomanek, what, in essence, did you say to him?

WILLIAMS: I also confronted him, on the same occasion, with his disruptive and, I believe I said, malicious behavior. And then I just said—I think I explained why he'd got that salary, and I said, "You've got to shape up," or words to that effect. I think I said "shape up."

Lerner's cross-examination of Williams goes on for forty pages in the transcript. He began with bullying questions, structured as accusations, jumbled in a grab bag. He characterized Williams as "hating" Tomanek, Kaelber, and Montgomery, which Williams denied. Lerner cast Williams as belligerently planning to sue everyone. Williams's responsive refrain was just right—he said he tried to heal a fractured department, but he did not succeed. Instead of a defensive reaction, his response humanized him.

Bob's objections were touched with giddiness.

ZEGLOVITCH: Objection. Outside the scope. And I guess I'll sit
down, because that probably is within the scope.
THE COURT: You just ruled on your own objection.
ZEGLOVITCH: I will pop up again. I will rise again.
THE COURT: Go ahead.

Williams's responses were careful, concise, clear, and convincing.
Bob did not ask any questions of him on redirect and did not need to,
as Lerner had not scored any points. Williams stepped down. *Whew!*

Day 12, November 29

On Wednesday morning, we had just two witnesses—Jean Jew and
Mary Jo Small—each for brief rebuttal of specific points. The remainder
of the morning was taken up with housekeeping details and everyone,
even Judge Vietor, relaxed. Judge Vietor asked the attorneys to submit
proposed findings of fact based on the testimony so far. "Don't make
them argumentative. I mean give me something I can use, not something I have to look over and ignore because it's a partisan argument.
Clear, clean straightforward proposed fact findings that you believe are
supported by the evidence."[24]

When a judge is the fact finder at trial, proposed findings of fact,
based on the evidence that came in at trial, are among the most important documents an attorney will submit. The proposed findings function
as a truncated transcript for the judge. The judge usually does not have
a transcript of the trial as a resource. Only if the case is appealed is the
expense of a full transcript warranted. The proposed findings help the
judge focus on the key facts as he reviews his notes from the testimony
and prepares his written decision. Done well, proposed findings of fact
anticipate the judge's concerns about the case and present factual statements that address them effectively. It is a partisan document that must
appear nonpartisan. Facts cited must faithfully adhere to the evidence
at trial. When persuasive, proposed findings are often incorporated
into the judge's opinion.

The judge moved on to scheduling. He pushed for an early due date for our proposed findings of fact. We agreed to provide them by January 2, 1990. *Another family holiday forfeited*, I thought. A few additional trial days for expert witnesses were scheduled for late April. After that, attorneys would have the month of May to prepare post-trial briefs to be submitted in early June. The judge's decision would issue at the earliest in July and more likely later, depending on his trial schedule, administrative workload, and summer vacation. A six-month period was not atypical to complete the tasks that follow a nearly three-week trial, especially given a chief judge's schedule.

As we worked, Judge Vietor said, his voice tinged with more than a little sarcasm, "I've never in my life had such a succession of high-powered, educated, intelligent people pass through this courtroom." I hoped he was referring to the many academics the university brought in. Had he seen through them, or was he referring to the ones we had called?

His last words stunned us all by foreshadowing his decision in the case. Perhaps he decided it would be unkind to make Jean wait six months for an indication of how he was thinking.

THE COURT: I might say this, and I can fairly say this, that at this time certainly part of my findings will be that there is not—and I realize this isn't controlling in the case or anything like that, but there is not credible evidence that would lead me to be able to find that there was in fact any sexual relationship between the plaintiff and Dr. Williams. And I'm going to have to look at it further. I may indeed find—and it may not be necessary to find but I may find, I am going to review it, that in fact the credible evidence leads me to find that it's been established by a preponderance of the evidence that there definitely was not a sexual relationship between the plaintiff and Dr. Williams. You might keep that in mind as you prepare your proposed findings, but I simply don't find anything here to—in this record to provide any factual basis for the rumors that circulated, and I think you can count on that being a part of my findings of fact.

Jean looked down at counsel table, hiding her smile, expressed rarely in twelve courtroom days. Here is what she most wanted—false smears supplanted by the truth. The judge had listened to all of Galenbeck's and Lerner's innuendos and did not believe that there was any sexual relationship.

The judge said, "Anything further? Very well. Thank you. And I'll see you again in the spring sometime, late winter or early spring."

Galenbeck and Lerner distractedly collected their papers, not making eye contact, nor we with them. We exchanged curt good-byes.

CHAPTER 9

Findings and Experts

IT WAS NOT possible for me to sashay back into family life that December. Seth, Leah, and Eric were reliably tethered to each other as they went through their days. Morning and evening carpools for the kids had been long scheduled with other drivers. I hadn't cooked a meal or shopped for groceries for weeks. I had to concentrate to cook the five or six dishes that all four of us could eat, now that Leah was a vegetarian, while Eric had memorized them. I did not recognize some of the kids' friends or know their names. Occasionally Seth or Leah, out of habit, addressed me as "Dad," which I considered a subconscious slip that indicated continuing affection for me notwithstanding my peripatetic interjections into their routines.

⁘

"How come the kids aren't practicing tonight?" I asked Eric. "Are they keeping up?"

"Tuesday is their night off. Yes, our diligent children are still at their violin and viola, for now. They'll quit cold turkey as soon as they get college acceptance letters."

⁘

"You just handed him a $20 bill when he asked for it? How will he learn the value of money if it's there for the asking?" I scolded.

"Soccer practice is late tonight. He needed money for pizza. I didn't have a $10 bill with me," Eric patiently explained, as if he had to.

⁘

"I don't want Leah going over to Lizzie's house after school, painting nails and doing make-up. Doesn't that middle school have any sports for girls after school?" I asked.

123

"Deep breath. Take it easy." Eric responded.

"I can't. I have to work."

I wish this had been an occasional response. But I recall it as a recurring one when I was asked to participate in family life.

⋮⋮⋮

Normally, our December holiday was spent with Eric's parents and his brother's family on the Gulf Coast of Florida. Unfortunately, long before the trial, Eric and I suggested a change in the routine for December 1989. Since his brother's family could not join us, our thought was to substitute a California eco lodge at year end 1989 and expose the kids to the ocean in an ecological environment, far from Disney playgrounds. Eric's parents were game.

At Sea Ranch in northern California, I was miserable, and so were the kids. We had neglected to take the cool weather into account, find substitute activities for the kids, or anticipate that I would be sitting for hours in a room on the third floor of a clapboard cottage typing into a computer to meet the January 2 deadline for submission of proposed findings.

Eric and his parents gave me a pass from the family hubbub, another to add to my stack of passes. Shmush . . . the sound of oranges being juiced for late-rising adolescents. Eric's father made fresh-squeezed orange juice for the kids, whatever the time of day. Tedious negotiations with teens wafted up.

"What should we do today?" Eric asked

"There's nothing to do." Seth expressed what, to him, was obvious.

"How about a brisk swim in the pool?" Eric tried.

"Too cold." Leah said. "The sun isn't even out."

"We can warm up in the sauna."

"Sitting in a small, hot, dark room with my brother and father?" Leah's rhetorical question was sarcastic. I pictured Eric's glare. I knew they were all together in the kitchen with his parents, Zelda and Phil. Leah's display in front of his parents would not be to Eric's liking.

"We can take a walk around the place. It's interesting to see how it was planned," Eric offered.

"Any movies nearby?" Seth was trying. No movies nearby. The internet and streaming services were years away.

Ensconced in the attic, at a table in front of a window, with an ocean view and the companionship of the tides, my task was to squeeze twenty-five pages of proposed findings of fact from hundreds of pages of notes and exhibits. A transcript of the trial did not yet exist. Even if the word processing software I was using had a rudimentary search capability (and I don't know if it did), it was of no use because the resource materials were not digitized. My goal was about a hundred paragraphs, give or take, individually numbered, laying out everything important to proving Jean's case, every paragraph with citations to supporting testimony or exhibits in the trial record. The task was overwhelming, and the short time in which to do it was panic-inducing. I breathed with the rhythm of the tide, observed how the ocean persevered, and slowly got started.

Once again, my job was to extract a narrative arc from a heaping mound of detailed raw material. In the first four pages I introduced the Anatomy Department, its place in the College of Medicine, and the cast of characters. Carefully crafted paragraphs describing particular incidents of harassing behaviors and speech followed for a dozen pages. Next, facts demonstrated that Jean was aware of the behavior although it rarely occurred in her presence. Several paragraphs documented that university officials had contemporaneous notice of the behaviors and did not respond, even after the receiving the panel report.

Judge Vietor had not asked us to draft proposed conclusions of law, which typically accompany proposed findings of fact. His goal was to capture the facts while they were still fresh in everyone's minds. Conclusions of law would have to await the expert witness testimony later in the spring. But the legal elements of a sexual harassment claim were the form on which I had to drape proposed facts—that Jean was denigrated in the workplace by slurs that were unwelcome, sex-based, pervasive and severe, known to her employer, and not corrected.

The uniqueness of Jean's sexual harassment claim had been very much on Judge Vietor's mind, and therefore on mine. The judge commented during trial: "I haven't found any case just like this" and Jean's case was "a very unique type of treatment case."[1] The question that troubled him was "Whether what happened here—assuming I find it to be as plaintiff contends—fits within Title VII."[2] Our proposed findings of fact had to help him see that a sexual smear campaign was cut from the same cloth as a quid pro quo demand for sexual favors, physical gropes, or stolen time cards. They all had in common one goal: excluding women from traditional male jobs by denigrating them. Title VII prohibited all of them.

⁝⁝⁝

Eric and I shared professional interests in the law. His experience as an advocate made him patient. He knew the responsibility of shepherding a client through the legal system, the worry of preparing for trial, the wearing attacks from opposing counsel, and the stage fright of court appearances. As a law professor, while his subject matter expertise was unrelated to employment discrimination law, he was practiced at drawing out main points from his students and honing their focus. He applied these skills to our discussions.

"I'm done for." I had come down to the kitchen in our cabin at Sea Ranch in the late afternoon. Eric was beginning to prepare dinner. We were alone. I perched on a stool. "We have to show this was sex-based even though it was not sexually inspired. That is, the bad actors were not seeking sex from Jean." The percussion of knife on onion on cutting board—chop, chop, chop—quieted my mind.

"The content of the rumors is sexual, so that helps," I mused. "But Jean wasn't the only one targeted. Heidger, a supporter of Williams, was a target. I'm worried about distinguishing him."

Eric put up the water for pasta. "Maybe Heidger is your comparable. Like Jean, he followed Williams up from Tulane, but was not subjected to ongoing harassment."

"He shows that, but for Jean's gender, she would not have been harassed in an ongoing way," I added. We made progress this way. I went upstairs and drafted.

Proposed finding number 22: "The hostile work environment for Dr. Jew was based on her sex. First, the hostility of the environment arose from speech that was explicitly sexual and explicitly referred to Dr. Jew in sexual terms. The speech encouraged Dr. Jew's colleagues to view her in sexual terms rather than as a professional physician and professor. It also sought to attribute Dr. Jew's professional accomplishments to a sexual relationship rather than to merit."

Proposed finding number 23: "Second, Dr. Jew was harassed because she was a woman. Similarly, situated males were not harassed. While there was evidence of an isolated incident of graffiti directed at Dr. Heidger, there was no evidence that either Dr. Heidger or Dr. Bergman, both of whom were viewed as supporters of Dr. Williams by the opposing faculty, were subjected to a continuing pattern of harassment."

Later, I returned to the kitchen in another quiet moment. "Let's talk about Williams. Their mantra is that it was all motivated by hostility toward Williams, a man, so could not be sex-based harassment of Jean. It's true that nearly all of it disparaged Williams." To prove discrimination, it was our burden to show that the offending conduct was motivated by sex bias, not departmental politics.

"Sex harassment of Jean was their weapon: they chose this weapon intentionally."

Eric noted, "If they chose sex knowing it would be injurious to Jean, so what if their principle purpose was to damage Williams? They still made the tainted decision to injure Jean and used her sex to do it."

"Never mind if the war was about something else," I agreed.

Back and forth we went. "Only Jean was accused of using her sex as a tool to gain favor with Williams. This slur was unique to Jean, the only woman in the group. Nobody accused Heidger of using sex to influence Williams," I added. "Sexual slurs have a different and more harmful impact on a junior woman than on a senior man, or a junior man, for that matter."

Eric responded, "Sexual rumors might even enhance the reputation of a successful male." *Hmmm.*

Proposed finding number 24: "Some of the harassing speech that was aimed at Dr. Jew also made reference to Dr. Williams. The fact that Dr. Williams, a man, was sometimes also a target does not mean that the harassment of Dr. Jew was not sex-based. Dr. Williams was not similarly situated to Dr. Jew. He was married and was a senior scientist; Dr. Jew was single, younger, and a junior scientist. Dr. Williams's professional reputation and stature were firmly established before he came to the University of Iowa. He was in the position of chair. The harassing statements did not suggest that his professional accomplishments were derivative of his sex or of sexual favors. None suggested that Dr. Williams received preferential treatment from Dr. Jew. Even if he had been similarly situated to Dr. Jew, the references to him would not have carried the same connotation as the references to Dr. Jew. In our society, statements about men's sexual exploits do not carry the same stigma as similar comments about women. While some of the harassment of Dr. Jew may have been initially motivated in part by animosity toward Dr. Williams, it nonetheless remained sex-based harassment of Dr. Jew."

"Few might see it this way, but I think what happened to Jean was as bad, and arguably, worse, than a direct sexual come-on," I said, still concerned about how Jean's circumstances differed from the fact patterns in other sex harassment cases.

"Why?"

"Because she couldn't fight back or say no." I added, "Not that it is easy to fight back or say no, and often circumstances make it impossible, but at least the woman is present and has that opportunity. Jean didn't have any opportunity or agency to stop this. She was totally dependent on the university to act."

Eric was listening but busy at the stove.

"Another thing," I continued, "The rumors were career killing. They eviscerated her accomplishments. Jean's work-related merit, achievements, and skills were made invisible. What she purportedly did was sex, not academic work. The sexual content of the slurs was perfectly designed to shut down her academic future."

"Works for me," Eric said.

Proposed finding number 25: "The nature of the speech regarding Dr. Jew was highly offensive, and it would be extraordinarily difficult for a reasonable person to work in the resulting environment. This is particularly so because of the nature of Dr. Jew's workplace, which necessitates interaction with colleagues throughout the university and with students from the department, the College of Medicine, and other divisions of the university. Vice President Remington admitted that the innuendo regarding Dr. Jew was something no human being should have to put up with. It clearly created a hostile work environment for Dr. Jew."

Eric continued preparing spaghetti sauce. Leah was only eating plain pasta with butter now, so the sauce was for the rest of us. I tried not to harangue her about being a vegetable-hating vegetarian.

On December 31, 1989, New Year's Eve, I sent Plaintiff's Proposed Findings of Fact by overnight mail from Sea Ranch in California to Leonard, Street & Deinard in Minneapolis. Sheila came into the office on New Year's Day, put the document into proper shape, and sent it by overnight mail to the Des Moines Federal Courthouse where it was filed January 2, 1990, copy to the Iowa Attorney General's Office.

⋄⋄⋄

We reconvened in Judge Vietor's courtroom months later on April 30, 1990. The critical issue for the expert witnesses was whether Jean was qualified for promotion as of 1983, and whether, if Judge Vietor determined Title VII had been violated, the appropriate remedy was to order her promotion to full professor retroactive to July 1, 1984. The judge had to be convinced.

Two distinguished neuroscientists from Anatomy Departments in the University of California system gave credible testimony with contrary conclusions. The thoroughness of their preparation made the difference. Our witness, Dr. Carmine Clemente, read Jean's entire dossier record, the promotion files of all faculty promoted to full professor in the Department of Anatomy since 1979, and promotion files for selected faculty promoted in other departments within the college in that time period. He read and annotated all of Jean's publications. He testified that his review showed that male faculty had been promoted with weaker qualifications than Jean's. Her qualifications were not the reason she was not promoted. Dr. Clemente evaluated Jean's teaching, service, and research accomplishments and concluded that her record as a whole so clearly demonstrated qualification for promotion "that factors other than those normally considered for promotion were responsible for the negative decision."[3]

The university's expert, Dr. Henry Ralston, was asked to evaluate Jean's research record, not her teaching or service contributions. He did not read all of her publications. He did not reach an opinion on whether her qualifications in all three areas—teaching, service, and research—satisfied promotion criteria. Acknowledging that Jean's research credentials should be compared to those of faculty promoted prior to 1984, Ralston only compared her credentials with Anatomy Department faculty promoted five years later. His opinion was full of holes.

After the experts concluded, we had one last chance to address the judge orally. We did not waive a closing argument as is sometimes done at the end of judge trial. Because we expected him to be cautious about substituting his judgment for the university's judgment on Jean's promotion, my closing argument focused on the need for Judge Vietor to order Jean's promotion to full professor. I began by likening the University of Iowa to an ocean freighter that would not alter its course even one degree unless it received a sharp blow on its prow from an even more powerful institution. I reviewed the direct evidence of discrimination at the 1983 faculty evaluation of Jean's progress, including Tomanek and Kaelber's participation in the discussion and vote, the graffiti, and sexist remarks made by senior faculty during the discussion. We argued that this direct evidence shifted the burden of proof to the university to show that Jean's promotion would have been denied even in the absence of discrimination. The university had not met that burden.

Title VII required a remedy that made Jean whole, and only an order promoting Jean to full professor retroactive to 1984 could accomplish this. I asserted that no good alternative was available. If Judge Vietor returned the promotion decision to the university with guidelines for a corrected promotion process, would Jean receive a fair review? No, as evidenced by the university's refusal to provide Jean with a corrected promotion process. Should the court order an outside review of Jean's credentials by academicians at other universities? No. This had already been done by Drs. Clemente and Ralston. No process seven years after the fact could be fair to her.

Finally, I argued that a court-ordered promotion rested on the university's favorable evaluation of Jean's credentials when it granted her tenure and promotion in 1979. This provided a solid foundation for the court to take the next step—promote her to the rank of full professor. Our supplemental proposed findings of fact and conclusions of law on the promotion issue followed. Final, post-trial briefs to the court were all that remained. Feeling satisfied that we had done good work in a challenging case, I anticipated putting Jean's case to the side for a time. We needed a breather. Instead, we got a surprise.

CHAPTER 10

A Jury Decides

WE HAD JUST returned from expert witness testimony in Des Moines when we got notice that the state court defamation lawsuit against Tomanek had been set for trial four weeks hence. After three years hibernating in state court, "Trial of the case of *Jean Y. Jew M.D. vs. Robert Tomanek* is set to begin on May 29, 1990 at 9:00 a.m. in the Johnson County Courthouse in Iowa City and continue for eight days." *Unbelievable!*

Originally, we filed one case in state court against two defendants—the university for sex discrimination and Tomanek for defamation. When the case against the university was dismissed by Judge Eads, we filed against the university in federal court under Title VII and left the defamation case against Tomanek on the docket in Johnson County. Three years of discovery in the federal action provided all the information we needed for both cases. To pursue discovery in the state court action would have been duplicative. So it sat more or less dormant for years.

In Johnson County Court, setting a case on for trial appeared to be at the initiative of one of the parties. Either party could call the clerk's office and ask for a trial date. If neither party wanted to push the case to trial, it could languish. And many did, which is why most courts have abandoned this laissez-faire approach to scheduling.

Normally a scheduling order setting a trial date is welcome. But that was not true here, especially not now. Per the scheduling order, the Tomanek trial was set to begin May 29 and continue for nearly two weeks. We had asked for a jury trial. This meant that on the last trial day, the judge would instruct the jury about the applicable law and send the jury off to deliberate about the facts. In a jury trial, since the judge does not issue a final written decision explaining the law and the facts, there is no need for the parties to submit proposed findings of fact and conclusions of law. The Tomanek jury would likely have a decision on June 8 or 9, months before Judge Vietor's decision could be expected.

The timing was terrifying because of a legal doctrine, collateral estoppel, which provides that when the same parties litigate the same contested issue in two different courts, the first court's ruling on a fact issue is final and binding on the other court. The doctrine precludes conflicting factual determinations in different courts about the same case. The defendants in Jean's cases were different, but both lawsuits turned on contested facts in common. Did Tomanek make statements about a sexual relationship between Jean and Williams? Were his statements true or false? Judge Vietor had told us he saw no credible evidence of a sexual relationship, but his conclusion was not yet incorporated into a final decision. If we lost this factual issue before an Iowa jury, our loss could raise complicated collateral estoppel issues that could bar Judge Vietor's anticipated ruling. I suspected Galenbeck and Lerner of pushing for a trial date in the Tomanek case as an attempt to intercept Judge Vietor's conclusion that there was no sexual relationship.

We were dealing with different lawyers in Tomanek's case, Chuck Traw and Tom Diehl of the Leff Law Firm in Iowa City. We believed they were being paid by the state of Iowa to represent Tomanek personally. We had come to know Diehl during the federal trial, which he attended most trial days. Now we came to know Traw. Both were cordial, professional, and skilled. Traw was an experienced trial lawyer before Johnson County juries. He knew these people. Diehl was his second chair.

A desperate campaign to delay the state court jury trial was our first response. Infused with more urgency than law, I argued, "The federal court heard fifty witnesses over fourteen days of trial in November 1989. Three additional days of expert witness testimony just ended. The university chose to defend the federal litigation on the theory that Drs. Jew and Williams had a sexual relationship and rumors about it were true. U.S. Judge Harold Vietor told us that the lack of credible evidence of a sexual relationship would be part of his findings of fact. Defendants are here trying to do an end run around the federal court."

Traw countered, "Plaintiff's motion is grounded upon contingency, superimposed upon supposition, layered on top of possibility and prediction." Denied.

We followed this defeat with a motion to Judge Vietor requesting an order staying the state court trial. It was an act of desperation since the federal court did not have jurisdiction to stay state court proceedings. Predictably denied.

Traw and Diehl filed a motion in state court to dismiss Jean's case against Tomanek without trial. Traw argued that Tomanek was immune from suit because his alleged statements, true or false, were made "in the course of his employment," for which he could not be held liable. In federal court the university had argued the opposite, that it could not be held responsible for Tomanek's misconduct because he acted "outside the scope of his employment." Whether Tomanek's conduct was within or outside the scope of his employment turned on facts to be developed at trial. Motion to dismiss denied. Tomanek appealed to the Iowa Supreme Court, requesting expedited consideration.

Bob and I had fear-laden disagreements about whether we should object to Tomanek's request for expedited appeal or should join his request. The silver lining of the appeal was it would likely delay the jury trial by weeks, maybe months—perhaps long enough to get us past August, when Judge Vietor's decision could be expected.

Standing in the doorway to my office, Bob said, "Let's just dismiss the case against Tomanek. Let it go." He was testing the waters from a safe distance.

I looked up, puzzled. "Why would we do that?"

"Because it would be smart?" he leaned against the door jamb with his arms crossed.

"We are going to finish this fight with Tomanek, or die trying," I said.

Bob kept at it. "Exactly. We may win this skirmish about an expedited appeal, go to trial on the defamation case, and put at risk all we worked for in the federal case against the university." I stubbornly refused his arguments. Tomanek would not have our assistance in escaping unscathed.

We would oppose Tomanek's request for an interlocutory appeal. The court sided with us and denied their appeal. Now nothing stood in the way of Tomanek's jury trial beginning on May 29.

A few days later, Bob was back. "I can't come to Iowa City."

"What?" I was shocked, then angry.

"I'm backed up with demands from other clients."

"That's not reason enough. All of us are dealing with that," I countered. "I'm not going down there without help!"

Bob's decision shook me. He wasn't the only one scared to death; I was, too. But backing out was not an option for me. Tomanek would add another notch to his belt and gloat. No. One foot in front of the other. Keep going. Find another associate lawyer to come—preferably one with jury trial experience.

Susan Robiner was available and willing to help us. In her midthirties, she had joined the firm in 1985. By 1990 she had trial experience comparable to Bob's. Like Bob, she was emotionally cool on the surface, easy to be with, bright, and efficient. She would be an excellent sounding board for the myriad pretrial decisions that were coming up. Susan would have a steep learning curve, whereas Bob knew the case from the ground up. But like Bob, Susan was an excellent writer. I was lucky to have her help.

On the phone with Jean, I took a deep breath and said, "Bob won't be coming for the jury trial. In his place, Susan Robiner, who has had jury trial experience, will join us." I said this with confidence—more than I felt. Bob had been so involved and had been so good at it. If Jean was dismayed, she did not show it. I explained that Bob was needed on another case. Much later, Jean confided that she had been taken aback. She hypothesized that the firm was pressuring me. She knew the firm couldn't dislodge me, but it could prevent Bob from working on the case.

⁂

As Jean and I were hauling banker's boxes into my motel room in Iowa City, I said, "The first thing we need to do is go through the questionnaires that prospective jurors have filled out, so we can select a jury. I've never selected a jury before. I don't know that I've ever told you that, have I?"

Jean looked up, a little startled, but received this news quietly with no remonstrance. Having little experience with lawyers, she had assumed, based on TV and books, that every lawyer had done jury trials. She accepted my confession as just one of many novel experiences that had rolled out over the years of litigation—Judge Eads's dismissal, Galenbeck and Lerner's attacks, and the way the litigation just kept growing. Unanticipated developments had become the new normal in both our lives. There was so much coming at us all the time, there was no occasion to think about juries, or my experience with them, until the time came. I added, "Susan and I met with the National Jury Project last week for their advice on picking jurors, simplifying our themes, and getting them across."

Jean may not have been disappointed in me, but I was. Occasional disappointments sprinkled the six years of working together. We were aging—wrinkles, a few gray hairs, softer muscles, more pounds— together. Together jumping off. Together wringing our hands. Together accepting our obligations to each other. She had full confidence in me and Bob. Since I did not want to undermine her confidence, I hadn't told her of my lack of jury experience. My mistake. Her acceptance.

$$\S\S\S$$

The Johnson County Courthouse in Iowa City was hot and muggy on May 29, 1990, and for two weeks after that. The atmosphere was damp from humans under stress—four lawyers, a couple of clients, eight jurors, two alternates, a judge, his clerk and bailiff, and several spectators. Since this trial was in Iowa City, home of the university, a dozen or more spectators attended daily. Narrow and long, the court-room had windows along the left side and behind the judge's bench, creating a glare that sometimes put the judge in shadow. The jury box ran along the wall on the right side. Benches for the public occupied the back half of the courtroom, the rows divided at the midline by an aisle that lawyers and witnesses used to enter and exit the courtroom.

Traw and Diehl had claimed the attorney table on the left side of the room—putting their backs to the windows and giving them a sightline that included the judge, the jury, and us. Tomanek sat with them. His face and its grimaces were outside the jurors' line of vision. Our table was on the right side of the courtroom in front of the jury box. Jean's chair faced the jury. She could see their faces during the trial. As the days passed, we saw Tomanek exhibit a succession of grimaces and frowns toward Jean. Wanting the jurors to be able to see this, midway through the trial, I lightheartedly suggested to Traw that we switch counsel tables for the remainder of the trial. He declined, replying with a smile, "How about we switch clients, instead?"

Defamation is the communication of a false statement about another that harms the person's reputation. If the form of the communication is in writing, it is libel; if spoken, it is slander. For Jean's claim of slander, we had to prove oral communications about her were made by Tomanek, even if only repeating the statements of others. Tomanek could defend himself by proving that the statements were true or substantially true. If we proved he made these statements, he failed to prove they were true, and we proved they attacked Jean's moral character, injured her in her profession, or impugned her chastity, the damage to Jean was presumed as a matter of law and need not be proved.

Over the next twelve days, nearly forty witnesses testified on the question of whether, by spreading rumors that Jean provided sexual favors to Williams, Tomanek had slandered her. No transcript of this trial has ever been prepared. A complete transcript is normally prepared only when a case is appealed, and this case was not.

On the first day of trial, we met Judge William Thomas in his chambers. The role of judge in a jury trial is more like a referee than an inquisitor. The jury would be deciding the fact questions, not the judge. Judge Thomas was lanky and tall. His all-business demeanor and manner made Jean uneasy. Her unease was discernible on her face. She recalls me giving her a gentle elbow to the ribs and whispering peremptorily, "Smile."

Our local counsel described Judge Thomas as "bright, moderate, fair, very even-tempered." His brusque directions were delivered with kind eyes. Over two weeks of trial, I came to appreciate his dry sense of humor. We discovered he and his wife lived nearby in Cedar Rapids, where she was a pediatrician. We hoped this was a good sign. She would likely be familiar with the challenges a professional woman faces and with sexism in medical school and the profession.

In Judge Thomas's chambers that morning, we argued about the evidence, what the jury would be permitted to hear, and what would be kept from them. Evidentiary motions were more significant in a jury trial than in a judge trial, where the judge is practiced at disregarding inappropriate information. Evidence about Jean's birth control medical records was excluded as irrelevant. Evidence about her real estate investment with Williams would come in on the issue of favoritism. Evidence that a lock was installed on the door to Williams's office was excluded because there was no evidence about who ordered the lock. Psychologists could testify as expert witnesses on the issue of pain and suffering damages, recoverable in a defamation suit.

When we returned to the courtroom, voir dire—questioning of potential jurors—began. Susan and I were looking for certain qualities in potential jurors: awareness that men in male-dominated workplaces, including a medical school, can resent women newcomers, thoughtfulness about why employees make complaints, and acceptance of the occasional necessity of lawsuits. We wanted to ferret out biased stereotypes of Chinese people, especially about Chinese women. When asked, "What has been your experience or perception of Chinese people?," one potential juror responded, "Someone in a rice field with a wide-brimmed straw hat." We exercised a peremptory strike to keep that person off the jury. Traw and Diehl struck from the jury a teacher who responded "yes" to their question "Do you support a multicultural curriculum?" By the end of the first day, eight jurors—seven women and one man—and two alternates (all ten white) were selected to hear the case.

Wednesday morning began with opening statements. Once the judge finished instructing the jury regarding the role of opening statements, I began. "This case is about a smear campaign. It is not about gossip in the workplace or academic freedom in a university. It is about Robert Tomanek systematically setting out to destroy Jean Jew's reputation in her workplace beginning in 1973. He has slandered Jean Jew by sowing lies among her coworkers that she has been having sex with the chair of her department, Dr. Williams, and that her accomplishments are due to sexual favors, not hard work. These lies have robbed Dr. Jew of the fruits of seventeen years of professional work and threaten to rob her of her future career. Dr. Tomanek has sown his sensational lies broadly. He initiated conversations with people he didn't even know. You will learn from the evidence that he told graduate students, lab assistants, and clerk typists. He told new faculty when they started at the university. He spread the lies directly and indirectly by asking pointed questions. He continued relentlessly, repeating statements about Dr. Jew—the same statements—year in and year out. It is his flagrant refusal to stop that brings us here to ask you for relief."

Traw's opening statement presented an effective defense. "Dr. Tomanek is the son of an immigrant tailor. The university context here is very important. The university's mission is to inform and educate. Faculty have a duty to foster free exchange of ideas, to question, and to dissent. The role of the chair is to exercise power fairly based on merit, not self-interest. This case is about Dr. Williams building his own little kingdom. Cronyism developed between Williams, Dr. Jew, and others who came from Tulane. Cronies got raises and financial support. Dr. Jew continued to research and publish with Williams. Many believed she was victimized by Williams." Traw continued, "Dr. Tomanek's talk about Dr. Jew was always a subissue in the larger Williams/department issue. It is true that Dr. Tomanek concluded that Dr. Jew and Williams were having an affair. Don't look at Dr. Williams as he is now, but as a younger man and the evidence that indicated they were having an affair. Dr. Tomanek passed on information reinforced by his observations and everyone else's. It was based on how they conducted themselves. It was appropriate for Dr. Tomanek to speak up if his boss was hurting the department."

Our witnesses went first. We began with several university staff, neutral with respect to the faculty cliques in the department, who testified to statements Tomanek made to them about Jean. Jean was our final witness. The first witness Traw called was Tomanek. He asked the jury to empathize with how unfairly he had been treated by Williams. He explained that he was only one among a crowd of gossip mongers.

⁙

We hunkered down in a tacky long-term stay motel on the edge of Iowa City. Our rooms opened directly to the parking lot. My room was outfitted with a raised hot tub as an unconvincing sign of luxury. We used the extra space in my room to store boxes of documents, binders, laptops, and printer—the supplies we needed for the upcoming contest. Every day we left this rudimentary shelter to enter downtown Iowa City and the Johnson County Courthouse. When we picked up the morning paper en route, we were reminded we were in hostile territory. The *Iowa City Press-Citizen*, the local daily, began reporting on the trial five days after it started. We had nearly finished putting on our witnesses when the reporter, Monica Seigel, showed up. As Tomanek's witnesses took the stand, so did the salacious news articles. From June 5 through June 9, front-page articles about the trial sounded Tomanek's themes:

"Prof Testifies in Harassment Trial" (June 5, 1990)
"UI prof takes stand in own defense" (June 6, 1990)
"Witnesses: we believed the rumors" (June 7, 1990)
"Anatomy Profs' gossip rampant witness says" (June 8, 1990)
"Defamation Trial: Witness saw man, woman in 'compromising' position" (June 9, 1990)

Scanning the newspaper each morning was a punch in the gut. Jean said later, "To have all this on the front pages was just sickening."[1]

Perhaps I should be faulted for not making more of Jean's case in the media. I was wary that a media contest would deplete our stamina and spirits. When the *Daily Iowan*, the campus newspaper, quoted Jean about filing her complaint in November 1985, Jean wrote me that she was quoted inaccurately. "Carolyn, this is the problem with speaking to the press." In September 1986, Jean forwarded a *Daily Iowan* article reporting on the federal court complaint with a sticky note. "I just learned that I was not selected for the U-wide awards for teaching for which I was nominated by the medical students. It's difficult to assess what impact, if any, my notoriety had on the selection process." The press attended to the case briefly at several turning points—the faculty panel in 1984, the complaint filed in 1985, dismissal of the university from the state case, amendment of the Iowa Civil Rights Act, and the Iowa Supreme Court decision. Even these press reports caused Jean distress and me distraction.

The cost-benefit analysis favored caution. The media's potential to injure Jean was palpable. The public's awareness of sexual harassment was limited. Modest public support for a woman complaining of sexual harassment had to await the Anita Hill and Clarence Thomas 1991 hearings. Even for those familiar with sexual harassment, Jean's was not a garden variety case that could be easily comprehended. These risks were not compensated for by the media's potential to help achieve our goal of stopping the slander campaign. Press coverage sympathetic to Jean likely would provoke defensive publication of the slurs she wanted quieted. As I saw it, publicity could contribute to achieving Jean's goals only after authoritative voices—those of judge or jury—publicly determined that the slurs were false. In the meantime, our strategy was to starve the media beast with silence. Largely it worked, up until the jury trial in Iowa City.

The decision to keep silent did not foreclose developing a media strategy to complement our litigation strategy, as lawyers frequently do today. But these were not skills that came naturally to me. I regret that I was not savvy enough to keep a few key reporters updated so that when the case was newsworthy they had some background from our perspective.

⁘

Susan and I split up responsibilities for witnesses, as Bob and I had. Since emotional distress damages could be recovered in a defamation suit, Jean and I faced the challenge of showing her emotional distress to the jury. It was a fine line to walk. If she were too distressed, she couldn't teach and conduct research at the level expected of a full professor. If she were not distressed enough, she looked stoic and uninjured. I hoped we would succeed in providing a glimpse of the pain she showed at her deposition in Iowa City months earlier. Tom Diehl asked Jean to read out loud for the record some of the obscene statements that had been directed at her. In the midst of this recitation Jean broke down in sobs and left the room to collect herself. The intensity of her pain was unmistakable on that occasion. We were unable to replicate it in her testimony.

Tomanek's attorneys called expert witnesses to rebut our claim of emotional distress—Robert Smith, a psychiatrist, and Robert Straight, a psychologist. Dr. Smith's diagnosis was that Jean had obsessive compulsive personality disorder and major depressive disorder with minor to moderate severity. She was biologically predisposed to depression, which she inherited from her family. Smith relied on her self-description as a perfectionist. Smith had asked his colleague, Dr. Straight, for a psychological assessment of these traits. Straight had not met with Jean. On the stand, when Straight described Jean's traits as paranoid, guarded, feeling misunderstood and unfairly blamed, he walked right into the buzz saw that was Susan's cross-examination.

Susan established that Smith's and Straight's diagnoses were based on Jean's answers to questions like: Do you sometimes feel that people are following you? Do you think people are trying to do you harm? Do you think people are looking at you? Then Susan pressed them: "Are you aware that for a week we've heard testimony about people following Dr. Jew? Saying untrue things about her? Sending anonymous lewd letters about her? Is it possible that her answers to these questions are yes because that is exactly what people are doing? Some people feel persecuted because they are persecuted? Feel misunderstood because they are misunderstood? Feeling depressed, misunderstood, and guarded would be a normal response in these circumstances, wouldn't it?" Sheila wrote later in the law firm's newsletter, "I never wanted to be cross-examined by Susan Robiner. She destroyed—and I mean destroyed—the testimony of their psychiatric experts. The attorneys for Tomanek even complimented her."

⁘

Many of the same witnesses examined in the federal trial gave testimony in Tomanek's case. On Tomanek's behalf, the university spared no effort or expense to comb universities across the country for witnesses to bolster his defense. Most tiresome was Jane McCutcheon's reappearance. Swatting her down did not defeat her. She righted herself like an anchored, helium-inflated caricature, with attention-getting bobbing arms and head, making her pitch. Jean and I knew what McCutcheon would say. Her steamy testimony could be particularly damaging with the jurors and the ever-present newspaper reporter. The stakes, high at the beginning of trial, inched higher.

The evening we prepared for McCutcheon's testimony, Jean and I sat cross-legged on the floor of my motel room. Hot, even with air-conditioning, we were wearing shorts. As we worked our way through transcripts of McCutcheon's previous testimony, I cast about for diversions.

"Jean, look at your legs," I said. She furrowed her brow, puzzled.

"Put your legs out straight." As she unfolded hers, we straightened our legs beside each other. We looked at them. Then I broke the silence, "Our legs are the same color. Your legs cannot be distinguished from my legs, at least not in color."

We went over to the window for natural light and looked again. There was no appreciable difference in the color of our legs. We had asserted Jean's legal right to be free from sexualized speech based on stereotypes about Chinese women. Yet stereotypes had crabbed our own factfinding. The stereotype of yellow skin had stopped us from looking at the actual skin color of Jean's legs. Years of viewing Jean's experience on the single axis of sex discrimination, and putting aside the race and national origin features of the harassment, had impoverished my powers of observation. McCutcheon had said she saw legs, "consistent with Jean's" and "darker than Caucasian legs." We assumed, just as she had, that there was a difference in color. That night in the motel, we came to our senses.

How could we use this insight? I was taller than Jean so my legs were somewhat longer, but not appreciably longer from the knee to the foot. McCutcheon would predictably assert that she assumed it was Jean on the library table by the color and length of the legs that she saw. Once she was committed, we decided to take a big risk and re-create for the jury what had happened to us this evening. We would hold out our legs to the jury, like a couple of Rockettes. Hopefully, the jurors would see for themselves, the defense attorneys would be caught by surprise, and Judge Thomas would not be unduly irritated by this unorthodox exhibit. The demonstration would have to be executed with confidence.

McCutcheon was poised on the stand—grown up from the nineteen-year-old who had worked in Tomanek's lab a decade earlier. Her testimony about the evening in the Anatomy Department was as we expected. She saw two legs hanging over the edge of the table on either side of the man—consistent with Jean's in length and color—and assumed they were Jean's legs. That she could not identify Jean as the person lying on the table did not discredit her testimony entirely. The jurors, unlike Judge Vietor, had not spent their working lives deciphering truth from falsehood.

By the time the mid-afternoon break came, the jurors were tired of McCutcheon and of our respective efforts to make much, or little, of her story. Jean and I searched for a private place to take off our stockings. The women's room was small, and we did not want to wait with jurors for two stalls to open up in time. One of the courtrooms on the floor was not in use, so we slipped in there. As quickly and discretely as possible, we took off our stockings and returned to the courtroom.

"With the court's permission, we have an exhibit for the jury," I said.

"What is it?" Judge Thomas's voice was flat and incurious. Just one more exhibit. Tedium was the dominant emotion on this Friday afternoon, the seventh day of trial.

"The color of the plaintiff's legs is central to this witness's testimony. We want permission to show the jury the color of Jean's legs," I said.

"Any objections?" The judge turned to Traw, who took one moment too long to collect himself.

"Go ahead," Judge Thomas said.

Jean and I stepped forward to the thick oak knee wall that fronted the jury box. We stopped about five feet from the wall. We raised our skirts to just above our knees and extended our bare legs, my left beside her right, side by side, toward the jury. The jurors leaned forward, bug-eyed. Jurors in the second row stood up and craned over those in the front row to get a better view. Tomanek's attorneys were too surprised to intervene in time to stop what took only a few seconds. With afternoon light, overhead lights, and our legs proximate to their eyes, the jurors saw what was indisputable. Jean's legs and mine were indistinguishable in color.

Tomanek's attorneys began objecting energetically, and the judge turned to the points they were making. It didn't matter because the jurors were not paying attention to them. All eyes were fixed on our legs, even after we sat down and they were partially camouflaged by the counsel table.

Saturday morning's story in the *Iowa City Press-Citizen* replayed McCutcheon's testimony as if our leg demonstration never occurred.

The reporter didn't stay in the hot courtroom to see our late afternoon demonstration. Maybe she rushed back to meet a deadline with
McCutcheon's account in her hand.

"It is this kind of attitude on the part of the press and the public
that makes women fearful of reporting cases of sexual harassment or
even speaking up for their rights," wrote Margery Wolf, a professor in
anthropology and chair of the Women Studies Program, in a letter to
the *Iowa City Press-Citizen* published that Saturday. Her letter had an
ameliorative impact. Articles thereafter were more neutral.

"Defamation Trial Arguments End" (June 12, 1990)
"Jury Weighs Evidence in Defamation Trial" (June 13, 1990)

⸭⸭⸭

It's hard to believe, looking back, that Jean and I did not focus on the
racial bias in McCutcheon's observations about the color of Jean's legs.
Our cursory treatment of race had several likely causes—all painful to
consider. Our racial difference was cloaked by what we had in common:
our gender, age, educational background, intellectual ambitions, economic resources, and values.

One cause was the structure of Jean's lawsuit. By June 1990, the legal
issue of race and national origin discrimination, which we put aside at
the outset of the case, had faded from my field of vision. My pattern of
thinking about the case was well established after years of litigation. It
had to do with discrimination based on sex, not race or national origin.
The narrowed focus left race indistinct.

Our reserved personalities may have contributed. Although I needed
to know just about everything that happened to Jean at the University
of Iowa, I did not need to know everything that happened before.
Neither of us was comfortable probing into what the other may have
considered private. We were well suited to each other in this regard.
Both of us were comfortable with silence on the deeply personal topics
of the differences in our race, ethnicity, and upbringing.

When these differences surfaced, they took me by surprise. After
it was all over, I learned that Jean had not told her parents about the
litigation and the incidents that led to it. On occasion she had intimated

this, explaining her reasons. In 1984 Jean told the faculty panel, "I have chosen not to speak with my family about it because my mother and father would suffer very much if they knew."[2] In 1989, she explained, "The thought of a woman doing something like this, having sex before marriage and on top of that, having sex with a married man, it's just totally inconceivable to my parents."[3] As a first-generation Asian American, Jean navigated an outside world where some people intended to hurt her and a personal world where her place was secure, determined by her family's culture and affection. This complicated balancing act was made a bit simpler by not telling her parents about the demands of her outside life.

Her parents' concern for her welfare would have worried Jean and required her to continually reassure them. The sexualized statements, precisely aimed to affront her family and cultural values, would have confused her parents. Sex was a taboo topic in Jean's family, no more appropriate for discussion than for indulgence. How or why could these things be said about a daughter who was not "that kind of girl?" Jean was always mindful that she might lose the case and if so, her parents' embarrassment and shame would deepen. The weight of their concern, confusion, and shame, when added to her own, would have been difficult to bear. It was easier for Jean if her parents did not know the distressing truth about her experience that despite her accomplishments, people still felt she did not belong at the University of Iowa.

Only in November 1990 after the case concluded and *Newsweek* magazine asked to take a photo of her, did Jean tell me that she had never told her parents. We were discussing whether she would agree to the photo. Key to her decision was the fact that *Newsweek* was sold in her parents' grocery store. She did not want her parents to be inadvertently blindsided by friends or acquaintances who saw the story. She permitted the photo and told her parents about the case in broad strokes. "It's nothing bad. People said some wrong things about me. I had to go to court. It's okay now." She never told her parents the full extent of what she went through.

Years later when we were talking about this, Jean teared up. She explained that her painful experience at the University of Iowa and in the litigation made her comprehend and appreciate what her parents had endured for so many years to raise the family and give their children opportunities. Her parents were deferential to white authority figures, patient while white customers were served ahead of them, and stoic when they were called "Chinamen" or "Chinks." They shielded her from seeing the prejudice they faced, just as Jean shielded them from seeing it when it surfaced in her work life.

⋄⋄⋄

Tuesday, June 12, was the last day of the trial. The judge and attorneys needed to finalize jury instructions on the applicable law, make closing arguments, read instructions to the jurors, and excuse them to deliberate.

My closing argument went first. I would speak for Jean—but how best to lay it all before the jury? Jean had trusted me, and I had led her to this precipice out of my conviction that she was in the right. I hoped we would not plummet right over. Could Tomanek convince these jurors that a totally innocent woman had no recourse for vile false statements? We were going to find out today. *Here goes.*

"Dr. Tomanek wants you to believe he is a bit player in this drama. There are other players, but Dr. Tomanek is the star of this show. All roads lead to him. He truly despised Dr. Williams. He was relentless and incorrigible in planting lies about Dr. Jew that damaged Dr. Jew's personal and professional reputation." I led the jury through the judge's instructions, repeating, distilling, and simplifying to make them more understandable. As to each, I urged the jury to answer "yes." I carried detailed notes in my hand and consulted them. My voice was tight and emphatic.

Susan and I had gone back and forth on Jean's damages. I chose not to ask the jury for a specific amount. I described the damage as a wound one could not see. "Jean's pain did not come from challenging work, attending to duty, putting the needs of others above her own. She was used to these. Pain came from knowing others say you are nothing but a slut and the institution you have given so much to won't take action to stop it." I told the jurors money was the only remedy the law provided for emotional pain and suffering and offered them some ways to think about it. There was no amount of money Jean would have accepted to be put through this. Since she continued to work in the environment Tomanek poisoned, should he pay perhaps $10,000 a year for the pain he caused her in each of the past seven years? Another approach was to compensate her for two or three years of productivity she lost because of his conduct, valued at one year's salary. Or consider the annual grant money that supported her research. If Jean lost just a year of funding because of Tomanek's damage to her reputation, she would lose $230,000.

Traw, conversational and relaxed, simply said, "Everything she's told you to do, do the opposite." He mounted a large chart—maybe three feet high by four feet wide. Perched on an easel, the chart dominated the courtroom. Titled "Non-Actionable Language," along the horizontal axis were years 1973 to 1983. The vertical axis listed people's names. From each name a Velcro strip extended horizontally across the years. As Traw's closing argument proceeded, he attached large index cards, oral statements spelled out on one side and a strip of Velcro on other, to the board, aligning them with particular speakers and dates until they were scattered across the board, most of them prior to 1983. It created a visual maelstrom of ugly statements about Jean and Williams. Traw argued that many people, not just Tomanek, made awful statements. Only the statements made by Tomanek after the October 1983 statute of limitations could be the basis for a slander verdict, and those few caused Jean no additional injury. "Remove Tomanek from the equation and the damage to Jean remains." Pointing to the cards on the chart, he added, "This is the reputation Jean Jew had in 1983." Traw characterized Tomanek as a true Iowan—simple, well intentioned, and devoted to his work. "Professor Tomanek earns a living wage, but no more. He has no deep pocket. Remember his testimony that he has just $30,000 in savings. As you decide what the truth is, please remember Dr. Tomanek's reputation. This is his town. This is his university." *But not his alone, as much as he wished it were,* I thought.

Some of the speakers identified on Traw's chart had not appeared at trial. Some statements were not testified to at trial. Some that had been testified to, when transferred to the cards were altered in misleading ways. It was against the rules to introduce new facts in closing argument that were not presented at trial. I saw this as a last-minute ambush. At the conclusion of Traw's argument he began to remove the chart to make room for me. I barked sharply, "Leave it there."

"You see all these slurs, lined up like cars on freeways. The problem is we didn't hear these statements at trial. You never heard from Erlandsen." I tore off a card purporting to be Erlandsen's slander of Jean. The grating sound of Velcro separating, and the soft thud as the cards hit the floor were my accompaniment. "... or from Halmi." I grabbed the edge of another card, ripped it off, and dropped it. "He didn't say..." Rip, rip, rip. "Nobody reported a statement like..." More cards piled up on the floor. With a spontaneous ferocity, I let them have it. The physicality of ripping Velcro apart, the rasping noise, and the insouciance of nonchalantly dropping cards to the floor were all very satisfying. "This chart is another manifestation of the malignant and virulent tactics Dr. Tomanek uses. It shows the slurs will continue unless you stop them. Go by what you remember being presented to you here, in this trial. For everything they say, ask: Where is the truth?"

I relished the taut stillness that hung in the air as I sat down. For a few seconds, neither the spectators in the room nor the previously restive jurors moved. Jean's eyes met mine, communicating appreciation. Slowly, normal bustling resumed. Traw took down his chart and collected his cards from the floor. By having let loose, I knew I would have fewer regrets if we lost.

After a break, Judge Thomas turned to the jury and read twenty-six instructions—beginning with the jury's duty to decide all fact questions. He instructed them on the law of slander, on the burden of proof. and on the challenge of deciding whom to believe. Exhibit A to the jury instructions was the heart of the matter (see Appendix C). It identified eleven statements that we alleged Tomanek made after October 30, 1983, the statute of limitations cutoff date. Statements made before October 30 could be considered for determining Tomanek's knowledge or motive or to provide context for other evidence. Only those made after October 30, 1983 could be the basis for holding Tomanek liable and ordering him to provide a remedy to Jean.

Judge Thomas instructed the jury to decide if Tomanek made and communicated each of the eleven defamatory statements. If yes, did the statement injure plaintiff's moral character or impugn her chastity? If yes, they must decide if any were true or were made within the scope of Tomanek's employment. If no, then the jury had the duty of determining the amount of damages. All eight jurors needed to agree, except "after deliberating for six (6) hours from 1:45 p.m., only seven of you need agree upon the verdict." Seven women and one man were sequestered mid-afternoon June 12, 1990.

Jean, Susan, Sheila, and I went to Jean's home to be near a phone and await a call from Judge Thomas. We didn't have much to say to each other as we waited. I recall gloom, maybe rain. A short time after the jury began deliberations, the judge called. "The jury has questions. I want the lawyers in my office in twenty minutes." When we were gathered, Judge Thomas read the first question the jury had given him, "What is the definition of 'impugn her chastity'?" He looked up at the four lawyers around the conference table. He asked, with a quiet chortle, "Anyone want to make a guess?" No. It was an antiquated phrase. "Impugn her chastity" appeared in Iowa cases predating the 1920s.

Susan broke the silence to everyone's relief, "Let's look it up in *Black's Law Dictionary*." That exhumed a definition as antiquated as the phrase. With everyone's agreement, Judge Thomas wrote, tongue in cheek, a supplemental instruction to the jury: "Interpret the words in their common ordinary meaning. There is no technical definition of the phrase you ask about."

The jury forwarded a second question to Judge Thomas. "What were Jean Jew's legal fees for this case?" Jean was not paying our fees, only reimbursing us for out-of-pocket expenses. In the event we won the federal case, we would ask Judge Vietor to order the university, pursuant to Title VII's fee shifting provision, to reimburse us for our fees and costs in the state case as well, assuming we won the state case. Judge Thomas dispatched this question with another supplemental instruction to the jurors: "You have received no evidence on this issue and will consider it no further in your deliberations."

The jury deliberated for the rest of Tuesday afternoon and most of Wednesday. I have no recollection of how we spent the time. We must have returned to our motel Tuesday evening after the jury had been excused.

Judge Thomas called Jean's home about 4:00 on Wednesday afternoon. When he had me on the phone, he said, "Well, you won." I gave a thumbs up signal to Jean and Susan. I waited. "Seven of the eight jurors signed the verdict form. Since they deliberated for more than six hours, a verdict of seven is in appropriate form and accepted." He continued, "They found plaintiff proved the elements of slander for statements 3, 4, 5, 7, and 8." Later we would see the handwritten notes of the jury foreman indicating, for each time a vote was taken, the number of jurors voting yes or no on each statement.

I waited. "They awarded $5,000 in actual damages and $30,000 in punitive damages," Judge Thomas said.

"Oh…" Disappointment coated my throat. "Oh, no…" Most options I offered the jurors for valuing the damage to Jean were in six figures. This felt like a slap in the face.

Judge Thomas pointed out dryly, "Winning is much better than losing," and went on to say, "Thirty-five thousand dollars is a lot of money to these jurors." He added, "Interest on the award at the statutory rate will begin to accrue tomorrow and court costs are taxed to the defendant, so get those in." I thanked him. We appreciated his steady hand as we had Judge Vietor's. I turned to Jean, Susan, and Sheila that Wednesday afternoon, deeply relieved. But glum.

We were very disappointed by the $5,000 award for emotional distress damages despite all that Jean had suffered. But the $30,000 punitive damage award was gratifying, both because of its amount (Tomanek testified he had only $30,000 in savings) and because of the judgmental message it sent. Per the judge's instructions, the jurors could only award punitive damages, "if the plaintiff has proven that the defendant's conduct constituted a willful and wanton disregard for the rights of Dr. Jew." They were also told that the intent of punitive damages was not to compensate but "to punish and discourage the defendant and others from like conduct in the future." By allocating all of Tomanek's savings to punitive damages, the jury said he deserved punishment.

We did not win everything. Our original complaint against Tomanek had two counts, defamation and invasion of privacy. The privacy count rested on the same facts as the defamation claim and, in time, appeared to us largely redundant. Jean would not receive additional or different relief from winning on invasion of privacy. Instead of voluntarily dismissing the invasion of privacy count when we lost interest in it, we left it in the case, languishing. We did not refer to it in opening statement or closing argument. We did not present evidence unique to the privacy claim. Our oversight forced the jury to sound a sour note among the gratifying messages it sent in its verdict; Jean had not proved her second count for invasion of privacy.

Sometime later, a controversy erupted over payment of Tomanek's judgment and attorney's fees. The university and the attorney general's office each thought the other was obligated. The Iowa Department of Management considered the question and determined that neither should pay—state funds could not be used because his conduct was not within the scope of his employment. Nevertheless, Iowa taxpayers were reported to have paid in excess of $200,000 for the Tomanek judgment, his attorney's fees, and expenses.[4]

"I'm really disappointed that one juror did not sign," Jean said. We speculated about which juror it was. Was it the sole man on the jury? When picking the jury, we had not thought women jurors on the issue of sexual slander of a woman were necessarily better for us. Women's judgments, just as men's, are shaped by sexual stereotypes about Asian American women. Iowa City residents, regardless of sex, lived in a nearly all-white culture. We could not conclude that the impact of stereotypes differed based on a juror's gender alone.

We had been profoundly affected by those twelve days in the courtroom. The abrupt end left intense emotions unresolved. We made a plan to collect and submit our court costs. Numbly, Susan and I packed our banker's boxes into my minivan and left Iowa City on Thursday morning for the five-hour drive back to the Twin Cities. Before leaving, we picked up the *Iowa City Press-Citizen* and read the front-page article "Jury Gives Prof $35,000 in Defamation Trial." Jean was quoted as expressing satisfaction in the decision and relief that it would put an end to what had been happening to her. She reminded colleagues of the burden she bore. "I think that this has probably been hard on the faculty members and students and everyone in the department. But it's important for them to know that it's been the hardest on me."[5] On Friday morning, June 15, 1990, the *Iowa City Press-Citizen*'s editorial was captioned "Jean Jew's Personal Trauma." Describing the jury's verdict as correct, strong, and needed, it went on to say, "Men and women have to have the privilege of being colleagues without being defamed by wagging tongues."[6]

The court forwarded a copy of the jury's verdict form a few days later. Handwritten notes annotated the list of statements in Exhibit A. Each juror signed the verdict form except the foreperson Helen Harker. We were surprised. An older woman, birdlike, with piercing eyes, Harker had attended closely to the proceedings. Yet she had been the holdout. Jean picked up the phone a few days later to hear Helen Harker introduce herself on the other end.

"I want you to know two things," she said. "I want you to know I agreed with the factual decisions of the jury—that Tomanek's statements were false and defamatory."

"I'm very glad to know that," Jean responded, not sure if she was permitted to talk with a juror, even afterward.

Helen continued, "But I could not agree with the low damage award. That's the reason I didn't sign."

"Can you tell me why the jury decided on $35,000 for damages? Is that appropriate for me to ask?" Jean said.

Helen responded, "The others felt your reputation was so badly damaged prior to October 31, 1983, that little additional damage resulted after that date. I looked at it the other way around. Even that little additional bit was worth a lot."

"Thank you so much for calling and telling me," Jean said.

"I hope things go better for you now," Helen added. Neither was comfortable having much conversation. And neither was comfortable with the constraints the legal process put on fully understanding their experience. Helen Harper wanted to explain herself and wanted Jean to understand the meaning of her vote. Jean wanted this, too.

Later, I spoke with Sarah May, another juror.

"The key for us was that we believed the statements about Dr. Jew were false. But to tell the truth, I felt bad for the guy. Dr. Tomanek was singled out. We added punitive damages so that it would stop. We wanted to deter everyone, not just Dr. Tomanek."

I asked her for observations about the lawyers. "I liked Chuck Traw's laid-back style." She added bluntly, "Your repetition of sexual slurs was off-putting to me." I mused about the challenges for a woman lawyer pursuing a sexual harassment case before women jurors. Specificity about the ugly words was necessary. But those words coming from my mouth, without forewarning the listener, ran afoul of Sarah's expectations of appropriate speech from a professional woman. In the years that followed, when teaching law students, I encouraged them to practice speaking in the lower tones that aging judges could more easily hear, to lighten the emotional intensity in their voices, and to echo crude language only after explaining the necessity for it and preparing the decision makers to hear it.

⁝⁝⁝

In the office at the end of the week, Susan and I fielded congratulations from colleagues. George Reilly, the firm's managing attorney who had run interference for me, struck a different tone. "It doesn't look like such a strong case now, does it?" he said, referring to the paltry damage award.

"Remember, the university was not a defendant in this case. There was no deep pocket here. Tomanek testified that he had $30,000 in savings and the jury made him give it up," I said, putting the award in its most positive light. "The federal case is fully submitted. We won't be investing more in that one, either. We just wait for Judge Vietor's decision, whatever it is." Reilly didn't respond one way or another.

I had come to the end of the rope the firm had extended to me. My visit from Reilly was followed in late July by a visit from the head of the Litigation Department. He wanted an analysis of the fees and costs in the case—federal and state. August 1, I sent a memo to the billing department requesting that data. The firm had nearly $800,000 in attorney time and expenses in the cases, much of which could be down the drain.

CHAPTER 11

A Judge Decides

I ARRIVED IN MY office about 8:45 on the Tuesday morning the week before Labor Day. Sun streaming through the large, south-facing windows forced a squint. The office was quiet. Many were away on vacation this last week of summer. Our family was preparing to head up north for Labor Day weekend on the edge of the Boundary Waters Canoe Area. We went annually with a group of twenty-five—law partners, spouses, and kids—all close friends.

I was settling in at my desk, looking out over south Minneapolis and wishing I had taken the week off, when Sheila strode through the open door, shut it, and came up to my desk. A dramatic entrance was very unlike her. Her purposeful stride got my attention.

Struggling to hold back what she wanted to tell me until she reached my desk, when there, out it came in a rush, "Judge Vietor has ruled for Jean on everything!"

"What?" I asked, as if I had not heard her. But I had.

"His clerk just called. Just a few minutes ago, before you got in. She said he filed his decision this morning. She is faxing it to us right now."

"What did she say, exactly?" I demanded.

Sheila handed me the pink "while you were out" slip she had used to record her notes of the conversation. "I wrote it all down. Everything she said. I asked her to repeat it to be sure," she assured me. On the sheet Sheila had written, "The judge is filing his order and I wanted to let you know that he has ruled for the plaintiff on everything. I'll fax the decision. Now I have to call the other side."

"What did she sound like?" I pressed Sheila for all of her impressions.

"Kind of proud of the decision. Excited to tell me," Sheila said.

"Not a word to anyone. Not even to Bob or Susan." I was firm, dictatorial in fact. Sheila was confused.

"Isn't this great?" she said. I glowered. I would not permit a premature celebration with Bob and Susan or even a shared smile with Sheila that might jinx us until we had read the judge's order. My instinct was to hold back every emotion until a victory was in hand.

"We'll see," I said. The clerk's report might be colored by her desire to tell us what she knew we wanted to hear and not what she knew we didn't.

Sheila went to stand by the fax machine, to make sure it didn't jam or disconnect, to prevent another staff member from sweeping one of our pages into theirs, and to capture one page at a time. The pages emerged at a slow and steady pace, impervious to the fact that a life-changing message was emerging.

I closed my door, returned to my desk, and called Jean. In private I told her, "Judge Vietor filed his order this morning. We haven't seen it yet but his clerk is faxing it now." My voice did not tremble, although I thought it might.

"Just tell me, is it good or bad?" Jean asked.

"It's good. Maybe very good. Vietor's law clerk told Sheila this morning on the phone that he ruled for you on everything. I'll call you as soon as I've read it." Jean, like me, knew that we had too little to go on to indulge in celebration. Speculating together would have been as painful as waiting. No reason to stay on the phone.

Forty-three minutes, one for each page, stretched out interminably. I couldn't wait. I walked to the fax machine, took the first ten pages from Sheila, returned to my office, and started reading. I skimmed. I couldn't settle my eyes enough to focus on individual words or proceed in an orderly way line by line. No need. Even from a quick scan I recognized words and sentences written in the loft at Sea Ranch. Once I had the complete decision in my hands, I saw that Judge Vietor had drawn heavily from our proposed findings of fact.[1]

Judge Vietor concluded that we had proved all the elements of a hostile work environment sexual harassment claim. The harassment was sex-based "both because it was sexual in content and because it was directed at Dr. Jew on account of her sex." While the sexual relationship rumors also implicated Dr. Williams, there was no suggestion that Dr. Williams was using a sexual relationship to gain favor, influence, and power with an administrative superior. Men who were supporters of Dr. Williams were not subjected to a continuing pattern of harassment. Were Dr. Jew not a woman, "there would not have been a rumor of gaining favor by a sexual relationship." Although it may have been motivated by hostility toward Dr. Williams, it "nonetheless remained sex-based harassment of Dr. Jew."

Judge Vietor found that the verbal denigration was highly offensive. Harassment was directed at Jean "in a concerted and purposeful manner." It was severe and pervasive and created a hostile work environment for Jean. A reasonable person would have found it extraordinarily difficult to work well in the resulting environment. It was all unwelcome to Jean, as demonstrated by her complaints to administrators.

The university had notice of the harassing conduct. Rumors were ubiquitous. Despite having notice of the harassing conduct, it failed to take appropriate corrective action.

"Jean, his decision is great," I crowed. I summarized key portions for her while she awaited the fax that was now en route from our office to her office—another hour's wait. "He found 'There has never been a romantic or sexual relationship between Dr. Jew and Dr. Williams.' He could have said there 'was not sufficient evidence to prove a sexual relationship,' which would imply there was some proof but not enough. Or he could have said that 'defendant did not bring forward any evidence showing a sexual relationship,' implying there might be evidence but defendant did not present it." Although we would have been satisfied with either of these iterations, his finding that there was no sexual relationship was thrillingly unequivocal on this crucial fact. "He added 'Dr. Jew did not, by word or deed, invite the type of comments made about her and Dr. Williams.'" As I reviewed his decision, I could feel, even over the phone, a balm settling and nourishing all the worn, raw, sore spots on Jean's spirit.

Among the paragraphs in his order that were so gratifying, there was one that wasn't. In one sentence Judge Vietor concluded that plaintiff "has failed to prove that defendants retaliated against her for pursuing her sex discrimination claims." I agreed. We had not proved retaliation under Title VII. The reason was simple: because we had not tried. One might think we ignored it, but the more likely explanation is that we forgot about it. In the crazy complexity that was 1989, it fell off our plate. We did not present evidence at trial, cite legal precedents, or support the claim in our proposed findings of fact. No wonder we lost on it.

Judge Vietor did not dither over the university's argument that Tomanek's comments were constitutionally protected free speech. He concluded that doctrines of free speech and academic freedom did not shield academics from consequences for slanderous false statements—or for sex discrimination.

The factual and legal conclusions in Judge Vietor's decision built to a stunning, two-pronged remedy—one we had strongly urged on him and the other he designed himself. Relying on the university's 1979 decision to grant Jean tenure as evidence of its high opinion of her academic merit, Judge Vietor ordered Jean's promotion to full professor retroactive to July 1, 1984, with back pay, without any further university deliberations.

Judge Vietor designed a second remedy to cleanse the stain from Jean's reputation and, simultaneously, to educate university administrators on their responsibilities to take prompt corrective action. We had proposed distribution of his order to faculty in the Department of Anatomy. Judge Vietor went further on Jean's behalf. His order for relief resonated with an authority that only a federal Judge can imbue. He ordered distribution of copies of his decision, together with copies of the 1984 faculty panel report, to the regents, the president, the vice president of academic affairs, the deans of all colleges, the chairs of all departments in the College of Medicine, and all faculty and staff in the Department of Anatomy. He went on to require the university to take all reasonable steps to assure a hostility-free work environment for Jean. This obligation was open-ended. There was no end date. He was signaling he would keep a watchful eye in the future.

By ordering the distribution of his order and the faculty panel report, Judge Vietor exposed the university's abysmal refusal to respond to the panel report six years earlier. By listing the university administration offices to receive these documents, he signaled where the responsibility lay for permitting the harassment of Jean to continue after the panel report.

On August 28, 1990, when I hung up from talking with Jean, I called

Figure 8: Bob Zeglovitch, Susan Robiner, Jean Jew, and Carolyn Chalmers, December 1990. Courtesy of the author.

Eric and whooped my joy. I floated through the office. First, down the hall to tell Susan and Bob. I plunked into a side chair in George Reilly's office and enjoyed being the crier of good news. We chuckled together over the appearance of "if" in the last lines of the Order: "If plaintiff seeks attorney's fees as part of costs, plaintiff shall move for the award of attorney's fees within 30 days." For certain, on September 28, we would submit an application for reimbursement of attorney's fees and costs. I sent a memo to the firm's attorneys and staff, spreading the news, thanking them for their help, and alerting them that we would be asking for more.

A senior lawyer in the firm came by and said, "Go home, now. Or for a bike ride. Or to the movies. Or find a great martini. Just get out of here before the next fraught task asserts itself and this moment of joy evaporates." Good advice—but unnecessary. Future problems stayed put under a closed lid for now. My elation did not evaporate. It had staying power. I relaxed into a deep feeling of well-being.

We thought we had crossed the finish line.

PART III

❖❖❖

Return to the University

CHAPTER 12

Another Shoe Drops

OUR REQUEST FOR reimbursement of our attorney's fees included $530,000 incurred in connection with the federal lawsuit and the faculty panel hearing, $230,000 for the state court case against Tomanek, and $108,000 for out-of-pocket expenses in both actions to be reimbursed to Jean. We also requested a 33 percent enhancement of our fees to compensate the law firm for the risk of loss. This brought our request to over $1 million. Thirty days was not much time to prepare a persuasive justification for such a large sum.

We were concerned by Judge Vietor's comment one day, midway through the trial. "Been an awful lot of expense in this case already. I really shudder to think of the total expense directly and indirectly to the Iowa taxpayers of this litigation to date and more expense for them in the future, the amount of that expense depending, obviously, on the final result. But it's been a very, very costly spat for the Iowa taxpayers." *Spat? Is that all this is? I don't think so. Note to self: our fee request will have to clear a very high bar.*

The optics were not good from a layperson's point of view. Unlike a Title VII plaintiff suing the University of Iowa today who, on prevailing, may receive a large award for emotional distress damages, when Jean's case was decided Title VII did not permit emotional distress damages. The only monetary recovery she could receive was back pay she had lost plus interest, an upward salary adjustment, payment of her attorney's fees, and reimbursement of costs. Jean's lost back pay totaled $176,000. Our attorney's fees significantly overshadowed her recovery. Judge Vietor at least had witnessed the work, whereas the public had not. Our application had to be so substantive, so detailed, so thoroughly justified, that it would explain and persuade not just the judge, not just university faculty, staff, and students, not just the media, but also the citizens of Iowa.

The disparity between the amount of the award and the size of the fee request was of no concern to Jean. She had seen the work on which the fee request was based. Throughout the case, she had supported the firm's need for reimbursement. The university had tested her, on those few occasions it discussed settlement with us, by making offers to her that were contingent on dropping the demand for reimbursement of attorney's fees. Jean had simply refused. She had been privy to the economic stress on the firm as fees and costs mounted. She believed reimbursement of our fees was only fair and essential for future plaintiffs to get quality representation in discrimination cases.

Regrouping in the office after Labor Day, tasks were assigned. Susan and I called lawyers, judges, and clients asking for affidavits attesting to the difficulty of the case and the quality of our legal work. The firm's billing department collated and formatted eight years of time sheets and disbursements. Bob and others scoured the pleadings and correspondence files looking for the best examples of wasteful defense strategies.

George Reilly was keenly interested in our preparations. The conversation he had with Hal Field, our law partner and his longtime chum, probably went something like this.

"We need a deeper bench for the fee request," George said.

Hal might have replied, "It's sensitive. So far, Carolyn's been solo lead on this."

"You have a good relationship and could partner with her on the fee application."

"I'll talk with her about it," Hal might have replied. When he talked with me, he did a good job of subtly telling me he had been assigned to oversee me. "George suggested that I be available to help however I can on the fee application," Hal said.

I resented Reilly's decision to add a new team member, a man, now that money was involved and without consulting with me. When Jean's rights and career were at stake, the firm considered me adequate. But when the claim was for the firm's money, a senior man was assigned. Yet Hal was the best choice Reilly could have made. My affection for him neutralized any resistance. A much-admired senior partner at Leonard,

Street & Deinard, Hal was not prepossessing. Balding, with a broad smile that dominated even the large lenses he always wore, Hal was a small man in his mid-sixties. After earning an engineering degree at MIT and a law degree at Yale, he returned to the Twin Cities in 1952 and joined the one firm in town hiring civic-minded Jewish lawyers. With a razor-sharp intellect and deft emotional intelligence, Hal brought a surprisingly gentle spirit to complex litigation. I knew he would be a benevolent supervisor. While he could override me, he wouldn't do it by fiat. The political upside was that his reputation would provide a safety net for me in the firm should the fee application fail or fall short. The office nearly hummed with activity aimed at presenting our best case for attorney's fees.

In the midst of the effort, Iowa's deputy attorney general, Gordon Allen, called and asked me to come to Iowa City to discuss settling the case with the president of the university, Hunter Rawlings. Although Jean had prevailed in both trials, risks remained. Tomanek had not appealed the jury verdict against him, and now it was too late. But the university had thirty days from the entry of Judge Vietor's order to file an appeal of his decision to the Eighth Circuit Court of Appeals. Regardless of my feeling that our chances of winning on appeal were good, an appeal injected uncertainty and risk that settlement would eliminate. Allen's manner was curt and preemptory. He was defensive. I was not put off by his rudeness. We agreed to meet.

Hal, Jean, and I joined Allen and Rawlings on September 21 in Iowa City. To settle, we insisted on all of the relief that Judge Vietor ordered; Jean's promotion, her back pay, distribution of Judge Vietor's decision, distribution of the 1984 panel report, and the university's assurance of a hostility-free workplace. Judge Vietor's decision was a public document, so the university did not demand confidentiality or a gag order. The contested issue for settlement was reimbursement of attorney's fees and costs. At the end of a long day of back and forth, we were cautiously optimistic. University leaders had tentatively agreed to all of the relief for Jean and were considering our proposal to submit the contested attorney's fees to Judge Vietor for a binding decision. Allen asked us to provide the data supporting our fee request. We did so and received no response.

On September 28, 1990, we filed our application for fees—a legal brief backed up by two weighty volumes of appendixes, neatly bound with seventy-six laminated, numbered tabs. The first 140 pages of the appendix were itemized lists of time spent, each entry noting the date, attorney or paralegal doing the task, amount of time spent, and the person's billing rate. Next were twenty-four affidavits by attorneys, law professors, state commissioners, and nationally known civil rights lawyers. As a group, the affidavits attested to our expertise, the unique difficulty of the case, the extraordinary risk of loss, the dearth of Iowa attorneys with expertise and willingness to sue the University of Iowa, the foreseeability of attorney's fees exceeding Jean's monetary damages, the appropriateness of our hourly rates, the need for the number of hours spent, and the need for an award enhancing the actual fees to compensate for the risk of loss. Susan Buckley, longtime University of Iowa staff member and administrator, commented on the value of Jean's case for university women. "The only visible, successful court challenge to the institution's treatment of women ... and an inspiration to women in the community to speak up and out."

Following the affidavits were twenty-seven pieces of correspondence reflecting settlement initiatives we took between 1985 and 1990 and the university's stony silence or curt rebuffs. A chart tabulated attorney's fees on the dates of these settlement initiatives. When the faculty panel report came out, attorney's fees were less than $4,000. In October 1985 when we filed suit, a year after the faculty panel report, attorney's fees were $15,000. Four years later, in August 1989, when we sent the settlement videotape, attorney's fees were about $250,000. In November 1989, when a U.S. District Court judge supervised settlement discussions on the eve of trial, the total of our fees and disbursements was approximately $400,000. Over the next eight months, fees doubled. The university's repeated attempts to hold Jean's individual relief hostage to waiver of attorney's fees were also documented, as were my repeated proposals to break this deadlock by submitting the contested attorney's fees issues to a judge to decide.

The last section of the application was devoted to showing how university intransigence drove up our fees and costs. Jean and I submitted our own affidavits detailing the university attorneys' unreasonable and costly litigation strategies—insistence on arguing motions in person and not by phone, refusal to number or otherwise order the documents produced in discovery, denials of undeniable facts, and identification of James Freedman, past president of the university, as an expert witnesses who, when I deposed him in Hanover, New Hampshire, at considerable expense, had no expert opinions. James Hayes, our Iowa City co-counsel, commented in his affidavit, "I observed a number of negative communications and incidents directed particularly and very personally toward Ms. Chalmers." He added that his firm was also on the receiving end of threats from Lerner, who after speaking in "derogatory terms" about Jean, me, and the case, "intimated that our firm was at risk because of sanctions due to the 'frivolous' nature of the case."

A copy of our settlement video that Jim Hayes delivered to Iowa Attorney General Tom Miller in the summer of 1989, completed our submission.

░░░

The deadline for the university's appeal, initially due the same day as our attorney's fees application, was extended for two weeks at the university's request. The press reported that the university was considering an appeal. The *Daily Iowan* published an opinion piece September 28 by Peter Shane, a law professor and chair of the Faculty Senate titled, "Harassment Is Not Privileged Speech."[1] He deftly summarized U.S. Supreme Court rulings: "If an agency can regulate speech to protect against insubordination, it can regulate to protect against harassment." Shane's piece publicly applauded Judge Vietor's opinion. "I can hardly do justice in these few words to the detail and nuance of Judge Vietor's opinion." Faculty and staff began to speak out opposing an appeal and supporting Jean.

With the university still undecided on appeal, I was quoted as saying I would not be surprised by an appeal. "They have to come to terms with what has happened. That's hard to do when you've been avoiding it for so long."[2]

The public learned on October 12 that the university had filed an appeal, coupled with a motion to stay all aspects of Judge Vietor's order pending consideration of its appeal. Although the university had not responded to us about settlement since our September 21 meeting, President Rawlings claimed the university had been trying hard to settle. Rawlings was quoted, "The primary difficulty that's being faced now is the claim for attorney's fees and since those are so substantial, I think they do pose real problems."[3] Resting their refusal to reimburse attorney's fees on their concern for fiscal responsibility was ironic in view of their readiness to spend seemingly unlimited amounts to defend the university and Tomanek. The regents' press release accompanying the appeal characterized Judge Vietor's ruling as "extremely disturbing," not because of the harassment it described but because it imposed a responsibility on the university "for policing the statements and behavior of faculty members in ways that appear inconsistent with academic life. A community dedicated to the free exchange of ideas and views—even unpleasant ones—requires that the Board and the University pursue the matter further."[4] Both statements were outrageous. The university had abandoned settlement efforts, and a campaign of lewd gossip was not a free exchange of ideas and views.

My response was reported: "UI has been found liable by a faculty panel, a jury and a federal court judge. This is round four. I hope there're not 15 rounds."[5] I noted that if the university had settled the case when a faculty panel found that Dr. Jew had been sexually harassed and defamed, her attorney's fees would have been $3,945.[6] Jean was quoted as saying she "was just really stunned. I'm extremely disappointed in the U. The U, despite what it says, is denying me justice."[7]

The university's appeal galvanized public opinion on campus. After news of the appeal, interested faculty gathered to discuss what could be done to stop it. Sue Buckley brought her keen sense for strategies that are effective in a university culture. Martha Chamallas and Peter Shane, law professors at Iowa and supporters of Jean throughout the trials, drew on their advocacy skills. The meeting generated a name—the Jean Jew Justice Committee—and a course of action—make copies of Judge Vietor's decision and distribute one to every faculty member in the university. With the permission of the Faculty Senate, Jean Jew Justice Committee volunteers divided up the campus buildings and stuffed all the faculty mailboxes. "Most faculty did not care about the

Figure 9. Brinley, *Daily Iowan*, October 16, 1990. Courtesy of the *Daily Iowan*.

case or were not aware of the case. Once they read the decision, things changed," said Sue Buckley.

Before a week had passed, 200 faculty and staff signatures were collected for a petition, published on a full page in the *Daily Iowan*.[8] The text of the petition was pointed. "Do you know the facts? Why should you care? Want to see the facts for yourself? Copies of Judge Vietor's decision are being distributed to all faculty. Ask any faculty member to see a copy."

Blanketing the faculty with Judge Vietor's decision was a brilliant strategy. University administrators lost control of the message. A letter to the *Daily Iowan* followed, signed by eighteen math faculty members, announced that they "categorically denounce" the behavior of the College of Medicine and supported an apology to Dr. Jew and an end of the appeal.[9]

Jean's reputation among her faculty colleagues was changing. She began to sense that people she knew and who knew her were not deliberately ignoring her or pretending not to know her. She no longer worried

DO YOU KNOW THE FACTS?

Faculty Panel for Jean Jew
In fall 1984 a University–appointed faculty panel unanimously found that Dr. Jean Jew was subjected to sexual harassment by some members of her department and recommended appropriate remedies. The University ignored the legitimate results of its own appeal process and totally failed to act on the panel's recommendations.

Jury for Jean Jew
A year later Dr. Jew filed suit in Johnson County District Court against the member of her department who had led the harassment against her. When this case finally came to trial in June 1990, the jury reaffirmed that Dr. Jew had been subjected to sexual harassment and awarded compensatory and punitive damages. These have yet to be paid.

Judge for Jean Jew
Also in October 1985, Dr. Jew filed suit in Federal District Court against the University and the Board of Regents. In September 1990, Judge Harold D. Vietor found, once again, that Dr. Jew had been sexually harassed and he ordered that the situation be remedied.

University Continues to Defend Harassment in Court
Since 1985 Dr. Jew and her lawyers have sought to negotiate a settlement. All of their efforts have been rebuffed. Now, after 6 years and thousands of hours of expensive legal research and court costs, the University of Iowa continues to ignore the consistent judgments in Dr. Jew's favor. Dr. Jew wants this case ended and is willing to allow the District Court to determine a settlement of legal costs. The University has refused to agree to this reasonable solution.

WHY SHOULD YOU CARE?

This could have been any one of us – male or female – faculty, staff or student. We are all potential victims of practices that effectively condone harassment and defamation of character.
Instead of defending harassment in court, the University of Iowa should be leading the effort to eliminate harassment in the community in which we all work and live. Sadly, in this case, the University's actions speak much louder than words.

WANT TO SEE THE FACTS FOR YOURSELF?

Copies of Judge Vietor's decision are being distributed to all faculty at the University of Iowa by our Committee. Ask any faculty member to see a copy.
Copies are also available at Zephyr Copy Center, 124 East Washington, at cost.

Paid for by the Jean Jew Justice Committee

Chris Africa
Christine Allen
Don Aller
Patti Ambrose
Brooks Ammerman
Diane Anderson
Gene Asprey
Florence Babb
Regenia Bailey
David Baldus
Susan Beckett
Ron Bergman
Susan Birrell
Fran Blanc
Florence Boos
William Boos
Sharon M. Bower
Chris Brenneman
Jennifer Britton
Marvin C. Brummel
Sue Buckley
Mary Bucklin
Peg Burke
Deborah Burger
Elizabeth Burns
Brenda Buswell
Kathy Carlson
Dee Ann Casteel
Tess Catalano
Hisuk Chae
Martha Chamelias
Rob Chametzky
Teral Champion
Phyllis Chang
Michael Chibnik
Russell L. Clochon
Susan T. Cook
Dan Corum

Jeff Cox
Lois Cox
Carolyn Cutrona
Betty Dasovich
Bill Davies
Chris Davis
Julie Davis
Alice Davison
Richard Delaurell
Ursula Delworth
Wendy Develbaum
Elanor Dilkes
Minnette Doderer
M. Patricia Donahue
Maria A. Duarte
Mary L. Dudziak
Carolyn Dyer
Michele Eliason
Vicki Fagen
Bernie Fairchild
Ronald Feld
Mary L. Fellows
Raul Ferrera-Balanquet
Mary Fisher
Peter Fisher
Shawn Flanagan
Norman Foster
Teresa Garcia
Consuelo Garcia
Kathryn Gerken
Kate Gleiter
Carol Girdler
Craig Gjerde
Mathew Glasson
Monica Gonzales
Christine H.B. Grant
Leslie Griep
Virginia Gross

Julie Gumbiner
Vickie Guzman
Laurie Haag
Marlene Hall
Sarah Hanley
Nancy Hauserman
Paul M. Heidger, Jr.
Elyce Helford
Steve Herbert
Ellie Herman
Ellen Heywood
Egyirba High
Mary Holland
Robert Hopp
Diana Horton
Becky Hurt
Judith Hurtig
Richard Hurtig
Tom Jacobs
Kathleen Janz
Michael A. Jogerst
Lynda Johnson
Jennifer Joslin
Kelly Julian
Sally Kenney
Barbara Kerr
Sherry King
Jean Koch
Dean Koster
Rita Krause
Elizabeth Kudsk
Valerie Lagorio
David Lair
Janese Lample
Becky Lane
Lynette Larson
Paula Laube
Wendy Lavertu

Alexis Leacock
Dana Leigh
Tom Lewis
Victoria Sy Lim
Jasmine Ujima Love
Richard MacNeil
Nan Macy
Mac Marshall
Jean Martin
Cheryl Mason
Staci Matthews
Mary McDonald
Margaret B. McDowell
Barbara McKenna
Pat Meyer
Jeanne Meyers
Jill Miller
Papusa Molina
Vicki Mongeau
Dennis Moore
Adalaide Morris
Cherry Muhanji
Gayle Nelson
Kristine Nelson
Dolores Nesbitt
John Nesbitt
Mary Neuhauser
Reta Noblett–Feld
Nancy Noyer
Paul Papak
Robert N. Parker
Catriona Parratt
Tana Perry
Dorothy Persson
Mary Pettit
Sandy Pickup
Terry D. Powell
Mary Anne Rasmussen

Jean Retzinger
Amy Reynolds
Cecilia Ridgeway
Catherine Ringen
Barb Robb
Tonja Robins
Jean Robinson
Linda Robinson
Mary Rohlfing
Thomas Rohlich
Mac Rohrbough
Nancy Romaiov
Marilyn Rose
Christopher D. Roy
Nora L. Roy
Dianne Rucinski
Daniel Russell
Jackie Russell
Shauna Russell
Abran Salazar
Gayle Sand
Leonard A. Sandler
Jane Saxton
Lois Sayrs
Jeannette Scohill
Liz Seim
Peter Shane
Timothy Shipe
Dana Shugar
Caroline Sierra
Marilyn Simpson
Bonnie Slatton
Robert L. Spenner
Mary Stevenson
Karen Stewart
Jeanne Stoakes
Sandy Stockman

Donna Stone
Monica Strom
Shelton Stromquist
Katherine H. Tachau
Christine Tade
Micheal Teague
Kris Terrel
Laurel Thorn
Francine Thompson
Sue Ann Thompson
Sue Tiardis
Roberta Till–Retz
Joan Tucker
Jon Van Allen
Diana Velez
Stephen Vlastos
Margaret Voelker
Barbara Waite
Henry A. Walker
Joyce A. Walker
Yanteng Wang
Kal Weatherman
Mary Weideman
Burns H. Weston
Mary Whelan
Irene Wherritt
Glenys O. Williams
Gregory H. Williams
Terence Williams
Roselie Wissler
Margery Wolf
Peggy Wood
Rebecca Woodard
Marge Wright
Barbara Xakellis
Sharon Zeck
Ming Quon Zhang
Lori Ziegenhorn

Figure 10. Petition in the *Daily Iowan* October 17, 1990, 12A. Courtesy of the *Daily Iowan*.

Open letter

To the Editor:

On Oct. 18, each professor on campus received a copy of the judgment in favor of Professor Jean Jew calling for the UI to retroactively promote Jew to full professor.

After reading the judgment, various members of the mathematics department felt compelled to speak out regarding the treatment of Professor Jew by various members of the College of Medicine and by the UI central administration.

We categorically denounce as unacceptable the behavior of the members of the College of Medicine who have subjected Professor Jew to years of sexual harassment.

It is beyond belief that events such as those described in the judgment could occur at an institution where bigotry and harassment by virtue of one's race, religion or ethnic heritage simply should not exist and cannot be tolerated.

The university-appointed panel that investigated the situation of Professor Jew in 1984 unanimously found that she had been defamed and harassed, and it made several recommendations to the UI, most of which have gone unaddressed. In fact, the UI has decided to appeal the judgment.

We strongly urge the UI not to seek further appeal.

We ask that the UI issue a statement affirming its commitment to a work place completely free of such harassment.

We urgently ask the UI to issue Professor Jew a public apology and exoneration.

Norman L. Johnson
Juan A. Gatica
and 16 other math
department faculty

Figure 11. Open letter to the editor from math faculty, *Daily Iowan*, October 24, 1990. Courtesy of the *Daily Iowan*.

that people meeting her for the first time had heard the salacious rumors about her, knowing they would hear about the outcome of her case. The shunning that conveyed she didn't belong was no longer apparent.

Press was overwhelmingly positive for Jean, with daily critiques of the university in editorials, political cartoons, letters to the editor, and opinion columns. On October 16, both the *Iowa City Press-Citizen* and the *Daily Iowan* ran editorials criticizing the university. Titled "UI Never Learns," the Viewpoints editor of the *Daily Iowan* noted, "Even dogs learn. . . . No mode of negative reinforcement has succeeded

Sordid episode at U of I

Delay justice no longer

U.S. District Judge Harold Vietor's ruling in the sexual-harassment suit against the University of Iowa is a model of judicial craftsmanship. In 76 prosaic paragraphs, which are excerpted on the opposite page, Vietor presents the story of Dr. Jean Jew's 10-year trial of bigotry, petty jealousy and vicious gossip at the university's College of Medicine.

She was accused by colleagues in the crudest terms of sleeping with her boss, of being a slut, a whore, a bitch. She was the target of nasty rumors, anonymous personal attacks, sexually suggestive cartoons posted in the department and cruel jokes scribbled on the men's room walls. These slurs caused her no end of pain, and retarded her career.

Throughout this shameful ordeal, Jew's superiors ignored the harassment. Even when U of I administrators were put on notice — and urged by a faculty committee to take prompt action — they ignored the advice, dawdled and generally failed to take the situation seriously.

Nowhere in the recitation of these facts or in the subsequent conclusions of law does the judge yield to the temptation to lash out at Jew's colleagues and superiors to say, "Good God! This is a university, and you're acting like a bunch of juvenile thugs." Instead,

Vietor let the record speak for itself.

The sordid details make painful reading. One wonders how Jew managed to function at all in such an environment, let alone prevail in her five-year effort to win back her self-respect, her dignity and her professional advancement.

Painful as those details may be, the judge concluded they should be held up for all to see. In addition to awarding her the promotion she was denied, Vietor ordered that the decision be distributed among the Board of Regents, administrators at the University of Iowa and the College of Medicine and be kept on file and accessible to faculty and staff for no less than five years.

Nowhere in the decision does Vietor put in words what prompted him to require the university to face up to this distressing episode. He did not have to.

The university is keeping its options open to appeal Vietor's decision, but an appeal would almost certainly be a waste of time and money, and it would send the message that such behavior could somehow be justified, or excused.

Whatever the cost of accepting this decision, it is a small price compared to what Dr. Jew has paid. It would be an outrage to delay justice in this case a moment longer.

Figure 12. *Des Moines Register* editorial, October 31, 1990. Courtesy of Enveritas Group, Inc.

Figure 13. Andy Brownstein and Diana Wallace, "UI, regents put case to rest."
Daily Iowan, November 13, 1990. Courtesy of the *Daily Iowan*.

in correcting the U's behavior."[10] Accompanying editorial cartoons, excoriating President Rawlings for continuing to squander resources on the case, were an ironic twist on the cartoons about Jean that had started it all.

The *Iowa City Press-Citizen*'s criticism was equally harsh. Under the line "Double or Nothing," the university's appeal to the Eighth Circuit Court of Appeals was criticized as a public relations disaster, legally shaky, and only pursued by an arrogant gambler backed by the state of Iowa's big bank roll.[11]

CHAPTER 13

Finally, a Coming to Terms

IN THE MIDST of this uproar, Deputy Attorney General for Iowa Gordon Allen called. It was his first word on settlement since our September 21 meeting. His message: the state of Iowa is never going to come close to $1 million in fees. But if I would reduce my fee demand to the range of $350,000 to $500,000, he would take it to the regents at their meeting Wednesday and discuss severing the fees and submitting them to Judge Vietor for decision. His condition that I reduce our fee demand was a nonstarter and I said so. Yet I was encouraged to finally hear some willingness to discuss submitting our attorney's fees to Judge Vietor for decision. I prepared a letter for Allen to take to the regents' meeting October 17, explaining our proposal: implement agreed-on relief to Jean and submit the contested issue of our attorney's fees to the court for the judge to make a binding decision.

The day the regents met, the faculty petition appeared in the campus paper and Jean Jew Justice Committee volunteers were walking around campus with armfuls of Judge Vietor's decision for faculty mailboxes. Allen called again. He asked for a meeting in Des Moines on Saturday, October 20, to negotiate a settlement that would include attorney's fees. He tabled his precondition that we reduce our fee demand. Hal suggested we charter a plane to take us to Des Moines to meet their schedule—something that would never have occurred to me.

The four-passenger, two-propeller plane bumped through a thunderstorm with occasional lightning visible through the rain rippling down the window. Hal's was a reassuring voice. He wasn't worried or, if he was, he didn't show it. He distracted me with stories of flying through midwestern thunderstorms with his father to check on his father's movie theaters in small towns. "We went through storms like this dozens of times." I didn't know anything about small planes but he apparently did.

That plane ride was a metaphor for the negotiating discussions the next morning—turbulent and laced with potential disaster. Jean met us at the Des Moines airport and drove us to the meeting.

Our October 20 meeting with Marvin Pomerantz, president of the board of regents, was in a conference room at his company, Mid-America Packaging. *Who knew one could make a fortune manufacturing corrugated cardboard?* Regent Marv Berenstein, a Sioux City attorney; Gordon Allen; and University President Hunter Rawlings were there. All the university representatives and Hal were white men, in their early sixties, and at the pinnacle of success in their careers. By comparison, Jean and I were junior in age, commoners in status, outsiders by gender, and for Jean, by race. Pomerantz was jovial, and Hal adopted an avuncular tone in response, something neither Jean nor I could do. We would have sat in silence if Hal had not been with us to engage in the social chitchat Pomerantz insisted on.

I don't recall anyone apologizing to Jean for what she went through, congratulating her on her result, or even addressing her directly. They had come to terms with the need to implement a remedy. The question for our meeting was whether they would hold her relief hostage for a substantial reduction in attorney's fees.

"Our chances for reversal on appeal look good," Berenstein said, turning to Allen, who nodded encouragingly. Berenstein was comfortable playing the bad cop role against Pomerantz's good cop. "You can lose on appeal, you know." He added in a patronizing tone, "I'm sure you have, as I have. It's a risk for your client." He provoked me.

"The appeal is little risk for us," I said. "Vietor's decision is heavily fact-based, and factual findings are not revisited by the appellate court. Legal developments have been getting better and better for our side. We'll make great new sexual harassment law at the expense of the university's reputation and the state's financial resources." I was aware, despite my bluster, that Judge Vietor's order to retroactively promote Jean to full professor could be at risk on appeal.

Pomerantz tried to change the tone with compliments. "Obviously you did one hell of a job . . . but we don't want to pay," Pomerantz said.

"Some reduction in fees in order to avoid delay for your client," Berenstein resumed—*here comes the wedge again*—"is only reasonable.

Some days you say you worked twenty hours out of twenty-four. You must have slept some of that time."

I retorted, "The ugly antics of your attorneys accounted for many sleepless nights. I won't discount those painful hours." We went on like this for a couple of hours. We wore ourselves out while getting no closer. They made no offer; we made no concessions.

Berenstein said to Jean, "Your lawyer isn't looking out for your best interests. You've got the back pay and the promotion. If we appeal, you could lose it all." Anger, so seldom seen in Jean, flared. She stood up and nearly walked out. I caught her wrist and stopped her. I reminded her, in a private sidebar, "Pomerantz is a person with power to make a decision." Later she explained her outrage, "He was saying, after all this time, and after all we've been through together, I should trust him, not you!"

Pomerantz, who sat quietly through most of this, bounced up out of his chair. "It's lunch time. Let's go to my club." Jean and I looked at Hal. He called for a break. When we were alone, I said to him, "I can't go to lunch with them. I can't stand it, to be paraded past his chums in his country club for no purpose. Let's just go home." Our chartered plane was in a hangar waiting for us. I was ready. They had not come to make a deal, and they never would.

Hal insisted, "We have to say yes."

"I can't stand it," I repeated. To have come through a harrowing flight and be badgered to a predictable impasse was maddening. Instead of the camaraderie I had experienced over the past six weeks in the office, muscle memory brought back the harsh experiences, the bad feelings, and the cheerlessness of it all.

"It won't be long. I'll handle the small talk." Hal made it clear, diplomatically, that it was his call. End of discussion. Jean drove Hal and me to the Wakonda Country Club. It was after noon when we arrived. Pomerantz was greeted warmly by the maître d', who assured him that a table for seven was ready for us by the window. To reach it, we had to cross the sparsely populated dining room. Pomerantz and Allen paused to greet people at the tables as we passed.

"Great to see you again." "The Hawkeyes are having a great season." "Let's play a round before the snow flies." "Give my greetings to Tom." "How's the family?" Objects of curiosity, Jean and I dutifully trudged after Pomerantz, Berenstein, Allen, and Rawlins, as if falling in behind our superiors. I felt co-opted by the staging—part of their group, led by them, subordinate to them. It was all wrong. I imagined the conversations we left behind in our wake. "Who are those two women? Hmm. . . . Maybe the Chinese one is Jean Jew. Isn't she the one at the U who just won that sexual harassment case? The other one might be the lawyer who is asking for all those attorney's fees. Maybe they are trying to make a deal?" Or, "I don't get how gossip has become sexual harassment. It's ridiculous."

Pomerantz played the jovial host at our table, chatting with the waiter, recommending menu items, and establishing a lighthearted tone. Hal continued to provide needed ballast to my intensity. At Pomerantz's request, the waitress brought a radio over to the table so the Iowa leaders would not miss the University of Iowa football game. Its steady rumble, occasionally provoking a "good going" from our table, contributed to a surreal tableau.

While I had done much of the talking at the meeting, Pomerantz did some talking at lunch. Conversation was sandwiched between reports of football plays. Pomerantz asked Jean what she had been doing during the past few years. When she answered, "Working—doing my research and teaching full time," he seemed surprised. Other questions followed. The care with which Jean considered her answers, her directness, her unfailing dignity—all were evident. Pomerantz may have seen in her something of what Judge Vietor had seen. The same could be said of what I had revealed of myself in the morning. Our responses to these decision makers were as authentic as they had been to Judge Vietor.

I was relieved when Pomerantz pushed his chair back, indicating lunch was over. *I don't know what Hal thought we could accomplish with this, but it's good we got through it,* I thought. As he got up to leave, Pomerantz motioned for Hal and me to join him as we walked out. In the vestibule, the three of us were a bit to the side of the others as coats were collected. Pomerantz shook Hal's hand and thanked him for coming, saying it had been a pleasure to meet him. He then turned to me and instead of offering his hand, stepped in and, on his tiptoes, whispered into my ear, "We are going to make this right. It's going to work out," and planted a dry kiss on my cheek.

His kiss was physically prickly, like an unexpected zip of static electricity. A fairy tale flashed through my mind—*will he turn into a prince or me into a frog?* There was nothing sexual or malevolent in it, but it was decidedly patronizing and unprofessional. He used an uninvited kiss to communicate to me his agreement to end a sexual harassment case on our terms. Maybe his message was that I should think of him as a chum—on the same side with respect to settling the case. If so, did he notice the disjunction between the content of his message and the means he chose to deliver it? Once the shock wore off, I welcomed the message, if not the means.

Pomerantz said, still looking directly at me, but loudly enough so Hal and the others could hear, that he would send one of his people up to our office in a few weeks' time. "Okay," I said.

On the uneventful flight home, I asked Hal, "What do you make of it?"

"He wants to make a deal. It's a breakthrough."

"And only because you insisted on lunch," I said.

Hal noted. "He chose an odd way to end a gender discrimination case. I, who did nothing on the case, get a handshake because I'm a man. You, who did everything on the case, get a kiss because you are a woman."

⋰⋱

Our October 20 meeting with Pomerantz had been confidential by mutual agreement. While hopeful, we had nothing concrete. The press and the Jean Jew Justice Committee continued the drumbeat. Kim Painter's opinion piece in the *Daily Iowan* on October 23 was intemperate. She titled it "So This Is Academic Freedom?" Excoriating the regents for their press release, she suggested: "House Tomanek's enterprise in a new academic building, the Tomanek Chink and Slut Center for the Free Exchange of Ideas and Views." The *Des Moines Register* covered the tumult. On October 31, a front-page article ran on Judge Vietor's decision. Continuing on the inside, extensive excerpts from the decision filled the page across from the lead editorial. The lead editorial, "Sordid Episode at U of I: Delay Justice No Longer," called the judge's decision "a model of judicial craftsmanship" that told a story of "Dr. Jean Jew's 10 year trial of bigotry, petty jealousy and vicious gossip at the University's College of Medicine." A commentary titled "Being Ashamed of the U of I" by James Flansburg followed in the *Des Moines Register*.

Seven senior faculty women, led by Martha Chamallas, met with President Rawlings a few days later to request that he take a public position on Jean's case by Friday, November 9. Their demand was strategic. Rawlings was scheduled to speak that weekend at an annual Iowa conference to promote the advancement of women in higher education. He didn't take a public position or speak at the conference, but Jean Jew Justice Committee members held a protest at the conference

Figure 14. Brian Duffy, *Des Moines Register*, November 14, 1990. Courtesy of Enveritas Group, Inc.

on November 9, urging the attendees to ask the university to stop the appeal. In the College of Medicine, about 150 medical students sent a petition to Dean Eckstein asking that the appeal be dropped. Unrelenting faculty, student, and public pressure was to be capped by an open public discussion organized by the Jean Jew Justice Committee on November 12. Rawlings was asked to address the audience. Instead, he sent the vice president for academic affairs, Peter Nathan, in his place.

Behind the scenes, Pomerantz's attorneys came to our Minneapolis law office. Gordon Allen was not present. Jean was not present, as she was needed for Jean Jew Justice Committee activities. Glass walls permitted law firm staff passing in the hall to observe, and many did. A few partners on my floor (by this time, the office occupied three floors of a downtown office building) urged me to hold out for more than $1 million, arguing that a multiplier over and above actual fees and expenses was only fair to compensate the firm for the risk of loss. When $895,000 was finally offered with the ultimatum that Pomerantz would not agree to pay anything more than our actual fees and expenses, we agreed.

Settlement had been reached by the time Vice President Peter Nathan attended the packed public meeting at the university on November 12. He read a statement announcing the settlement and withdrawal of the appeal. Nathan also asserted to the audience, "I can guarantee that this kind of thing will not happen again."[1] Margery Wolfe, a professor and a leader of the Jean Jew Justice Committee, noted wryly, "Perhaps there should be an exam." The *Iowa City Press-Citizen* reported that Nathan's announcement of settlement was met with "cheers, applause and teary eyes."

Gordon Allen and I had a phone conference with Judge Vietor, informing him of the settlement and its terms, including withdrawal of the appeal, full relief for Jean as he had ordered, continuance of the permanent injunction to create a hostility-free workplace for her, and payment of attorney's fees and costs. Drafts of a settlement agreement were exchanged November 13 and finalized November 15. I sent a copy to Judge Vietor, and he wrote back a few days later, thanking me for it. "I think settlement is in everybody's best interest." In our office on November 16 was a check, drawn on the state of Iowa, for $895,000. The firm reimbursed Jean for the more than $100,000 in fees and costs

Diagnosis: Harassment

A medical-school prof overcomes sexual slurs

PAUL JENSEN
A five-year battle in the courts: *Dr. Jew*

For more than a decade, a male professor at the University of Iowa medical school spread lies about a female colleague. She was trading sexual favors for career advancement, the stories went—sleeping with her boss, sometimes in a motel, sometimes in his office. He told these tales to faculty members, graduate students and staff members. She complained repeatedly about the harassment. And what did the university administration do? Nothing.

Last week the school paid for its laissez-faire attitude. Settling a five-year-old lawsuit, the university issued a humbling public apology and agreed to pay Dr. Jean Jew $50,000 in back pay, $126,000 in damages and $895,000 in fees and expenses to her attorney. "Dr. Jew deserves our apologies and our respect for her stand," concluded Iowa's president Hunter Rawlings III.

The case has created sharp divisions in the university community. Jew's supporters thought the school should have settled sooner—as an example to other institutions involved in sexual-harassment suits. Others argued that settling the case limited academic freedom and freedom of speech on campus. The suit has brought much negative publicity to Iowa City, a town proud of its reputation as a liberal, sophisticated community. Last month The Des Moines Register printed a full page of excerpts from a federal district court ruling in Jew's favor and urged university officials to give up their plan to appeal. "It would be an outrage to delay justice . . . a moment longer," the Register said in an accompanying editorial.

In her suit, Jew claimed that a fellow anatomy professor, Robert Tomanek, spread a rumor that she was having an affair with Terence Williams, a former chairman of the department. Williams had been a professor at Tulane University in New Orleans before taking the Iowa job in 1973; Jew met him when she was a medical student there. She and two male doctors came to Iowa with Williams; Jew became a tenured assistant professor in 1979.

No comment: In a 34-page ruling issued in late August, U.S. district Judge Harold Vietor wrote that Tomanek "told faculty, graduate students and staff members of the department, sometimes in locker-room language, that Dr. Jew had been observed having sexual intercourse with Dr. Williams in Williams's office, that she was a 'slut,' that she and Dr. Williams were having an affair, that they had been seen coming out of a motel together, and that Dr. Jew had received preferential treatment based on a sexual relationship with Dr. Williams." Tomanek is still at the university; he declined to comment. In a 1985 defamation lawsuit brought by Jew, a jury returned a $35,000 verdict against Tomanek.

Others in the department joked about her ethnic background. Jew is an American of Chinese descent. Explicit sex-based graffiti about her appeared on the walls of the department's men's room when she was being evaluated for promotion. In 1979, another professor, apparently drunk, yelled at her as she walked down a hallway in the department, calling her a "slut," a "bitch" and a "whore."

Before filing suit, Jew protested several times to university officials. She says they told her to endure the insults; her life might be "hell," but she was assured she would continue to progress. Last week she said that "the hardest part of all is still to come"—correcting the problem. "It's so much easier to hand over money than to do what's right." Rawlings promised that the school would "provide a hostility-free environment for Dr. Jew," and "not tolerate" any other cases of harassment. That's a tough assignment, and one that no university can afford to fail.

BARBARA KANTROWITZ *and*
HEATHER WOODIN *in Iowa City*

Figure 15: Barbara Kantrowitz and Heather Woodin, "Diagnosis: Harassment."
Newsweek, November 26, 1990. Courtesy of Enveritas Group, Inc.

she had paid over the seven years. Sometime after the settlement was reported, I had occasion to call Judge Thomas. I could hear his smile over the line. "I trust you are calling from a gold-plated telephone."

Jean's case received national attention in the *New York Times,* the *Chronicle of Higher Education,* and *Newsweek.*[2]

The firm made the largest deposit ever with the help of the check from the state of Iowa. Reilly gave me a framed a copy of the check as a memento. Eric and I designed a T-shirt as a thank-you gift to some supporters. Its logo: "International Coalition for Academic Freedom and Gender Justice. Iowa Campaign. First Stage: 1983–1990." Some years later I was amused to find the T-shirt noted as among the contents of the Women's Archives in the University of Iowa Library.

⁂

The findings of fact and legal analysis in Judge Vietor's decision provided a rock solid foundation for faculty activism. The university's subsequent appeal and its self-serving press releases were inflammatory. The Jean Jew Justice Committee seized the opportunity. Its actions were guided by the insight that faculty, acting together, have sufficient power to overcome university intransigence. Judge Vietor's decision, the result of years of aggressive, creative litigation, was the tool the committee used to catalyze faculty opinion, motivate faculty activism, and push the university to settle. Law, litigation, judicial decision, and grassroots political advocacy were instrumental in producing the outcome.

The appeal, together with Judge Vietor's decision, educated people about the facts of the case and the wrongs done to Jean by individual actors and the institution. The university hadn't intended, by its appeal, to clear Jean's name. Rather, it sought to regain the upper hand by first threatening appeal, then filing one, and putting the remedy for Jean on hold while the appeal was pending. The unintended, unforeseen result of its action was an outcry against this power play.

Even after this comeuppance, a year later the university lapsed into long-established habits by filing an application for determination of compliance. The application asked Judge Vietor to find that the university had complied with his order and dismiss Jean's case.

Applying for a determination of compliance was a tone-deaf move,

Jean Jew: After the battle

Professor looks to the future

By Julie Creswell
The Daily Iowan

With a slight laugh and a sideways glance, Jean Jew will tell you she fought the UI because she knew she was right.

Admired and respected, she shrugs off the label of "courageous," citing that the most difficult part of her 17-year sexual harassment ordeal was making the decision to fight the university. After that, she never looked back.

"To get to a point where you would challenge authority was a very big step for me," Jew said. "But once I made the decision, that was that."

Jew, an anatomy professor, won a sexual harassment suit against the UI last August in a scathing ruling delivered from Federal District Court Judge Harold Vietor. The ruling criticized the university's handling of the case and ordered that Jew be promoted to full professor and paid nearly $100,000 in back pay and benefits.

As an American of Chinese ancestry, Jew said she is not a stranger to harassment and discrimination. She often encountered and fought racial discrimination growing up in the South.

"Growing up in a system like that prepares you for discrimination. It makes you accept it more readily because you've put up with it all your life, but it does give you strength," Jew said.

"I never told my family until two or three months before the federal trial because the nature of the allegations were something so abhorrent to them. I didn't feel I could burden them with this."

Today Jew, the anatomy department, and the UI are working toward healing the scars left from several years of turmoil. While Jew says she is not bitter, she feels a sense of loss over the number of years of her life that

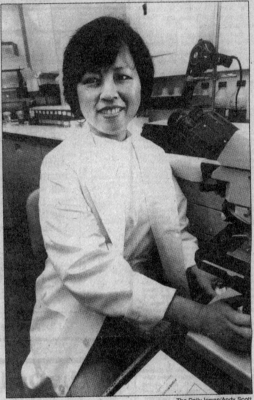

The Daily Iowan/Andy Scott

She hoped to become known for her research, but anatomy professor Jean Jew instead found herself the focus of a sexual harassment suit which brought the national spotlight on the UI.

were spent fighting the university in and out of court.

"You just don't lose 10 years and make it up. I feel a sense of grieving over that. But after all this time, I still don't understand why the university fought me tooth and nail — the stakes became very high," she said.

Iowa state Board of Regents President Marvin Pomerantz said the "perceived delay" in ending the suit was the result of a long litigation period.

"We were involved in a lawsuit and that takes time, unfortunately and regrettably," Pomerantz said.

Jew's suit stemmed from incidents within the anatomy department dating back to 1973. Occurrences which met deaf ears or easy explanations when she complained.

"I complained to the administration and had been told essentially there was nothing they could do,"

See Jew, Page 6A

Figure 16: Julie Creswell, "Jean Jew: After the battle," *Daily Iowan*, April 4, 1991. Courtesy of the *Daily Iowan*.

and like the appeal, it had an unintended outcome. In preparing to oppose the application, we learned that the university had not distributed copies of the 1984 faculty investigative panel report to administrators and faculty as Judge Vietor had ordered. Failing to distribute the report was not an oversight, as the university claimed. It was more likely a defiant act. The university had successfully resisted our requests for a periodic accounting of steps that it was taking to establish a hostility-free work environment for Jean. In the absence of oversight, administrators' refusal to distribute the panel report was not discovered until it requested a determination of compliance.

There were other flaws in implementing Judge Vietor's order. Jean had been promoted to full professor effective 1984, but university electronic records still showed her as an associate professor. Her research funds were delayed six months. Sexual harassment training for the Anatomy Department, lasting little more than an hour, was not scheduled until new graffiti (not about Jean) appeared in spring 1991. Tomanek's tenure home remained in the Anatomy Department, and he continued to vote on departmental decisions that affected Jean's research program. Because granting the application would bring an end to judicial oversight, Judge Vietor declined to rule on the application, and judicial oversight continued for several years.

The university's reversion to type after the case ended was part of the aftermath, but not the whole story. At a personal level, the case made all the difference to Jean. On August 28, 1991, exactly one year after his order, Judge Vietor summoned counsel to his chambers "to explore the possibility of a nonlitigation resolution" of the university's application for a determination of compliance.[3] We sat around a table in his chambers as we had on the first day of trial. After greeting us, he turned to Jean and asked, "How are things going now?"

Jean paused, thinking, and said quietly, "I feel like I've been in a state of grace."

CHAPTER 14

Jean's Legacy

A LAWSUIT ASKS a judge to finish a story. But a lawsuit is rarely the last word. Stories don't end when a case closes. Jean's story continues, along with efforts by others to stop discriminatory bias in universities.

The Jean Jew Justice Committee pondered how Jean's ordeal and the success of their grassroots efforts could be put to good use in the future at the University of Iowa. An award was established in Jean's name, to be given annually to a faculty or staff member who demonstrated a commitment to women's rights. Intended to keep Jean's story alive in a community where people come and go, for nearly thirty years the Jean Jew Women's Rights Award and its recipient are celebrated at an annual reception. New students and faculty in transit through the university wonder, who is Jean Jew? Her story is retold. The narrative encourages women. Some say Jean's case and the regular reminder of it make women braver.

Jean was honored outside of the university as well. At the end of 1990, the Feminist Majority Foundation selected eleven people who "demonstrated tremendous courage, creativity and conviction in publicly standing up for women." Derrick Bell, a professor at Harvard Law School, and Jean Jew were the two winners in education.[1] In a retrospective occasioned at the end of the twentieth and the beginning of the twenty-first century, Jean was one of the individuals the *Iowa City Press-Citizen* honored for her contribution in the outgoing century.

I happened upon a 2009 interview of Susan Johnson, the 1999 recipient of the Jean Jew Women's Rights Award. She worked in several roles at the university—as a faculty member, associate dean in the College of Medicine, and, at the time of the interview, associate provost for faculty in the medical school. Jean's lawsuit "has had a profound influence on the way the university has approached the whole issue of sex harassment. . . . It is a particularly public example of how things can go wrong and you just can't forget about that."[2]

I don't suggest that the Jean Jew Women's Rights Award and other recognitions have been unmixed blessings. Encouraging others to remember doesn't let them or Jean forget. It brands her as it honors her. She doesn't have the option of separating herself from her history as a litigant. Use of her name reminds university people that there was a time when Jean was not institutionally approved.

Its blessings are that for Jean, for me, and for her supporters, friendships forged years ago are kept strong by these contemporary recognitions. Memories thrive on annual nourishment. Honoring her work protects it from piecemeal deconstruction over time and helps keep the work of gender equity strong. In Iowa, her name stands for the ongoing struggle against sexual harassment that, when she first experienced it, had no name. Title VII requires a woman be made "whole" for the damage of sex discrimination. The movement to keep Jean's story resonant has helped make her whole.

In 2018, Jean was inducted into the Iowa Women's Hall of Fame. In her letter of support, Sue Buckley wrote, "While the United States had Anita Hill, the state of Iowa had Jean Y. Jew. Jean Jew modeled incredible courage and personal perseverance in the face of inequity and injustice. She has actively served as a mentor to others who desire to raise their voices, and she has provided both an inspiration and a map for girls and women who seek legal redress."[3] Honored along with Peggy Whitson, an astronaut who spent nearly two years at the International Space Station in three visits, and Ruth Harkin, a lawyer and the first woman in several national public service leadership roles, Jean's presence and accomplishments held their own.

Jean's black eyes took in the audience. She shared a memory from the trial. "The attorneys for the university argued that I had not been damaged because I only learned of these things said about me after the fact and only in connection with my lawsuit. I had brought the harm on myself. Judge Vietor listened and then asked, 'Are you saying that if poison gas is pumped into a room and a person who is there is not aware of it and dies, the person is not injured because she did not know of it?'" After some appreciative laughter, she continued, "The university attorneys said yes. That's what they had meant." She paused, "The people who supported me during the case and after the decision and in giving me this award pumped oxygen into that room. I am so grateful."[4]

⁙

As an emerita professor at the University of Iowa, Jean looks back on a distinguished career, which includes some (but not all) of the scientific accomplishments she foresaw for herself. The case "meant a lot of my youth and energy were gone. I wanted it all. I wanted both science and fair treatment. I liked that I played a part advancing women and was appreciated for that. But only by a segment. Another segment is missing. Even now there are young people in the university who are dismissive of women's rights. They ask what did Jean Jew accomplish research-wise?"

In the years that followed Judge Vietor's decision, Jean was called on to be a spokesperson for women's issues and an advisor to women seeking help. She rarely said no to these entreaties. In the university, she sat on the Council on the Status of Women and was appointed to numerous other committees. Outside the university, she was a founding member of the Iowa Women's Foundation, where she helped begin a grant program to support projects to overcome the barriers that women and girls in Iowa face in striving for economic self-sufficiency. She continues this volunteer work.

Since retiring in 2010, Jean has put her medical training to work as a clinician, taking care of elderly family and friends. When Williams's multiple sclerosis deepened and Glenys Williams developed Alzheimer's disease, Jean was their case manager, recruiting and supervising home health aides and accompanying them to medical appointments. Glenys died in early 2018 and Terry Williams died in late 2017. Jean's mother (recently deceased at the age of eighty-nine) and father (approaching one hundred) lived to see their hopes for Jean realized. They bragged to relatives and friends (though not to Jean herself) that "our daughter, the doctor, takes such good care of us and our medical problems."

⁙

Jean's case held a special place in Judge Vietor's assessment of his life's work. For his official portrait, painted near the end of his judicial career, he chose to appear in his judicial robe holding a case book, the spine of the volume legible to the viewer. His portrait hangs in the main hallway in the U.S. Courthouse in Des Moines. From the hundreds of volumes lining his bookshelves, he chose to hold for his portrait the volume containing his decision in Jean's case. His choice suggests the importance he accorded this decision in his nearly fifty years serving as a judge in Iowa.

Figure 17: Portrait of U.S. District Court Judge Harold D. Vietor, ca. 1996. Courtesy of the U.S. District Courthouse in Des Moines.

⁙

In 2014 Leonard, Street & Deinard merged with the Stinson law firm headquartered in Kansas City and became one of its fourteen offices with over five hundred lawyers.

Bob Zeglovitch, who worked on Jean's case from its inception through the federal trial, left the Stinson law firm in 2016. He subsequently started a firm, KZ Workplace, that conducts neutral workplace investigations (including of sexual harassment allegations) and training. He studies and practices mindfulness meditation and teaches it to lawyers and in workplace settings.

Susan Robiner left Leonard, Street & Deinard when she received a judicial appointment to the Minnesota District Court bench in 2006. She has been reelected three times. Her current term as a state court judge expires in January 2027.

Sheila Canard, who accompanied us for both trials and assisted throughout, has continued to work at the Stinson law firm. In her spare time, she resumed partnering with me on Jean's case by formatting and processing the manuscript for this book.

Hal Field, the senior partner who joined us for the attorney's fees application and negotiation, retired from the law firm in 2007 and passed away in 2014 at the age of eighty-seven. I was out of town when his funeral was held. In my condolence note to his wife and family, I recalled how he adroitly helped others, including me, navigate the obstacles on the way to becoming our better selves. His wife generously wrote back that Hal admired the way I handled the case and was very aware of the insensitivity and irony of "how the regent shook hands with him at the end of the luncheon and hugged and kissed you."

⁙

The two vice presidents for academic affairs whom Jean approached with her complaints, May Brodbeck and Richard Remington, have since passed away. Both were sympathetic to Jean's plight, if unable to effectively address it. Like Jean, Brodbeck remembered "too well being virtually the only tenured woman in liberal arts in a huge university."[5] She died in 1983 at the age of sixty-six. Remington died in 1992 at the age of sixty-one.

Dean Eckstein reportedly was never reconciled to the outcome in Jean's case. He passed away in 2011 at the age of eighty-seven.

Julia Mears's university career was upended. She left her position as assistant to the president in 1992 and joined the Mears Law Office in Iowa City, where she practices law, including representing clients on university employment matters.

Robert Tomanek has retired from the University of Iowa and is an emeritus professor of the Department of Anatomy. His family origins in the Bohemian-Moravian highlands led him to take several trips to the region and write a book on the history of the Czech Sokol gymnastics movement.[6]

⁂

After retiring from her assistant attorney general position in 1987, Merle Wilna Fleming passed away in 2006 at the age of eighty.

Dean Lerner went on from the attorney general's office in the mid-1990s to various leadership positions focusing on oversight and accountability for nursing home/assisted living quality of care and other issues of elder justice.

Scott Galenbeck spent more than thirty years in the Iowa Attorney General's Office in a variety of roles before going into general law practice at the firm of Sellers, Galenbeck & Nelson.

The Iowa Attorney General's Office apparently practices law much the same way as it did in the 1980s. In a 2021 ruling, U.S. District Court Judge Stephanie Rose ordered Iowa to pay nearly $5 million in legal fees to plaintiffs' attorneys in a constitutional challenge to abuses at the Boys State Training School in Eldora, Iowa. The judge reported that the attorney general's office "fiercely defended," "opposed the requested relief every step of the way," and produced documents "in a manner that was disorganized and lacking identification."[7]

⁂

The Universities of Iowa and Minnesota, despite searing experiences with the tangible and intangible costs of sex discrimination in the 1970s and 1980s, have been in trouble again. Discrimination complaints brought by two women employed in the Athletic Department at the

University of Iowa and later terminated, Jane Meyer and Tracey Gries-
baum, belied Vice President Nathan's guarantee that the injustice done
to Jean would not be repeated at the University of Iowa.[8] Despite a
scorching defense put up by the Iowa Attorney General's Office, a Polk
County jury awarded Meyer $1.43 million in damages. Subsequently
the university settled with both defendants for a total of $6.5 million,
of which $2.7 million was for attorney's fees.[9]

At the University of Minnesota, a winning women's hockey coach,
Shannon Miller, sued over her termination in 2014. In 2018, a jury
awarded her $3.4 million in damages. The university appealed. Shortly
after Joan Gabel was installed in 2019 as the University of Minnesota's
first woman president, a settlement was reported—$2.1 million to the
plaintiff and $2.43 million to her attorneys.[10]

⁑

The academy continues to be a hard workplace for women research
scientists to crack. Larry Summers, former president of Harvard University, illustrated this in 2005 when he theorized about why women scientists are not well represented on university faculties. He said women
were less likely to work the long hours necessary for advancement,
particularly if they were married. Suggesting that women did not have
the intrinsic aptitude necessary to succeed in a top research university,
he discounted sex discrimination as a factor holding women back. In
response to the furor that arose after his talk, he issued several public
apologies, noting that "progress overall has been frustratingly uneven
and slow," and called for clear thinking to "understand all the various
factors that might possibly bear on the situation."[11]

An outstanding woman scientist offers a simpler hypothesis. "Public
and private organizations all over the world have studied the mechanics
of sexism within science and have concluded that they are complex and
multifactorial. In my own small experience, sexism has been something
very simple: the cumulative weight of constantly being told that you
can't possibly be what you are."[12] Everyone loses when women are sent
messages that they are not wanted in scientific and academic work.
Katalin Kariko moved from lab to lab in temporary positions at the
University of Pennsylvania. Without her perseverance, her scientific

talent would have been lost and the scientific breakthroughs that led to vaccines for COVID-19 might have been as well.[13] For Asian American women in the academy, sex shaming is not yet a thing of the past, as Prageeta Sharma found at the University of Montana.[14]

⁂

I resigned from litigation and my law firm in 1994. My interests turned to advising and mediation. By representing both plaintiffs and defendants in employment cases, I had gained a three-dimensional perspective on employment disputes. I served as Carleton College's consultant on sexual harassment and assault prevention, taught at the University of Minnesota Law School, conducted investigations of complaints of sexual harassment, and served as a mediator in employment cases. Professionally I was squarely in my comfort zone during these years — doing work I knew how to do well. I was independent, accepting work I was interested in and declining everything else.

After eight years of this work, I was recruited to the University of Minnesota as the director of the Office for Conflict Resolution, an office

Figure 18: Jean Jew and Carolyn Chalmers at dinner in Minneapolis, February 2020. Courtesy of the author.

charged with helping resolve employment disputes among nonunionized faculty and staff. From 2002 to my retirement in 2014, I helped academic employees and administrators at the University of Minnesota navigate workplace conflicts.

⁝⁝⁝

Jean's story about a woman's fight for dignity was not accompanied by high monetary stakes or celebrity personalities. Her complaint was human-sized, not outsized, yet it was brought to bear against a powerful institution. Perhaps this asymmetry, an individual wrong versus institutional indifference and worse, is why so many feel so deeply about the injustice done to Jean.

Neither of us knew what would be required of us when we started; that this would be a case fraught with danger and played out along a ridge line. As we journeyed, the arduous struggle forced us to summon strength, skills, and courage we otherwise might never have known we had. The justice and grace that resulted continues to sustain.

Afterword

MARTHA CHAMALLAS

Robert J. Lynn Chair in Law, Moritz College of Law
The Ohio State University

IN THE DECADES since Jean Jew's case was decided, much has changed in the law governing sexual harassment and in the norms, discourse, and practices in academic and other workplaces. If Jean's case were decided today, her lawyers would argue her case on an altered terrain, citing different precedents and doctrines and encountering some different obstacles. At the same time, the case seems oddly contemporary, a vivid example of the adage "the more things change, the more they stay the same." Despite all the legal and cultural changes in the intervening years, the kind of bias that Jean faced as a female scientist, as a young woman in academia, and as an Asian woman in a white institution stubbornly persists. That is why her story still resonates and why it seems so pressing to assess the legacy of her long legal struggle against the University of Iowa.

In 1990, when Judge Vietor wrote his opinion, sexual harassment law was in its early stage. Only ten years had passed since the influential federal guidelines on sexual harassment had been issued,[1] and it had been only four years since the U.S. Supreme Court decided its first sexual harassment case.[2] Courts were just beginning to fashion the elements of the hostile environment claim, the kind of claim that Jean brought against the university. Perhaps most important, Jean's case predated the famous Anita Hill and Clarence Thomas confirmation hearings that riveted the nation as it listened to Hill's account of a sexually hostile workplace created by the man who was being judged to sit on the nation's highest court.

In the wake of the Thomas hearings, Congress finally amended Title VII, in part to bolster the rights of sexual harassment victims who pursued their claims in court. The new law gave harassment victims the right to a jury trial and allowed them to seek compensatory and punitive damages. This reform meant that for the first time, Title VII law recognized the emotional toll that harassment takes on its victims, even when individuals, such as Jean Jew, manage to keep their jobs and paychecks. Three years later, Congress amended the federal rules of evidence, enacting a sexual harassment shield law that prohibits defendants from prying into a plaintiff's past "sexual history" or casting aspersions on plaintiff's character by asking questions about her "sexual predisposition."[3] Each of these reforms might have been useful in Jean's case and might have given her attorneys a bit more leverage as they negotiated with the university.

However, it soon became apparent that these legal fixes to sexual harassment law were not nearly strong enough to place sexual harassment victims on an even footing with institutional or business defendants. Instead, the strong institutional impulse to resist charges of sexual harassment did not dissipate, even as hostile environment claims proliferated. Many institutional defendants continued to side with harassers and to fight tooth and nail once their employees' claims reached the courts, all while professing a commitment to equal opportunity and diversity. To make matters worse, by the century's end, courts took a sharply right turn in civil rights cases, erecting new procedural and substantive barriers to recovery. In a series of important cases, the U.S. Supreme Court created an affirmative defense for Title VII defendants that allowed them to defeat liability if they could prove they had internal grievance policies and procedures in place that plaintiff did not fully make use of.[4] Strict limits on punitive damages were imposed, letting institutions off the hook if they could point to "good-faith efforts" to comply with Title VII.[5] Most relevant to Jean's case, courts demonstrated that they were more reluctant to impose liability if plaintiffs only suffered verbal harassment from peers, as opposed to physical harassment from supervisors with official power to hire and fire employees.[6]

Tracing the legacy of Jean's case is thus not as simple as pointing to a specific legal reform that was enacted in response to her case or others like hers. Indeed, it is debatable whether it would be easier now than it was thirty years ago for a faculty member confronted with similar bias to prevail. Rather than look to legal developments, we can only appreciate the imprint and impact of Jean's story when we see it juxtaposed against the still-unfolding cultural and intellectual movements that have taken place largely outside the law. These influences may yet force institutions to finally side with sexual harassment victims and stop trying to defend the indefensible in court.

Looking back, we can view Jean's case as a harbinger of core complaints about women's vulnerability to sexual libel and sexual shaming only now coming to light through the #MeToo movement. Her case can also be seen as an early example of a distinctive form of "intersectional" bias inflicted on women of color in the workplace, directed specifically at her as an Asian American woman. When Jean's case was tried, we did not yet have the vocabulary to describe what she went through—we did not speak openly about slut-shaming as a weapon of harassment or recognize that women of color were disproportionately likely to be harassed through the use of racialized stereotypes and tropes. In so many ways, Jean's case was ahead of its time. What is remarkable is not that it was so difficult for her to win her case but that she was actually able to convince a federal judge and a state court jury that the law—as it was then understood—afforded her redress. In 1990, Jean's lawyers could not tap into a cultural backdrop that made her grievances legible and familiar; they had to improvise as they went along, pushing on every front to seek justice for their client.

Although it is not so easy to trace, the law of sexual harassment has been affected by and shaped by the #MeToo movement.[7] Catalyzed by the sexual assaults of women in the U.S. entertainment industry, the #MeToo hashtag first went viral in October 2017 when millions of women took to social media to tell their stories of sexual assault, harassment, and exploitation and to describe how employers and institutions that were complicit or indifferent did little or nothing to support them or stop it.

The narratives of victimization that flooded the internet as part of the #MeToo outpouring provided texture and structure to various kinds of oppressive behaviors that harassers engage in to humiliate and intimidate their targets. One recurring weapon of harassers is what is known as "slut-shaming," defined by one scholar as the "act of criticizing a woman for her real or perceived sexual promiscuity."[8] To be sure, for centuries women have been afraid to come forward with charges of rape or sexual assault, lest they open themselves up to accusations of being immoral or loose women unworthy of respect and protection. In the contemporary critique of the slut-shaming phenomenon, however, women have turned the tables, embracing and appropriating the "slut" label,[9] and calling out men who use such tactics, in an attempt to shift the shame onto the perpetrators rather than the targets.

A poignant example of slut-shaming recently surfaced when the #MeToo movement arrived in Australia and exposed the discriminatory treatment of women who serve in Australia's Parliament.[10] Women senators described how the "low hum of disrespect" from their male colleagues greeted them on a daily basis and revealed that slut-shaming was used as a political weapon to discredit female politicians and staff members. One woman senator, for example, remarked that "male rivals would often shout across the chamber the names of men she was falsely accused of sleeping with," and on one occasion a male colleague shouted "stop shagging men" at a female colleague while he was on the floor of the chamber. The women in the Australian Parliament regarded the tactic of slut-shaming as a kind of "weaponized gossip," designed to drive them out of their elected positions and make their lives miserable.

The similarity between the disrespect and slut-shaming experienced by these contemporary members of Parliament and Jean's case is unmistakable. Like the Australian women, Jean was repeatedly accused of sleeping with the chair of her department and vilified as a promiscuous woman who had slept her way to the top. The rumors were so widespread that many in the Anatomy Department and in the larger university simply accepted them as true. The rumors also played a pivotal role in discrediting Jean's professional accomplishments and providing a reason she should not be promoted to full professor. Her opponents portrayed her as unethical and conniving—as someone who simply placed her name on a "joint" publication that was the product of her chair's research and used her sexual relationship to obtain tenure and a high salary. For her detractors, Jean's case was one of sexual favoritism, not sexual harassment.

Significantly, the university's defense strategy hinged on these rumors and false accusations of sexual conduct. The university tried to reframe Jean's case as the unfortunate fallout of a private sexual affair, rather than a clear-cut case of sexual harassment. The "logic" behind the defense was that if the rumors were true, that would somehow excuse Jean's treatment, employing a not-so-subtle form of victim blaming. Although many in the university believed that Jean's treatment was inexcusable, regardless of whether she had a sexual relationship with the chair of the department, the defense proceeded as if her private sexual conduct was highly relevant. To counter this strategy, Jean's lawyers not only had to negate the rumors but also had to convince Judge Vietor that instigating and propagating sexual rumors could itself be a form of sexual harassment. Their job was made all the more difficult because they could not readily point to other cases of "weaponized gossip" where perpetrators had used sexual libel and slut-shaming as their preferred means of sexual harassment.

In addition to the use of sexual slander and gossip, Jean's harassment traded on what we now recognize as distinctively racial stereotypes and tropes. Although her case was widely regarded as a case of sexual (not racial) harassment, as a plaintiff Jean stood at the intersection of gender and race, and her harassment cannot be separated from her identity as an Asian American woman.

When Jean's case was tried, intersectionality theory had just surfaced in the legal academic literature and had not yet made its way into the courts or litigation.[11] Intersectionality theory posits that women of color are sometimes discriminated against in the same ways that white women or men of color are discriminated against, exposing them to a kind of double discrimination because of their complex identities. However, women of color also face a kind of distinctive discrimination that neither white women nor men of color are subjected to. When courts and other legal actors insist on employing mutually exclusive thinking—and treating cases as either sex or race discrimination cases—they can lose sight of the intersectional nature of the bias and fail to appreciate the full extent of the harm that a plaintiff may suffer. Because intersectionality theory had not yet appeared on the legal radar screen, Jean's case was poured into the sexual harassment mold, losing some of the outrage that might have accompanied a charge of racialized harassment. Although Jean was clearly subjected to explicitly racist name calling, the case proceeded solely as a sexual harassment case, erasing its racial character.

One important legacy of Jean's case is the stature it has gained in academic circles as a pioneering intersectional discrimination case. Legal scholars have pointed out that Jean's harassers traded on two pernicious stereotypes of Asian women that, although seemingly in conflict, in tandem provided the defamatory script for the vicious rumor campaign against her. Jean was at once the "lotus blossom," the stereotype of the passive Asian prostitute who would do anything for her brutal Chinese proprietor and the "dragon lady," cast as "a conniving, predatory force who travels in tandem as a partner in crime with men of her own kind."[12] Once Jean's detractors planted the rumor that she was having a sexual relationship with the despised and feared department chair, the racialized stereotypes did the work of explaining what was "really" happening in the department. The rumors made it seem like Jean both passively did the bidding of the chair and brazenly used her sexuality to get undeserved, favored treatment. Of course, lost in this account was Jean herself, the scientist and professor who had spent her adult life acquiring the credentials and doing the painstaking research that landed her a coveted tenure-track position at a top-rated research university.

The virulence of discrimination against Asian Americans, including Asian American women, is only now sinking into the American consciousness. The March 2021 shootings of six Asian women in three spas and massage parlors in Atlanta has sent journalists and scholars searching for the roots of Asian bias in the United States and discussing intersectionality theory in the mainstream media. As we discover once again how sexual violence can be intertwined with racism in a toxic mix, Jean Jew's case may now rightfully take its place as a forerunner of a kind of sexualized racism that can infect the behavior of university professors as well as a rampaging gunman.

As a law faculty member at the University of Iowa and a member of the Jean Jew Justice Committee, I remember my grave disappointment when I learned that the university intended to appeal Judge Vietor's decision on the grounds that the criticism and derogatory comments directed at Jean were protected under the First Amendment as part of faculty members' constitutional free speech and academic freedom rights. Like many of my colleagues, I believed that free speech and academic freedom did not extend to sexist and racist name calling and vicious rumors. Although faculty members were free to criticize the policies and actions of the chair and debate the merits of Jean's academic writings and teachings, to claim that the actions of her harassers were protected under the First Amendment distorted the Constitution and undermined the integrity of the university. The university's ultimate decision to drop its appeal was an unusual move, reflecting not only the strength of Jean's legal case but also the widespread support she received across the university and the state.

I must confess that I am still a bit shocked that the harassment that Jean endured occurred in an academic environment. Although it is now clear that competition among faculty and lack of oversight may facilitate sexual harassment even in "polite" university settings, Jean's ordeal still seems unbelievable to me. At the same time, it was entirely predictable, once we consider that she was the only Asian woman faculty member in the Anatomy Department. The combination of her vulnerability and her strength is sobering and inspiring. After all this time has passed, I can only say once again that her victory was richly deserved.

Appendix A

TIMELINE OF SIGNIFICANT EVENTS

FEBRUARY 1973 ⁚ Dr. Williams is appointed chair of the Anatomy Department, University of Iowa College of Medicine.

MAY 1973 ⁚ Dr. Jew receives her M.D. degree from Tulane Medical School.

JULY 1973 ⁚ Dr. Jew is appointed as an associate in the Department of Anatomy, University of Iowa.

JULY 1974 ⁚ Dr. Jew is appointed as an assistant professor of anatomy.

FALL 1974 ⁚ A colleague tells Dr. Jew of Dr. Tomanek's allegations of a sexual relationship.

1974–1978 ⁚ Dr. Jew receives many reports that Dr. Tomanek and others are making allegations of a sexual relationship.

DECEMBER 1978 ⁚ Majority of senior faculty in Anatomy Department recommend tenure and promotion to associate professor for Dr. Jew and promotion to full professor for Dr. Heidger. Both promotions become effective November 1979.

JANUARY 11, 1979 ⁚ Dr. Kaelber shouts slurs at Dr. Jew as she passes in the hall.

JANUARY 1979 ⁚ Dr. Jew reports Dr. Kaelber's vilification and past incidents of sexual harassment to Dean Eckstein. She meets with Vice President Brodbeck and with Dean Eckstein.

JANUARY 4, 1982 ⁚ Graffiti appears on the men's room wall: "Jean Jew is a lesbian."

FALL 1982 ⁚ Dean Eckstein receives anonymous letters containing sexual slurs about Dr. Jew.

SEPTEMBER–OCTOBER 1983 ⁚ At Eckstein's request, Dr. Williams resigns as chair of Anatomy. Associate Dean Rex Montgomery is named acting chair.

NOVEMBER 1, 1983 ⁛ Senior faculty meet to evaluate junior faculty. Graffiti limerick alleging sexual activity between Dr. Williams and Dr. Jew is written on the men's room wall.

NOVEMBER 9, 1983 ⁛ Dr. Jew meets with Vice President Remington about graffiti and faculty bias in her evaluation.

NOVEMBER 1983 ⁛ Dr. Jew retains Carolyn Chalmers as her attorney.

JANUARY 12, 1984 ⁛ Chalmers writes to Vice President Remington stating a complaint of sexual harassment on Dr. Jew's behalf.

AUGUST–SEPTEMBER 1984 ⁛ A faculty investigation panel conducts hearings on Dr. Jew's complaint of sexual harassment.

NOVEMBER 27, 1984 ⁛ The faculty investigation panel report concludes that Dr. Jew has been sexually harassed and recommends corrective action.

OCTOBER 30, 1985 ⁛ Dr. Jew files a lawsuit in Johnson County Court against the university and Dr. Tomanek.

MARCH 10, 1986 ⁛ Judge Eads dismisses Dr. Jew's claims against the university, citing the Iowa Administrative Procedure Act.

AUGUST 1, 1986 ⁛ The Iowa Civil Rights Act is amended to clarify that state employees can bring civil rights suits notwithstanding the Iowa Administrative Procedure Act.

SEPTEMBER 18, 1986 ⁛ Dr. Jew files a Title VII suit against the university in federal court. The suit against Dr. Tomanek remains open in Johnson County Court.

JANUARY 14, 1987 ⁛ The Iowa Supreme Court holds that state employees were not barred from suing under the Iowa Civil Rights Act even prior to its amendment.

NOVEMBER 1989 ⁛ Federal trial is held on Dr. Jew's claim against the university.

MAY 1990 ⁛ Federal trial continues for expert witnesses.

JUNE 1990 ⁛ Jury trial of defamation suit against Dr. Tomanek takes place in Iowa City.

JUNE 13, 1990 ⁚ Jury verdict is reached in Dr. Jew's favor and against Dr. Tomanek.

AUGUST 28, 1990 ⁚ Judge Vietor's decision is in Dr. Jew's favor and against the university.

SEPTEMBER 28, 1990 ⁚ Dr. Jew's application for attorney's fees is submitted.

OCTOBER 13, 1990 ⁚ The university appeals Judge Vietor's decision to the Eighth Circuit Court of Appeals.

MID-OCTOBER 1990 ⁚ The Jean Jew Justice Committee forms and distributes Judge Vietor's decision to faculty. University and press criticism of the university's appeal builds.

NOVEMBER 12, 1990 ⁚ A settlement is announced.

AUGUST 28, 1991 ⁚ The university files application for determination of compliance.

Appendix B

FACULTY INVESTIGATION PANEL REPORT

The University of Iow

Iowa City, Iowa 52242

Department of Industrial Relations and Human Resources
College of Business Administration

(319) 353-5037 *Nov. 27, 1984*

Richard Remington, Dean of Faculties
and Vice President for Academic Affairs
111 Jessup Hall
University of Iowa
Iowa City, Iowa 52242

Re: Complaint of Dr. Jean Jew

Dear Vice President Remington:

Pursuant to your charge to this panel, dated August 27, 1984, we have prepared
and now submit our response.

Statement of Facts

Dr. Jean Jew, a member of the Department of Anatomy since 1973, filed the
complaint of harassment based on sex through her attorney, Ms. Carolyn
Chalmers, on January 12, 1984. The letter details the basis of the complaints
including pertinent prior court decisions. On January 27, 1984, Ms. Julia
Mears replied to Ms. Chalmers. Dr. Jew then sent a letter dated July 1, 1984
to Ms. Laura Douglas presenting her complaint of harassment. Ms. Julia Mears
prepared background material on August 22, 1984. Dr. Jew proposed witnesses
and topics of inquiry in August, 1984.

The Charge to the Panel was drafted by Richard D. Remington, Vice President,
on August 27, 1984. The request is for an investigation of harassment based
on sex and defamation.

The proceedings were recorded by a court stenographer who supplied copies of
the transcript to Dr. Jew, her attorney, the Panel and Laura Douglas. No ex
parte communication occurred by Panel members or Laura Douglas. All testimony
was taken under oath and witnesses were assured that no part of their
testimony would be used in any legal action against them.

It seems clear that there has been a pattern and a practice of harassment in
Department of Anatomy, a pattern which has existed for more than a decade.
While determination of all of the exact causes of such harassment is beyond
the scope of this Panel, it does appear that the harassment stems in measure
from the fragmentation and polarization which has existed in the Department at
least since the arrival of Dr. Terry Williams as Chairperson. The Department
has been plagued by gossip, jealousies, various innuendos and insinuations,
and a considerable amount of litigation.

This Panel has been asked to consider the complaint filed by Dr. Jean Jew
alleging that she has suffered sexual harassment and defamation as a result of
various activities and statements made by members of the Department. In order

211

to render an opinion about such complaints, this Panel has interviewed the persons listed on the appended list and examined several documents. The Panel's conclusions follow; its statements and recommendations follow the order presented in Vice President Remington's Charge to Panel (see appendix).

Findings of Fact and Conclusions

I. To what extent has Dr. Jew been subjected to a pattern of defamation and harassment?

A. Statements were made in the university community to the effect that Dr. Jew was engaged in a sexual relationship with Dr. Williams. The Panel heard testimony which suggested that the relationship between Drs. Jew and Williams was "common knowledge." In essence, virtually every witness save one admitted to having heard, if not participated in, conversations about the alleged relationship. Furthermore, such statements were not confined to the Department of Anatomy, but were reported to have taken place at national meetings, on the "cocktail circuit," and between students. The panel did not receive testimony that these allegations specifically suggested any benefit(s) received by Dr. Jew as a result of the relationship. Many of the witnesses stated implicitly or explicitly that Dr. Jew had received favors or special treatment because of her "friendship" with Dr. Williams.

The Panel assumed the validity of the facts as contained in Dr. West's letter to the Dean regarding Dr. Kaelber's pronouncements with regard to Dr. Jew. This included obscenities and defamation directed against Dr. Jew.

B. A few of Dr. Jew's colleagues admit to have seen graffiti about her. None admitted to have written the same. While the nature of graffiti is childish, it was nonetheless intended as a derogation of Dr. Jew's character.

C. Anonymous letters were sent to various university personnel which impugned Dr. Jew's moral character and her professional integrity.

D. To the extent that a person's private nonacademic life should be her own, Dr. Jew's privacy was clearly disrupted by the persistent gossip and continuing monitoring of her behavior. In addition, witnesses and documents allude to faculty members who claim to have followed Dr. Jew's car, watched her home, and seen her enter a motel in the company of Dr. Williams. Other testimony suggests that faculty members themselves did not follow Dr. Jew but had heard of someone who did or someone who said he did.

The Panel was unable to adduce that any person actually did follow Dr. Jew or spy on her (with the exception of a lab assistant who claims to have "walked in" on Drs. Jew and Williams). Dr. Black was not available for verification of the contents of his letter. No faculty member who was reported to have done such spying admitted this to the Panel.

E. The grievance proceeding of Dr. Oaks was not available for perusal by this Panel. The reasons for such lack of availability were not clear and in the light of the not infrequent references to it, that is regrettable.

The grievance proceeding of Dr. Black does refer to Dr. Jew. However, the references to Dr. Jew are reasonable in light of the nature of Dr. Black's

grievance. Since he was complaining of an unfair denial of promotion and
tenure, it is logical that he would cite Dr. Jew as the colleague with whom he
should be compared. Her promotion decision was relatively recent history and
it is likely that he would expect and suggest that the standards to which he
would be held would be the standard evinced by the favorable decision in her
case. While Dr. Black does allude to the business relationship between Drs.
Heidger, Williams, and Jew, such reference again does not seem inappropriate
or malicious in light of the context of Dr. Black's grievance and his
assertion that his record favorably compared to that of Dr. Jew. There is no
explicit or implicit reference to any sexual relationship in Dr. Black's
grievance material.

    F. Clearly Dr. Kaelber publicly defamed Dr. Jew. This Panel heard
testimony that he was drunk at the time; however, his statements before this
Panel were of such a nature that his feelings and pronouncements are thought
to be independent of his sobriety. Testimony suggests that Drs. Tomanek and
Maynard were involved in conversations in which they assailed the moral
character of Dr. Jew. Dr. Tomanek is repeatedly identified as the initiator
for much of the defamatory suggestion about Dr. Jew. Neither Dr. Azzam nor
Dr. Halmi were mentioned as having made statements impugning Dr. Jew's moral
or professional character.

    G. Statements impugning the reputation of Dr. Jew were made to Drs.
Heidger and Bergmann according to their own testimony. Dr. West claimed only
indirect knowledge of any such statements. The Panel did not meet with Drs.
Black, Affifi and Thompson.

II. To the extent that the persons involved in any incidents of defamation or
    harassment identified above are not already known, can they be identified
    and, if so, who are they?

The Panel was able to identify a graduate student as one source of the rumor
that Dr. Jew and Dr. Williams had sexual relations in the workplace. A lab
assistant for Dr. Tomanek in 1980 claims to have entered the departmental
library and to have seen a man she positively identified as Dr. Williams
presumed (based on his state of undress) to be having sex with a woman she
presumed to be Dr. Jew (based on the lack of dissimilarity of physical
characteristics between the woman she saw and Dr. Jew). The lab assistant
claims to have told this only to one other lab assistant and Professor
Kalnitsky; the latter she met while vacationing in Mexico. There was nothing
in her testimony suggesting veracity.

Apparently no attempt has been made to determine the author(s) of either the
graffiti or the anonymous letters. This is regrettable and should be
corrected. While it might be difficult or impossible to track the author(s)
of the graffiti in light of the erasure of the same, tracking the author(s) of
the anonymous letters or at least attempting to do the same should be
possible. Both letters are handwritten and most likely by the same person.

Dr. Kaelber suggested that Dr. Yarmat was responsible for a statement that
Drs. Jew and Williams had been seen entering a motel in Coralville. Dr.
Yarmat was not interviewed because he no longer resides in Iowa. Dr.
Kaelber's testimony was not convincing.

III. Were any of the statements made about Dr. Jew in incidents of defamation or harassment identified above substantiated?

No. Drs. Jew and Williams denied to the Panel the existence of a sexual relationship.

The repeated allegations that the Head of the Department treated Dr. Jew with favor could not be substantiated. Rather it seemed that Dr. Williams used Dr. Jew to carry out responsibilities which other members of the Department were unwilling to accept. Dr. Jew did have her salary increased somewhat more than others in her rank, but this may be explained by the fact that she is a physician and by the assignments given to her. The number of graduate students or fellows who worked with her was not unusual and could be explained by her preference to use funds from grants for that purpose.

IV. What was the response of University administrators (i.e., the Department Head, Dean and Vice President) to the incident referred to in answer to question Number I above?

A. The department head, Dr. Williams, and, since 1983, the acting head of the department, Dr. Montgomery, Dean Eckstein, and Vice President Brodbeck as well as, since 1982, Vice President Remington, were made aware of the graffiti and the anonymous letters. In addition, in a letter from Dr. West, Dean Eckstein was made aware of Dr. Kaelber's verbal attack on Dr. Jew in January of 1979. Dr. Jew claims to have told both Vice President Brodbeck and Dean Eckstein about the allegations about her in the Department. Clearly Dr. Williams was aware of the harassment taking place. Dr. Montgomery had been alerted to the problem by Dean Eckstein as well as by faculty of the Department. The dates of such information are uncertain but not later than January of 1979. Dr. Williams reviewed the situation with Dr. Jew on a number of occasions but no overt action followed from those conversations. Dean Eckstein discussed the matter with several members of the Department on an individual basis and once with the department as a group.

B. It does not appear that any of the administrators took any steps to improve the situation for Dr. Jew, with the possible exception of the replacement of Dr. Williams as Head of the Department. It is unclear to what extent the harassment of Dr. Jew was a factor in this replacement decision. Subsequently, the acting head of the department, Dr. Montgomery, attempted to foster an atmosphere of open discussion among the faculty of the Department of Anatomy. The establishment of the present Panel may be seen as an affirmative attempt to quell the harassment, although the Panel is the result of the filing of Dr. Jew's complaint and her engaging an attorney. Notably there is no evidence that Dr. Jew's immediate superior, Dr. Williams, did anything to investigate or repudiate the conduct or comments.

C. Dr. Jew was the only witness who testified that she was discouraged from pursuing a remedy for the harassment. It does appear, however, that the various administrators failed to investigate actively the harassing behavior.

V. Was the treatment which Dr. Jew experienced related to her sex?

A. With the exception of one graffiti and one cartoon which involved Drs. Williams, Tomanek and Heidger, the Panel learned of no male faculty

member who had been subjected to the same treatment as Dr. Jew experienced.
The Panel went to some length to determine if the attacks on Dr. Jew's
character were the result of an attempt to "get at" Dr. Williams and not
intended as personal attacks on Dr. Jew. No male faculty member who came to
the Department with Dr. Williams had received comparable adverse treatment.
Dr. Williams himself was subject to vilifying comments.

Clearly there was a bias in the testimony given to the Panel by certain
faculty members. This bias was to the effect that Dr. Jew had not proved
herself as an independent investigator, able to functon apart from Dr.
Williams. None of these witnesses was able to explain why they thought Dr.
Jew was the junior, rather than the senior partner in the research team. It
would appear that in the absence of any evidence to support their assumptions,
their judgment was in fact based on a conscious or subconscious sex bias. The
effect of the assumption was to take away the credit Dr. Jew would otherwise
have earned for her publications and to provide reasons for those who felt
that she did not deserve to be promoted to full professor.

The attempt to discredit Dr. Jew as a private person by accusing her of an
extramarital sexual relationship also implies a sexist bias. The Panel doubts
that the defamation would have harmed Dr. Jew had she been a man and Dr.
Williams a woman. Much of our society condemns women's sexual affairs but
condones the same behavior in men.

B. The only instance cited was the remark of Dr. Longo during a recent
evaluation of the Department's faculty. Dr. Longo admitted to saying
something like "women and blacks have it made." Some members of the faculty
took this as a shockingly biased comment, but Dr. Longo tried, unconvincingly,
to put the comment in a positive light.

The Panel declined to call as witnesses any female or male staff or student
member who might receive unfavorable treatment as a result of such an
interview. Assurance of administrative protection seemed inadequate. The lab
assistant who claimed to observe Drs. Jew and Williams in the departmental
library was an exception in large measure because (1) she is no longer at
Iowa, (2) she is not a student in the Department of Anatomy, and (3) the Panel
had received testimony which directly cited her as a crucial witness.

VI. Have the incidents identified in answer to question I above tainted
Dr. Jew's work environment?

A. Based on the testimony of Drs. Tomanek and Kaelber, it is unlikely
that either of them could judge Dr. Jew objectively. The tone of Dr.
Kaelber's testimony was bitter and hostile. Dr. Tomanek was evasive, but the
Panel has reason to think that he has been the initiator or one of the
initiators of the defamation of Dr. Jew.

B. This question is answered in part under VI-A above. There is no
reason to assume that the conflict which has engulfed the Department, and the
polarization that has resulted, is likely to abate in the near future. An
objective evaluation of Dr. Jew will require a diligent appraisal of the
validity of comments made by some members of the Department of Anatomy.

C. The harassment had a destructive effect on Dr. Jew's professional and personal reputation both locally and nationally. Moreover, it probably has affected her productivity and the quality of her teaching. As she pointed out, it is difficult to face a large audience of students on the morning after your name has been linked with scandal on a local television news station. It is likely that Dr. Jew's evaluation last year was biased and the defamation may well have compromised her ability to find a position in another medical school. Whether the University's "failure to repudiate a pattern of harassment" is partly responsible for this situation is difficult to assess. Certainly, the absence of University response and support may have contributed to the stress felt by Dr. Jew and to a lowering of her morale and self-respect. Unfortunately, it is not clear that repudiation by the University could have undone the damage done to Dr. Jew, particularly the damage to her national reputation. The appointment of an acting Head for the Department of Anatomy from outside of the department may be an important step to control the condition within the Department, but it does not specifically reflect a concern for Dr. Jew.

VII. In view of its findings, does the Panel recommend any sanctions or remedies?

A. Dr. Jew's promotion process should include the current procedure with review by the full professors of the Department. Any conclusions reached within the Department should be subject to the strictest scrutiny by the Head of the Department of Anatomy, the Dean of the Medical College and the Vice President for Academic Affairs. The administration should seek consultation with other members of the College of Medicine outside of the Department of Anatomy. Dr. Jew should be provided with a written set of standards detailing what would be necessary for promotion including a definitive procedure for demonstrating "independence."

B. The President of the University of Iowa, James Freedman, should immediately issue a strong, public statement to the effect that the University of Iowa condemns sexual harassment of any form and, further, that the University reaffirms its commitment to provide a work and educational environment free of any form of sexual harassment. The administration should make clear to the members of the Department of Anatomy that no further harassment will be tolerated by any member of the Department. The faculty and members of the Department should also be warned against encouraging, either by action or inaction, harassing or defamatory statements outside the Department. The faculty of the Department of Anatomy, its staff, and its graduate students should have an opportunity to meet with the appropriate administrators to be informed of the findings and the expectations for the resolution of the problem.

Finally, the Panel recommends that a public statement be made on behalf of the University of Iowa which exonerates Dr. Jew. The specific content of such a statement should be determined by mutual agreement of Dr. Jew, her attorney, and the appropriate administrator(s) from the University of Iowa.

C. Immediate steps should be taken to ascertain the author(s) of the anonymous letters and, to the extent possible, the graffiti. If the author(s) is found, appropriate sanctions should be imposed. Because of their clear involvement in the defamation, Drs. Tomanek and Kaelber should have individual

conferences with the Head of the Department of Anatomy, the Dean of the
Medical College, and the Vice President for Academic Affairs. They should be
admonished to cease and desist any harassment and defamation of Dr. Jew and
should be warned of the consequences of persisting.

Respectfully submitted,

N. R. Hauserman, Chairperson

H. E. Kolder

M. A. Stewart

November 27, 1984

Appendix C

EXECUTED JURY VERDICT FORM, SELECTED PAGES

EXHIBIT A

Pat Palmer   1. Dr. Williams and Dr. Jew were caught on the sofa fucking.

Pat Palmer   2. Dr. Williams and Dr. Jew were caught on the sofa screwing.

Ron Bergman   3. She [Jane McCutcheon] is the one who found Jean and Terry in a compromised position on the library table.

James Searls   4. Jane McCutcheon found Dr. Williams and Dr. Jew in a compromising position in the departmental library.

James West   5. She [Jane McCutheon] saw Jean and Terry in a compromising position in the department office or the department library.

James West   6. Jane McCutcheon was the one who saw Dr. Jew and Dr. Williams in the library incident.

Pat Palmer   7. Dr. Williams and Dr. Jew were caught on the sofa in Dr. Williams' office.

Pat Palmer   8. Someone looked thorugh an apartment or condominium window and saw Dr. Jew and Dr. Williams in the clutches.

Pat Palmer   9. If I said I saw you [Dr. Jew] with Terry Williams on the sofa, you would have to drop your case, wouldn't you?

James West   10. Dr. Jew and Dr. Williams were getting ready to leave a restaurant in Kalona and Dr. Jew walked by with her head down acting like she was trying to avoid us [Dr. Tomanek and his wife] and not speak to us.

Ron Bergman   11. Jean and Terry were seen holding hands at the Kalonial Town House Cafe in Kalona

((

I - SLANDER

1. Has plaintiff proved elements 1 and 2 as set forth in Instruction No. 11?

yes _X_   no _____

(If you answer question No. 1 "yes," proceed to questions 2, 3, and 4. If you answer question No. 1 "no," proceed to question 5.)

2. Which statements numbered 1-5 of Exhibit A do you find defendant made and communicated?

_____3,4,5_____ (Place the numbers on this line.)

3. Which statements, contained in your answer to question 2, has defendant proved the truth of?

_____none_____ (Write each number. If none, write none.)

4. Which statements contained in your answer to question 2, has defendant proved were made and communicated in the scope of his employment?

_____none_____ (Write each number. If none, write none.)

II - SLANDER

5. Has plaintiff proved elements 1, 2, and 3 as set forth in Instruction No. 12?

yes _X_ no ____

(If you answer question No. 5 "yes," proceed to questions 6, 7, and 8. If you answer question No. 5 "no," proceed to question 9.)

6. Which statements numbered 6-11 of Exhibit A do you find defendant made and communicated and were defamatory?

_____7, 8_____ (Place the number(s) on the line.)

7. Which statements, contained in your answer to question 6, has defendant proved the truth of?

_____none_____ (Write each number. If none, write none.)

8. Which statements contained in your answer to question 6 has defendant proved were made and communicated in the scope of his employment?

_____none_____ (Write each number. If none, write none.)

((

III - INVASION OF PRIVACY

9. Has plaintiff proved elements 1, 2, and 3 as set forth in Instruction No. 15?

yes _____ no _X_

(If you answer question No. 9 "yes," proceed to question 10.)

10. Has defendant proved that the statements which form the basis of your answer to question No. 9 were made and communicated in the course of his employment?

yes _____ no _____

(You will determine damages pursuant to Instruction Nos. 18 and 21, if you find that defendant has made any statements, as set forth in answer to questions 2 and 6, concerning which the defendant has failed to prove truth pursuant to questions 3 and 7, or if you find plaintiff has proved elements of invasion of privacy under Instruction No. 15.)

IV - DAMAGES

We find plaintiff's damages as follows:

$ _5,000 ⁰⁰_ per Instruction No. 18

$ _30,000 ⁰⁰_ per Instruction No. 21

Dated this _13th_ day of June, 1990.

_____
Foreman*

*To be signed only if verdict is unanimous

Kathleen B. Zehrbach
Juror**

Linda J. Frauenholtz
Juror**

Janice M. Akre
Juror**

Lyle A. Swenson
Juror**

Sarah J. May
Juror**

Elaine M. Fink
Juror**

Dot a al
Juror**

**To be signed by the jurors agreeing thereto after six hours or more of deliberation.

Date: _6-14-90_
Mailed To: _Carolyn Chattros_
James Maues
Alan Lerner
Charles Traw & Thomas Diehl

_PK_

BY: _____
Clerk's Office Personnel Responsible
for Mailing Document

Executed Jury Verdict Form, Selected Pages ⁞ 223

Acknowledgments

MY GRATITUDE goes to Jean Jew for permission to excavate and recount this chapter in her life. She has very generously given her time to answer my questions, share her observations, and review and edit drafts. This is a better book because of her input. Errors or inaccuracies in my descriptions of her experience must be attributed to me.

Special thanks go to two distinguished professors. Throughout her career, Martha Chamallas has advocated for women and produced feminist scholarship that has influenced lawyers, judges, and policy makers. Her activism on Jean's behalf was decisive. Her afterword is a most appropriate last word. I am also indebted to Barbara Y. Welke. She valued this story long before I began writing it by inviting me to talk to her students. She shared her time and wisdom to review the manuscript and provide nuanced, insightful comments and detailed line-by-line edits. Her thinking has enriched this book.

I want to extend a thank you to the original members of the Jean Jew Justice Committee and their successors for their advocacy for Jean's rightful place at the university and for their message to other women and people of color that they are wanted there.

Thank you to staff at the Leonard, Street & Deinard and Stinson LLP law firms for organizing the record of Jean's case, storing it securely, and delivering all fifty-three boxes to my door. Without this archive, the story would not have been told.

I thank those whose legal talents and diligence were instrumental: Sheila Canard, Susan Robiner, Bob Zeglovitch, and Harold Field. I am grateful for the support of my law partners at Dayton Herman & Graham, particularly Chuck Dayton, John Herman, and Kathleen Graham, and at Leonard, Street & Deinard, particularly George Reilly.

This book began in creative writing workshops at the University of

Minnesota, where my earliest efforts were critiqued. I am grateful to the professors in those classes—Kirsten Fisher, Jacqueline Nasseff Hilgert, Madelon Sprengnether, and Kim Todd. Discussing the themes of this book with young students was great fun.

My gratitude to everyone who read drafts of this manuscript and provided guidance and encouragement: Sue Buckley, Sheila Canard, Ilene Carver, Jinny Chalmers, Martha Chamallas, Ellen Currier, Chuck Dayton, Mary Dunnewold, Sara Evans, Kathleen Graham, Margaret Green, Eric Janus, Leah Janus, Ann Rhodes, Susan Robiner, Ellen Sampson, Connie Starns, Margaret Swanson, Rosann Tung, Jay Weiner, Barbara Welke, and Bob Zeglovitch. I am particularly grateful for the close read and detailed comments by Rosann Tung, Jay Weiner, and Barbara Welke.

Thank you to everyone at the University of Iowa Press. I appreciate the resolve reflected in the press's decision to publish this book. I particularly thank my editor there, Meredith Stabel. Her insights and encouragement made critical contributions at critical times.

Sheila Canard, Ellen Currier, and Margaret Green attended to the detailed work of getting the manuscript and citations into proper format. Not my strong suit, it could have been my downfall without their assistance.

Heartfelt thanks go to my family—Eric, Leah, and Seth—for living through it, helping me live through it, and encouraging me as I wrote about it.

Notes

PREFACE

1. Susan Faludi, "She Said," *New York Times*, September 8, 2019, https://www.nytimes.com/2019/09/08/books/review/she-said-jodi-kantor-megan-twohey.html.

CHAPTER 1

1. Katherine Turk, *Equality on Trial: Gender and Rights in the Modern American Workplace* (Philadelphia: University of Pennsylvania Press, 2016), 126.

2. During the 1980s, more than three hundred women faculty at the University of Minnesota pursued sex discrimination claims, and fourteen hundred joined together in a salary discrimination petition. *In Re: Rajender Salary Settlement*, No. 3-89-464 (D. Minn. October 12, 1989).

3. Suzanne Perry, "Discrimination Claims at Minnesota Cost over $5-Million in Past 3 Years," *Chronicle of Higher Education*, August 31, 1983.

CHAPTER 2

1. Dayton, Herman & Graham is the firm name used throughout this book, although the firm was also known as Dayton, Herman, Graham & Getts and Pepin, Dayton, Herman, Graham & Getts.

2. Jean Jew in Celia Morris, *Bearing Witness: Sexual Harassment and Beyond—Everywoman's Story* (Boston: Little Brown, 1994), 130.

3. Cathy Park Hong, *Minor Feelings: An Asian American Reckoning* (New York: One World, 2020), 16.

CHAPTER 3

1. Kate Manne, *Down Girl: The Logic of Misogyny* (New York: Oxford University Press, 2018), 263–67.

2. News Broadcast KCRG-TV Channel 9, 6 p.m., September 13, 1984.

3. Faculty Investigation Panel Transcript, Jew testimony, August 29 and September 25, 1984, 83–135, 704–38.

4. Faculty Investigation Panel Transcript, Tomanek testimony, August 30, 1984, 342–93.

5. Faculty Investigation Panel Transcript, Kaelber testimony, September 25, 1984, 693–704.

6. Faculty Investigation Panel Transcript, Williams testimony, August 30, 1984, 224–49, 256–68.

7. Hope Jahren, *Lab Girl* (New York: Knopf, 2016), 274.

8. Faculty Investigation Panel Transcript, Eckstein testimony, August 30, 1984, 288–340.

9. Faculty Investigation Panel Transcript, Montgomery testimony, August 29, 1984, 136–74.

10. Faculty Investigation Panel Transcript, McCutcheon testimony, August 31, 1984, 397–416.

CHAPTER 4

1. Faculty Panel Report to Vice President for Academic Affairs Richard Remington (November 27, 1984). See Appendix B.

2. Faculty Investigation Panel Transcript, panelist discussion, August 28, 1984, 2–75; panelist discussion, August 29, 1984, 174–200; panelist discussion, August 30, 1984, 268–86; panelist discussion, August 31, 1984, 532–631; panelist discussion, September 28, 1984, 738–55.

3. Mark A. Stewart to Richard Remington, May 1, 1985.

CHAPTER 5

1. Malcolm Gladwell, "The Gift of Doubt: A. O. Hirschman and the Power of Failure," *New Yorker*, June 17, 2013, https://www.newyorker.com/magazine/2013/06/24/the-gift-of-doubt.

2. *Bradwell v. Illinois*, 83 U.S. 130 (1873).

3. Fred Strebeigh, *Equal: Women Reshape American Law* (New York: Norton, 2009), 110–14.

4. Civil Rights Act of 1964, 42 U.S.C. § 2000e et seq.

5. Equal Employment Opportunity Act, 20 U.S.C. §1681 et seq. (1972).

6. H.R. Rep. No. 92-238, 1971, as reprinted in 1972 U.S.C.C.A.N. 2137, 2155.

7. Carrie Baker, *The Women's Movement against Sexual Harassment* (New York: Cambridge University Press, 2008), 27–35.

8. Enid Nemy, "Women Begin to Speak-Out against Sexual Harassment at Work," *New York Times*, August 19, 1975, 38.

9. Baker, *Women's Movement*, 15–26.

10. *Corne v. Bausch & Lomb*, 390 F. Supp. 161, 163 (D. Ariz. 1975).

11. *Corne*, 390 F. Supp. 164.

12. *Barnes v. Costle* (D.C. Cir. 1977); *Tomkins v. Pub. Serv. Elec. & Gas Co.* (3d Cir. 1977); *Garber v. Saxon Indus., Inc.* (4th Cir. 1977); *Miller v. Bank of America* (9th Cir. 1979); *Corne v. Bausch & Lomb* (9th Cir. 1977); *Williams v. Saxbe* (D.C. Cir. 1978).

13. *Barnes v. Costle*, 561 F.2d 983 (D.C. Cir. 1977).

14. See *Williams v. Saxbe*, 413 F.Supp. 654, 660 (D. D.C. 1976), rev'd in part, vacated in part sub nom. *Williams v. Bell*, 587 F.2d. 1240 (D.C. Cir. 1978); *Barnes v. Costle*, 561 F.2d 983 (D.C. Cir. 1977); *Miller v. Bank of America*, 418 F. Supp. 233 (N.D. Cal. 1976), rev'd, 600 F.2d 211 (9th Cir. 1979). Barnes's and Miller's original complaints alleged both race and sex discrimination.

15. *Bundy v. Jackson*, No. 77-1359, 1979 WL 197 (D. D.C. Apr. 25, 1979), rev'd, 641 F.2d 934 (D.C. Cir. 1981).

16. *Meritor Savings Bank v. Vinson*, 477 U.S. 57 (1986).

17. Catharine A. MacKinnon, *Sexual Harassment of Working Women* (New Haven, CT: Yale University Press, 1979).

18. Guidelines on Discrimination Because of Sex, 29 C.F.R. § 1604.11 (1980).

19. *Bundy v. Jackson*, No. 77-1359, 1979 WL 197 (D. D.C. Apr. 25, 1979), rev'd, 641 F.2d 934 (D.C. Cir. 1981).

20. For example, *Green v. Board of Regents of Tex. Tech Univ.*, 474 F.2d 594 (5th Cir. 1973) (deferring to university's decision to deny tenure); *E.E.O.C. v. Univ. of Notre Dame Du Lac*, 715 F.2d 331 (7th Cir. 1983) (holding peer review documents were not discoverable); *Kumar v. Bd. of Trustees, Univ. of Mass.*, 774 F.2d 1, 12 (1st Cir. 1985) (Campbell, J. concurring) (noting that "courts must be extremely wary of intruding into the world of university tenure decisions").

21. Title VII was amended in 1991 to provide for emotional distress and punitive damages in certain circumstances and a right to trial by jury; 42 U.S.C § 1981(a) (1991).

22. *Hishon v. King & Spaulding*, 467 U.S. 69 (1984).

23. Monica Hesse, "'It's Race, Class and Gender Together': Why the Atlanta Killings Aren't Just about One Thing," *Washington Post*, March 18, 2021, https://www.washingtonpost.com/lifestyle/style/hesse-atlanta-asian-women/2021/03/18/183b3f00-8749-11eb-8a8b-5cf82c3dffe4_story.html.

24. *Rajender v. the University of Minn.*, 546 F. Supp. 158 (1982).

25. *DeGraffenreid v. General Motors Assembly Div.*, St. Louis, 41 F. Supp. 142 (E.D. Mo. 1976), aff'd in part, rev'd in part on other grounds, 558 F. 2d 480 (8th Cir. 1977).

26. Kimberlé Crenshaw, "Demarginalizing the Intersection of Race and Sex: A Black Feminist Critique of Antidiscrimination Doctrine, Feminist Theory and Antiracist Policies," *University of Chicago Legal Forum* 1989, no. 1 (1989): 139.

27. *Lam v. Univ. of Haw.*, 40 F.3d 1551, 1562 (9th Cir. 1994).

28. Sumi K. Cho, "Converging Stereotypes in Racialized Sexual Harassment," *Journal of Gender, Race and Justice* 1 (Fall 1997): 197.

29. Iowa Civil Rights Act of 1965, Iowa Code § 601A.1–15 (1973) (current version at Iowa Code § 216.1–22 (2021)).

CHAPTER 6

1. 1986 Iowa Acts, Ch. 1245, sec. 263, available at https://www.legis.iowa.gov/docs/publications/iactc/71.2/CH1245.pdf.

2. *Jew v. Univ. of Iowa*, 398 N.W.2d. 861 (Iowa 1987).

CHAPTER 7

1. Kate Manne, *Down Girl: The Logic of Misogyny* (New York: Oxford University Press, 2018), 101.

2. *Meritor Savings Bank, FSB v. Vinson*, 477 U.S. 57 (1986).

3. An affiant reported seeing a plaque on Lerner's desk reading *Thanks for fighting those witches*. Affidavit of Mary Lou Fellows, September 20, 1990.

4. Claudia Dreifus, "It Is Better to Give than to Receive," *New York Times Magazine*, December 14, 1997, https://www.nytimes.com/1997/12/14/magazine/it-is-better-to -give-than-to-receive.html.

5. Memorandum in Support of Defendant's Motion for Summary Judgment, 5.

CHAPTER 8

1. Trial Transcript, November 13, 1989, vol. I, 3–38.

2. Trial Transcript, Remington testimony, November 13–14, 1989, vols. I–II, 36–280.

3. Remington deposition, August 25, 1988, 216.

4. Trial Transcript, Remington testimony, November 13–14, 1989, vols. I–II, 38–287.

5. *Univ. of Penn. v. E.E.O.C.*, 493 U.S. 182 (1989).

6. Trial Transcript, Eckstein testimony, November 14–15, 1989, vols. II–III, 288–379.

7. Rosabeth M. Kanter, *Men and Women of the Corporation* (New York: Basic Books, 1977), 73, n.18.

8. Trial Transcript, Dawes testimony, November 15, 1989, vol. III, 388–406.

9. Trial Transcript, Perry testimony, November 15, 1989, vol. III, 497–510.

10. Trial Transcript, Glenys Williams testimony, November 16, 1989, vol. IV, 721–41.

11. Trial Transcript, Palmer testimony, November 16, 1989, vol. IV, 742–71.

12. Trial Transcript, Jew testimony, November 16, 1989, vol. IV, 774–77, 844–56; November 17, 1989, vol. V, 860–981, 998–1059; November 20, 1989, vol. VI, 1133–1225; November 29, 1989, vol. XII, 2372–415.

13. Trial Transcript, November 16, 1989, vol. IV, 856–57.

14. Hope Jahren, *Lab Girl* (New York: Knopf, 2016).

15. Trial Transcript, McHenry testimony, November 17, 1989, vol. V, 982–98.

16. Trial Transcript, Azzam testimony, November 20, 1989, vol. VI, 1094–133.

17. Asa Black was a faculty member. Evelyn Jew, Jean's sister, worked as a lab technician in the department. Williams walked with a cane due to multiple sclerosis.

18. Trial Transcript, McCutcheon testimony, November 22, 1989, vol. VIII, 1472–95.

19. Trial Transcript, Tomanek testimony, November 24, 1989, vol. IX, 1790–842.

20. Kate Manne, *Down Girl: The Logic of Misogyny* (New York: Oxford University Press, 2018), 49–54.

21. Trial Transcript, Kultas-Ilinsky testimony, November 27, 1990, vol. X, 1955–75.

22. Trial Transcript, Mears testimony, November 27, 1990, vol. X, 1993–2107.

23. Trial Transcript, Williams testimony, November 28, 1989, vol. XI, 2276–337.

24. Trial Transcript, November 29, 1989, vol. XII, 2447–51.

CHAPTER 9

1. Trial Transcript, November 28, 1989, vol. XI, 2367–68.
2. Trial Transcript, November 28, 1989, vol. XI, 2269.
3. Clemente expert opinion, plaintiff's exhibit no. 150.

CHAPTER 10

1. Jean Jew, in Celia Morris, *Bearing Witness: Sexual Harassment and Beyond—Everywoman's Story* (Boston: Little Brown, 1994), 137.
2. Faculty Investigation Panel Transcript, September 25, 1984, 737.
3. Trial Transcript, November 17, 1989, vol. V, 931.
4. Kelly David, "U of I Accused of Ignoring Sexual Harassment Ruling," *Cedar Rapids Gazette*, May 2, 1993.
5. Monica Seigel, "Jury Gives Prof $35,000 in Defamation Trial," *Iowa City Press-Citizen*, June 14, 1990, 1A.
6. Editorial, "Jean Jew's Personal Trauma," *Iowa City Press-Citizen*, June 15, 1990.

CHAPTER 11

1. Judge Vietor's complete decision is accessible at *Jew v. Univ. of Iowa and the Bd. of Regents of the Univ. of Iowa*, 749 F. Supp. 946 (S.D. Iowa 1990), https://law.justia.com/cases/federal/district-courts/FSupp/749/946/1616794/.

CHAPTER 12

1. Peter Shane, "Harassment Is Not Privileged Speech," *Daily Iowan*, September 28, 1990, 8A.
2. Andy Brownstein, "Appeal Deadline at Hand for UI Harassment Ruling," *Daily Iowan*, September 25, 1990.
3. Diana Wallace and Andy Brownstein, "University to Appeal Sexual Harassment Case," *Daily Iowan*, October 12, 1990.
4. Press release, Board of Regents of University of Iowa, October 12, 1990.
5. Diana Wallace and Andy Brownstein, "University to Appeal Sexual Harassment Case," *Daily Iowan*, October 12, 1990.
6. Linda Hartmann, "UI Faculty Say Appeal Sends Bad Message," *Iowa City Press-Citizen*, October 13, 1990.
7. *Cedar Rapids Gazette*, October 13, 1990.
8. Petition, *Daily Iowan*, October 17, 1990.
9. Norman L. Johnson, et al., "Letter to the Editor," *Daily Iowan*, October 24, 1990, 8A.
10. Michael Lorenger, "UI Never Learns," *Daily Iowan*, October 16, 1990, 6A.
11. Editorial, "Double or Nothing," *Iowa City Press-Citizen*, October 16, 1990.

CHAPTER 13

1. Andy Brownstein and Diana Wallace, "UI, Regents Put Case to Rest," *Daily Iowan*, November 13, 1990.

2. "Iowa: Judge Finds U Liable in Harassment," *New York Times*, September 2, 1990, 49; "University of Iowa Found Liable in Harassment," *New York Times*, September 3, 1990; "Iowa Told to Promote Faculty Member in Defamation Case," *Chronicle of Higher Education*, September 19, 1990; Debra Blum, "The University of Iowa to Pay $1.1 Million to Settle a Sexual Harassment Lawsuit," *Chronicle of Higher Education*, December 5, 1990; "Diagnosis: Harassment," *Newsweek*, November 26, 1990; Debra Blum, "Medical Professor, U. of Iowa Face Aftermath of Bitter Sexual-Harassment Case," *Chronicle of Higher Education*, March 13, 1991, A15.

3. Judge Vietor did not order the determination of compliance the university had requested.

CHAPTER 14

1. Susan Heller Anderson, "Top Feminist? Derrick A. Bell Jr." *New York Times*, January 19, 1991.

2. University of Iowa, "Women at Iowa: Susan Johnson," *YouTube*, February 17, 2014, https://www.youtube.com/watch?v=6zFhbL2qIHw.

3. "2018 Iowa Women's Hall of Fame Honoree: Jean Y. Jew, MD," Iowa Department of Human Rights, https://humanrights.iowa.gov/jean-y-jew-md; quoting from letter of support from Susan Buckley.

4. Iowa Department of Human Rights, "2018 Iowa Women's Hall of Fame," *YouTube*, October 15, 2018, https://www.youtube.com/watch?v=tbF4RLnn6l8.

5. Office of Strategic Communication, University of Iowa, "UI's First Female Vice President Honored," January 14, 2015.

6. Robert Tomanek, *Czech Immigrants and the Sokol Movement* (Iowa City, IA: Penfield Books, 2020).

7. Tony Leys, "Iowa Ordered to Pay $4.9 Million in Attorney's Fees after Lawsuit on 'Torture' at Eldora Boys State Training School," *Des Moines Register*, January 8, 2021, https://www.desmoinesregister.com/story/news/2021/01/08/judge-who-ruled-last -year-state-employees-inflicted-torture-teens-says-iowa-must-pay-5-million-attor /6599002002/.

8. *Meyer v. Univ. of Iowa*, Iowa Dist. Ct., No. LACL 133931 (2017).

9. "Jane Meyer Wins $1.43M in Case against Iowa," *Des Moines Register*, May 4, 2017.

10. "Jury Backs Ex-UMD Hockey Coach in Discrimination Suit, Awards $3.74M," *Minnesota Public Radio News*, March 15, 2018, https://www.mprnews.org/story/2018/03/15 /minnesota-duluth-hockey-shannon-miller-wins-lawsuit.

11. Lawrence H. Summers, "Letter from President Summers on Women and Science," Harvard University, January 19, 2005, https://www.harvard.edu/president/news -speeches-summers/2005/letter-from-president-summers-on-women-and-science/.

12. Hope Jahren, *Lab Girl* (New York: Knopf, 2016), 182–83.

13. Gina Kolata, "Kati Kariko Helped Shield the World from the Coronavirus," *New York Times*, April 8, 2021.

14. Cathy Park Hong, *Minor Feelings: An Asian American Reckoning* (New York: One World, 2020), 24.

AFTERWORD

1. 29 C.F.R. § 1604.11(a).

2. *Meritor Sav. Bank v. Vinson*, 477 U.S. 57 (1986).

3. Federal Rule of Evidence 412.

4. *Burlington Inds. v. Ellerth*, 524 U.S. 742 (1998); *Faragher v. City of Boca Raton*, 524 U.S. 775 (1998).

5. *Kolstad v. Am. Dental Ass'n*, 527 U.S. 526 (1999).

6. *Vance v. Ball State Univ.*, 570 U.S. 421 (2013).

7. See Tristin K. Green, "Feminism and #MeToo: The Power of the Collective," in *Oxford Handbook of Feminism and Law in the U.S.*, edited by Deborah L. Brake, Martha Chamallas, and Verna Williams (forthcoming 2022).

8. Wendy N. Hess, "Slut-Shaming in the Workplace: Sexual Rumors and Hostile Environment Claims," *NYU Review of Law and Social Change* 40 (2016): 581.

9. Deborah Tuerkheimer, "Slutwalking in the Shadow of the Law," *Minnesota Law Review* 98 (2014): 1453.

10. Damien Cave, "'The Most Unsafe Workplace'? Parliament, Australian Women Say," *New York Times*, April 5, 2021.

11. The foundational article on intersectionality theory is Kimberlé Crenshaw, "Demarginalizing the Intersection of Race and Sex: A Black Feminist Critique on Antidiscrimination Doctrine, Feminist Theory and Antiracist Policies," *University of Chicago Legal Forum* 1989, no. 1 (1989): 139–67.

12. Sumi K. Cho, "Converging Stereotypes in Racialized Sexual Harassment: Where the Model Minority Meets Suzie Wong," *Journal of Gender, Race and Justice* 1 (1997–1998): 185.